APPROACHES TO ANCIENT JUDAISM
Volume VI
Studies in the Ethnography and Literature of Judaism

Program in Judaic Studies
Brown University
BROWN JUDAIC STUDIES

Edited by
Jacob Neusner
Wendell S. Dietrich, Ernest S. Frerichs, William Scott Green,
Calvin Goldscheider, David Hirsch, Alan Zuckerman

Project Editors (Projects)

David Blumenthal, Emory University (Approaches to Medieval Judaism)
William Brinner (Studies in Judaism and Islam)
Ernest S. Frerichs, Brown University (Dissertations and Monographs)
Lenn Evan Goodman, University of Hawaii (Studies in Medieval Judaism)
William Scott Green, University of Rochester (Approaches to Ancient Judaism)
Norbert Samuelson, Temple University (Jewish Philosophy)
Jonathan Z. Smith, University of Chicago (Studia Philonica)

APPROACHES TO ANCIENT JUDAISM

Edited by
William Scott Green

Editorial Board
Alan J. Avery-Peck
Paul Virgil McCracken Flesher
Ernest S. Frerichs
A.J. Levine
Jacob Neusner
Gary G. Porton

Volume Six

STUDIES IN THE ETHNOGRAPHY AND LITERATURE OF JUDAISM

EDITORS FOR THIS VOLUME
JACOB NEUSNER
AND
ERNEST S. FRERICHS

APPROACHES TO ANCIENT JUDAISM
Volume VI
Studies in the Ethnography and Literature of Judaism

edited by

Jacob Neusner
and
Ernest S. Frerichs

Scholars Press
Atlanta, Georgia

APPROACHES TO ANCIENT JUDAISM
Volume VI
Studies in the Ethnography and Literature of Judaism

© 1989
Brown University

Library of Congress Cataloging in Publication Data

Studies in the ethnography and literature of Judaism / edited by Jacob Neusner and Ernest S. Frerichs.
    p. cm. -- (Approaches to ancient Judaism ; v. 6) (Brown Judaic studies ; no. 192)
    ISBN 1-55540-411-1 (alk. paper)
    1. Judaism--Middle East--Customs and practices. 2. Rabbinical literature--Historiography. I. Neusner, Jacob, 1932-
II. Frerichs, Ernest S. II. Series. IV. Series: Brown Judaic studies ; no. 192.
BM173.A66 vol. 6
[BM700]
296'.09'01 s--dc20
[296'.09'015]   89-10934
                                                                              CIP

ISBN 978-1-930675-73-5 (paper : alk. paper)

Printed in the United States of America
on acid-free paper

In memory of
the mother of our colleague and friend,
Wendell S. Dietrich

MARY WILLETT DIETRICH
1902-1989

Servant of God in this life,
"Her children arise and call her blessed."

Table of Contents

Preface ix

Part One
ETHNOGRAPHY OF JUDAISM

1. Evergreen Elijah: Ritual Scenes from Jewish Life in the Middle East. By E. S. Drower. With a Preface by Emile Marmorstein. Edited, with an Introduction by Jorunn Jacobson Buckley..3

       Introduction by Jorunn Jacobsen Buckley 3
       Preface by Emile Marmorstein 8
       Prolegomena 11
     i. Domestic...12
     ii. New Year: *Rosh Hashana*......................................22
     iii. The Day of Atonement (*Yom Kippur*) and the Feast of Tabernacles..29
     iv. The Feast for the Blossoming of Trees....................38
     v. Purim...43
     vi. Passover 46
     vii. Evergreen Elijah 58
       Postscript...62

                 Edited by Jorunn Jacobsen Buckley
                 Massachusetts Institute of Technology

Part Two
INSTITUTIONS OF ANCIENT JUDAISM

2. Palestinian Synagogues before 70 C.E.: A Review of the Evidence..67

                 Paul V. McCracken Flesher
                 Northwestern University

Part Three
THE LITERATURE OF ANCIENT JUDAISM

3. The Three Stages in the Formation of Rabbinic Writings.........85

                 Jacob Neusner
                 The Institute for Advanced Study and Brown University

4. Documentary Hermeneutics and the Interpretation of Narrative in the Classics of Judaism 107

Jacob Neusner
The Institute for Advanced Study and Brown University

Part Four
SOME SCHOLARLY CLASSICS ON ANCIENT JUDAISM REVISITED

5. Louis Jacobs, *Studies in Talmudic Logic and Methodology* 137

Oren Joseph Tversky
Brown University

6. Adin Steinsaltz, *The Essential Talmud* 149

Eli Ungar
Brown University

7. E. E. Urbach, *The Sages: Their Concepts and Beliefs* – Twenty Years Later 155

Jacob Neusner
The Institute for Advanced Study and Brown University

8. Why Schechter, Moore, and Urbach Are Irrelevant to Scholarship Today 173

Jacob Neusner
The Institute for Advanced Study and Brown University

EPILOGUE

9. The Language and Structure of the Babylonian Talmud: Its Influence on its Readers' Mode of Thought 197

Jhonatan Rotberg
Brown University

Index 201

Preface

These free-standing essays lay no claim to cogency, other than in topic and approach to the topic. But in that matter, they hold together in a more coherent way than collections of papers in annuals commonly do. For the papers concern themselves, beginning to end, with the reconsideration of what we know, with special interest in the heritage of learning that we have received from former generations of scholars. When we study Judaism, after all, we do not invent the subject; our task is to receive and make our own the received invention of the subject and the conventions on how the subject is to be studied. That is why time and again we read the scholarly classics of an earlier age and also study the lives and examine the context in which those classics were composed. These classics of learning did not fall from heaven; people thought them up and worked them out, and in doing so responded to the intellectual challenges of disciplined learning. And even while we go about the task in response to different challenges and another definition of discipline – and of learning – we seek in the inheritance of scholarship to preserve the good and to learn the lessons of the bad.

No one proposes to ignore what has been done, to invent the wheel in the study of Judaism. But surely better ways in which to pay our homage to the past, when it has earned that homage, exist than piling up bibliographies of useless titles and writing long footnotes of materials essentially unexamined and lacking all insight. But that is what people do who deem bibliographies of everything on a subject to be required in monographs on a subject, and who compose endless footnotes of information that plays no role in the argument of an article or a book. For so far as an article proposes to make a point, a book to set forth and analyze and demonstrate (or refute) a proposition, information must serve the purpose of argument, and argument must pertain to the proposition. The uncrafted and merely erudite works that tend to win approbation ordinarily collect masses of information, without point or purpose or plan.

There is a better way to make our own what has been given to us, and that is the way of sustained and on-going rereading of the classics in their terms, not in ours; that is, as models for learning, rather than as mere vessels of information. The purpose of such a rereading is to find out two things: what do we (already) know and how do we know it? No one begins fresh, so we want to know what others have had to say and the basis on which they propose to say it. But all learning stands in a tradition; we do not create ourselves any more than we invent the wheel. That is why in finding out what we know and how we know it, the task draws us ever deeper into the context of learning: the models by which our predecessors for two hundred years defined their task, the paradigms of learning that told them what was worth knowing ("what do we know") and how one finds out what we know ("how we know it").

In my view, the answers to those questions lie in not reading discrete articles or books, that is, items on the same topic as that on which we work. They are to be found, rather, in reading in context the bulk of the *oeuvre* of a scholar, in finding out under what circumstances she worked (in the case of Lady Drower, for instance), or to investigate the methodological presupposes in which he framed his questions and undertook to answer them (in the case of Professor Urbach and Rabbi Steinsaltz and Dr. Jacobs). Does this interest in context invite gossiping about personalities and trading insight information about politics – in power struggles among people who today are corpses? I think not, though it can. Context is intellectual and institutional, but above all, it is cultural. For the cultural setting in which we conduct our professional lives to begin with defines our minds and the structure of our intellect, long before we have used our minds to frame questions of interest to that intellect.

In these pages, therefore, we review over and over again the evidence and the argument in the setting of the mind-set and method of the scholar. Our principal paper, which called the project into being, is that of Professor Jorunn Jacobsen Buckley; she had nearly as much trouble finding a publisher as did Lady Drower in presenting the original work. I am proud of having created this and other media to break all the monopolies and make possible speedy publication of monographic writings. In this regard scholarship presented in the English language in the study of Judaism today enjoys far greater freedom of expression than it has at any time in the past, or than it does even now in the Hebrew language, where the journals are closed to unconventional viewpoints, and the monograph series virtually moribund anyhow.

Reviewing evidence over and over again, comparing evidence against proposition, questioning the premises of method and the givens

Preface   xi

of inquiry – these processes form the heart and lifeblood of learning. Paul V. McCracken Flesher's paper does just that in reference to the synagogues of the Land of Israel before 70. We call attention to another paper, printed just now, cited by Flesher, that of Lester Grabbe; between these two papers, the premises concerning the existence and character of synagogues prior to 70, placed on display most recently by Lee Levine in his introduction to the book edited by him, *The Synagogue* (New York, 1987: The Jewish Theological Seminary of America), are shown to be utterly without foundation.

The papers by my undergraduate students at Brown University in 1988, Oren Joseph Tversky on Louis Jacobs, Eli Unger on Adin Steinsaltz, and, in a different way, Jhonatan Rotberg on the impact of the Bavli on its audience, show how the youngest generation can and should read the mature works of earlier times. Jacobs was a pioneer and he remains a formidable figure. But this young mathematician has asked some questions out of his training in mathematics and applied mathematics that Jacobs will surely wish to rethink. Steinsaltz is today celebrated and a major personality in the living study of the Torah, in all its phases. But he (and perhaps those who celebrate him) will all the more wish to take to heart the honest observations of a young scholar of religion of tomorrow; he is not the first, nor, if God shows grace to the future, he will not be the last, to ask whether the emperor is wearing any clothes. Jhonatan Rotberg, a young Jewish student from Mexico City, lives in three cultures, the Mexican-Latin American, the Jewish-Yiddish and Hebrew, and the American. He is well equipped to investigate, if haltingly and with much anguish, how the works of one age and place make an impact, intended and fully conscious, upon all ages and places.

My own rereading of Urbach is now joined by a statement of why, in my view, we have nothing whatsoever to learn from Urbach and the others whose line of learning – method, premise and, as a matter of fact, result as well – he continued and concluded, except for episodic observations on this and that. I have systematically reread the entire corpus of writing in European languages and in modern Hebrew on Judaism in antiquity, which is my field of specialization. The papers presented here take their place alongside those in the following, where the work is done systematically and in an orderly way:

Ancient Judaism. Debates and Disputes (Chico, 1984: Scholars Press for Brown Judaic Studies).
Struggle for the Jewish Mind. Debates and Disputes on Judaism Then and Now (Lanham, 1988: University Press of America).

Paradigms in Passage. Patterns of Change in the Contemporary Study of Judaism (Lanham, 1988: University Press of America).

In this same context I call attention, also, to my paper "What Happens to Scholarship When Paradigms Shift: Does the End of the Old Mark the Beginning of the New" in *History and Theory,* October, 1988, reprinted in *Paradigms in Passage.* There I deal with the two most influential figures in Judaic scholarship in the USA in the mid-twentieth century, Saul Lieberman (1898-1982) and Salo W. Baron (1895-). If there is nothing of consequence to be learned about ancient Judaism from Urbach, who at least made the effort, all the more so do I find it possible to dismiss the ideas on that same subject by Saul Lieberman, a philologist with a vastly inflated opinion of the value of his own opinions, and Salo W. Baron, whose *Social and Religious History of the Jews* (Philadelphia, 1952: The Jewish Publication Society of America), Volume II, scarcely makes contact with anything we today can recognize as "religious history," if he means, "history of religion."

Lieberman's legacy of exegesis of texts is valuable; as a labor of free association carried on in a well-stocked mind, it is a monument to how much can be accomplished even in a complete vacuum of method: good guessing raised to a high level. But in contrast to Urbach, Schechter, Moore, and the others, Lieberman's legacy will endure, if not in the center of learning, then at least in an honored corner, because, after all, facts do matter, and meanings of words and phrases, while enjoying far greater importance for the past century and a half than they intrinsically merited, still make a difference, even now – not half the difference that they did when Lieberman reigned supreme over much of the realm of Judaic learning. That accounts for the inflation of his reputation while he lived; today he appears a mere mortal, and a merely useful, but not a very memorable, scholar at that. He left a lot of information, but not a single interesting idea.

Baron, by contrast, has nothing to tell us, other than the titles of the articles and books in his overblown footnotes; but these articles and books only rarely tell us something we need to know, and still more rarely are they right about what their authors claim to know. When people speak of publishing "too much," there are books and articles of Baron that provide a fine case in point. These are the ones that are either uninformed of vast stretches of scholarship done in Baron's own time, or that merely collect and arrange enormous globs of undigested information around banal and platitudinous propositions, or both (as is mostly the case). I do not know precisely when Baron stopped learning, but I can show, with his writings on history and religion in antiquity,

Preface   *xiii*

that he simply did not open any books other than those in his own library, for which he must have stopped acquiring books in this field when he had printed his Volume II. Twenty years later, it can be demonstrated chapter and verse, he had learned absolutely nothing in this area. What the work is like elsewhere I do not know.

So turns the wheel of learning: their day will come again, I suppose. Meanwhile, we are in charge. That is not by reason of politics, but only by reason of publication: we are here, we are doing the work, and we are taking the risks. When others come along, now in other places, or in time to come, to do the work their way, to make the judgments within their conventions of thought and canons of evidence and reasoning, they will be in charge, and they will dispose of our heritage. I hope we give them more reason to treat with respect – if, in the nature of things, also reserve – than our predecessors have given us; that is, I hope they will find reason to read what we write, in ways in which, alas, after a fair go at survey and reprise, we find it difficult to justify spending a great deal of time on what our predecessors have left us.

But survey and reprise, criticizing the results of others who have worked on our subject, hardly suffice. We owe ourselves the effort at construction and reconstruction. It is not enough to criticize the received. We have also to give something of our own over to the readership for whom we claim to write. Otherwise the entire enterprise is sterile and academicistic: a mere rehearsing of opinions and a trading of politics, ours for theirs. That is why I set forth two papers of work of mine that is quite current. These papers are sketches of large-scale conceptions with which, at present, I am experimenting. They can of course stand a fair amount of refinement. But since I maintain we have nothing to learn from Urbach, Schechter, Moore, and their friends, I owe it to my readers to show what I wish to know. For without a clear statement of what I want to find out, I can hardly have made an adequate statement of why, in the received corpus of learning, I am not able to find what I want to know – and, let me say very bluntly, also, what I think is *worth* knowing.

The senior editors of this series dedicate this volume to the memory of the mother of one of our colleagues in Judaic Studies at Brown University, who died in the very week in which the book went to press. Through her son, we know her, and we are therefore confident that, had she received this small tribute in her lifetime, she would have been touched and pleased by it. It is a very American transaction, and can have taken place, in our view, only in this country, and only today. That is where the son has made his mark, and one of the many reasons the mother will have had very profound reason for pride in him and respect for the life that he has made out of the life that she made possible.

JACOB NEUSNER
For the Editors

September 1, 1989

School of Historical Studies
The Institute for Advanced Study
Princeton, New Jersey 08540
and
The Program in Judaic Studies
Brown University
Providence, Rhode Island 02912

Part One
ETHNOGRAPHY OF JUDAISM

1

Evergreen Elijah: Ritual Scenes from Jewish Life in the Middle East

Edited by Jorunn Jacobsen Buckley
Massachusetts Institute of Technology

Editor's Introduction

Lady E. S. Drower (1879-1972) is best known as this century's foremost fieldworker among the Mandaeans and as procurer and translator of literature by this still-surviving Gnostic group in Iraq and Iran. A number of Mandaean texts were unknown to the West before Drower made them available. Her interests and experiences in the Orient extended far and wide even before she started living in Baghdad in the 1920's (Drower's husband had a post as juridical adviser to the government there). Already in the year 1909 Drower (then Stevens) published her first in a series of novels set in the Orient. Some of these books became bestsellers. Drower also published travel accounts from Iraq, Syria, Sudan, and other countries, books that include a wealth of folkloric and religious material.

In her *Water into Wine* (London: Murray, 1956), a comparative work on Near Eastern "sacred foods" symbolism and practices, Drower originally intended to include a substantial section on popular, Oriental Judaism as she had observed it, particularly in Iraq. In her Introduction to this book, Drower acknowledges, "In Palestine and Iraq Jewish families welcomed me to Passover, New Year and other ritual feasts, and explanations were freely and generously given" (p. 4). However, only bits and pieces of Jewish material but no sustained treatment of Jewish practices occur in *Water into Wine*, for Drower was forced to omit it. She states this in a letter of 6/20/1962 to J. G. Weiss, then the

Editor of *Journal of Jewish Studies*. The reason for the exclusion was that the Jewish part "had aroused much hostile criticism... amongst some orthodox readers which hindered acceptance by publishers. I therefore removed it from the book and set it up as a separate piece of genuine research....It lay by for years" (Drower to Weiss 6/20/62).

Why did it "lay by for years"? Drower had conducted her research on Jewish rituals on and off between the two World Wars, and into the years of the Second World War. In 1943, she asks Dr. S. D. Goitein in Jerusalem about certain unclear areas in her research. Generally supportive of Drower's first attempts to pull her work into publishable form, Goitein nevertheless doubts some of her observations, especially on two points. First, the bits of donkey-skin tied to the tip of the oxhide rod used by the scourger on the eve of Yom Kippur (see iii, below) are "hardly believable," and, second, Goitein doubts that Drower really has attended a *Hashkavah* Prayer during the Sukkot week, because mourning is not allowed then (Goitein to Drower 1/4/44). But Drower holds on to her observations; in an undated list of responses to Goitein's letter she insists on the existence of the donkey-skin bits and she says that Hashkavah is not thought of as mourning (she refers to an article in J. de Haas, *Encyclopaedia of Jewish Knowledge*, to support her second point).

Goitein's objections to these details foreshadow the later, more massively negative reactions toward Drower's manuscript. On 3/3/53, she writes to her friend E. Marmorstein, headmaster of a Jewish school in Baghdad (after the Second World War, he worked in England, in BBC's Arabic Department), about the Jewish section that was excised from *Water into Wine*. She says,

> I find that [that] part arouses indignant denial amongst non-Oriental orthodox Jews. I feel nervous, yet cannot retreat about scenes which I witnessed.
>
> Now, *you* were in Baghdad and have European eyes and a mind both critical and tolerant. Would it be possible...for you to go through the manuscript?
>
> I wondered further whether it would stretch your generosity too far to ask you to write a brief foreword? You know that Judaism there [i.e. in Iraq] has its own bright and vivid colouring – just as the Eastern Churches have, and you could corroborate that what I saw was not only the result of a fertile imaginative eye!" (Drower to Marmorstein 3/3/53)

Marmorstein *did* write the Preface (which I include here), and he remained an unswerving supporter of Drower in her attempts to find a publisher for the Jewish material – whether in long article or book form. Matter-of-factly, Marmorstein replies to Drower, "Parochialism is, of course, one of the faults of orthodox Jews everywhere." He also includes a story he has heard about a European Jew who appeared in the Albert Sassoon synagogue in Baghdad. The European "knew no Arabic, was suspected of being an imposter and possibly a missionary in disguise" (Marmorstein to Drower 3/9/53). So, *who* is suspicious *to whom* remains an issue of cultural relativity.

The manuscript is rejected, twice. Drower writes to Marmorstein, "I feel sure that these ancient and most important survivals in ritual will be carefully 'ironed out' by zealous Israelis with little interest in *ancient* but a burning interest in modern history." She also tells Marmorstein about one of the two readers' reports accompanying the rejected *Evergreen Elijah,*

> The reader is obviously *furious* that I should have been invited to view these ceremonies, at the same time, he hopes that all these heretical and backward manifestations of differences should have been *by now* eradicated! I am afraid that I laughed joyfully over his unconscious self-revelation. (Drower to Marmorstein 7/21/53)

Drower may have laughed in exasperation, too. The reader dismissed Drower's book because "it was written before the British *cleared out*" (i.e. it depicts an old, now uninteresting, way of life); the Jewish rites are *"a thing of the past";* Drower's descriptions constitute "a personal chronicle of Babylonian Jewry as it survived into the Author's day." (To this last statement Drower adds, acerbicly, in her own green ink, "Yes, that happened to be its value"). Further, the reader doubts "if *Jews* here [i.e. in Europe?] would pay much attention to the sketches by a foreigner of ritual scenes from Jewish life in far away lands." Neither would Gentiles be interested; they ought rather to "consult the standard text books and the *Jewish Encyclopaedia.*" Drower's *real* sin is spelled out in the reader's last, swiping attack: she has been *"poking into Jewish synagogues where strictly speaking she has no right to be present and into Jewish households* in search of data."[1]

Drower thinks that it is her data on the Jewish beliefs and practices regarding the transmigration of souls that particularly set off the reader's (and probably others') ire. In the same letter of 7/21/53 to Marmorstein she adds, "The Israelis are not going to root out Kabbalism and belief in transmigration as easily as they imagine." In a letter to Drower, Marmorstein concedes that "the things which you have observed are part of general Jewish usage – 90 per cent of them are

---

[1] The reader shall remain nameless.

practised in my own household – and it is the remaining 10 per cent that are of such interest to me" (Marmorstein to Drower 9/4/53).

Evidently, Marmorstein was one of the few who could so magnanimously accept Drower's fieldwork. In the years after the formation of the Israeli state, few Jewish scholars there and in Europe wished to be reminded of the clearly *Oriental* Jewish beliefs and practices. Preferably, these (including Sephardic) traditions should quietly melt or mold themselves into the idealized, dominant, Western-oriented Jewish identity.

In the same letter of 9/4/53, Marmorstein advises Drower to read David Sassoon's *History of the Jews in Iraq*. But in her reply to Marmorstein, Drower is unimpressed by Sassoon: "He seems entirely unaware that some of the folklore and superstitions are not exclusively Jewish but are local Arab" (Drower to Marmorstein 9/9/53). Here, she also wonders whether scholars will get upset over the three-part auctioning of Torah-readings in the synagogue (see notes 53 and 60 in iii, below), for one or two of Drower's European Jewish friends have already "exclaimed 'impossible'" at this information.

In subsequent letters, Marmorstein gives Drower patient advice about rewriting *Evergreen Elijah*, and he suggests new readers for it. Drower acquires another Jewish supporter in these years, the American Rabbi O. Lehmann, who spent time in Oxford in 1955 researching a Biblical manuscript belonging to Rabbi S. D. Sassoon.[2] Lehmann is delighted by Drower's book, and shows it to Sassoon, who is the son of the author of *History of the Jews in Iraq. He* offers to send Drower a copy of his father's work (Sassoon to Drower 3/29/55) – a gesture Drower could probably do without, given her previous reaction to the book.

Clarendon Press rejects *Evergreen Elijah*, and *Journal of Jewish Studies* drags out its decision for a year and a half. Drower asks Weiss for a Jewish expert to go through the manuscript, jauntily closing her letter in this way: *"l'homme propose* etc.! At 83 it is a corollary that must be added!" (Drower to Weiss 9/27/62). The Jewish expert is probably the one who cut the length of the original manuscript, leaving out the *Rosh Hashanah* section, the *Purim* material, and other sections. During the next year or so, Drower produces a second draft, based on these editorial suggestions.

However, as she grows tired of the drawn-out decision process, Drower confesses, "I sometimes feel inclined to scrap the whole thing"

---

[2] Lehmann published the result of his research as *The Damascus Pentateuch and its manuscript tradition (according to Ben Naphtah)*, Oxford: Blackwell 1962.

(Drower to Weiss 3/11/63). But in the summer of 1963, Drower writes from Jerusalem and Baghdad to England for notes she needs in yet again revising the manuscript. But *Journal of Jewish Studies* must have made a negative decision on the book sometime late in 1963 (although I know of no letter to this effect). *Evergreen Elijah* was not published during Drower's lifetime.

About half a year after Drower's death, her daughter, Dr. M. Hackforth-Jones (a Near Eastern archaeologist), writes to the scholar J. B. Segal regarding her mother's manuscript. He suggests taking it to Israel, although he considers "the chances of its being published...slim" (Segal to Hackforth-Jones 7/29/72). However, at the end he adds, "who knows? – its time may come."

In the summer of 1986, M. Hackforth-Jones asked me to take a look at the *Evergreen Elijah* manuscripts, wondering if I could help in having the book finally see print. I had no time for the project then, but in January 1988 I took the two large folders containing the two versions of the manuscript, along with the correspondence spanning the years 1944-1972. Then, I chose what was essentially Drower's second draft, added some of the excised parts of the first, and thus made a "combined" version which to me seemed closest to Drower's original intentions for *Evergreen Elijah*.

I believe the gist of the correspondence, as I have excerpted it here, gives some indication of *why* Drower's book could not reach print earlier. The scholarly world was still stuck in its stereotypes regarding Judaism. Oriental magical aspects seemed too embarrassing. In the aftermath of the establishment of the state of Israel, the country's westernized, modern vision overshadowed the "Judaisms" of other, variegated inhabitants and immigrants to the new country. The orthodox, Jewish scholarly establishment in Europe evidently had no need to be informed of the "ten per cent," the parts of Oriental Jewish life that so intrigued Marmorstein.

Drower's offense was to have experienced and testified to Oriental forms of Judaism that Western scholars wished were extinct. The "insider-outsider" question also played a role – as seen in a part of the reader's report quoted above. Nobody seems to have minded Drower's fieldwork among Mandaeans, Christians, Yezidis, Zoroastrians, and Arabs – but her not being a Jew suddenly set Judaism up as forbidden territory to her. The Jewish scholars hostile to Drower's book were not really defending their fellow-believers; rather, they were offended *at* the Oriental beliefs and practices, and they wished that Drower would have left well enough alone. Drower's pressing on with her material is, to me, admirable, and her experience with the *Evergreen Elijah* manuscript writes its own little chapter in the history of recent scholarship on Judaism. I met Drower once, less than a year before her death, and she still had a glint in her eyes that I imagine she flashed during her years of stubborn commitment to *Evergreen Elijah*.

Preface
By Emile Marmorstein

I first met Lady Drower in 1936, when I took up my duties as headmaster of the Shamash Secondary School in Baghdad. As a result of personal experience of the kindness and hospitality which she dispensed to members of all communities, I began to appreciate the extent of her influence on the social and intellectual life of the city where, for nearly three decades, she represented the standards of Western civilization so worthily. Defying the lethargical influences of the climate, she found time to make valuable contributions to Mandaean studies, and her interest in folk lore and religious customs, which she studied industriously at first hand, resulted in the collection of a great deal of material leading to the publication of a number of scholarly works from her pen.

The Baghdad Jewish community, with which this book is largely concerned, is one in which I have taken an affectionate interest not only in my professional capacity but as an observant Jew. I think that I felt the first stirrings of this affection on my first Sabbath afternoon when I wandered round the old Jewish quarter, perhaps, if the truth must be told, desolately and a little homesick, after having attended a Sabbath morning service in which the decorous conduct of Oriental worship contrasted acutely and even painfully with the vigor of the fervent devotions to which I am accustomed, in a synagogue where my solitary hat appeared to be spiritually isolated amid a crowd of turbans, tarbooshes, and sidaras. On that afternoon I was passing by a decayed looking building – it was afterwards burnt down as a result of a short circuit – when I heard the strains of Talmudic argument emerging from one of the small barred windows. I went into this place, which was known as Beit Zilkha, and was welcomed and invited to join the group. I noticed a participant scanning the text in advance in order to create an impression by anticipating a question that was to be asked later. This reminded my of one of my fellow students at home. From that time on, the barriers were set aside and I attended that weekly Sabbath afternoon study circle throughout my first year in Baghdad, that is to say, until I moved to a house some miles away and joined another group.

Yet, it would be dishonest to convey the impression that the Jewish community of Baghdad in my day had remained a citadel of the faith.

The walls had been breached many years before when the schools of the Alliance Israélite were founded apparently with the purpose of teaching young men and women to speak French, and to ape Europeans who, they were led to believe, were staunch secularists. During the British occupation and mandate, the process was hastened. Rabbinical responsa and commentaries ceased to be published. Parents wanted their children to become doctors, lawyers and Government officials rather than Rabbis. The Jewish shops were all closed on the Sabbath with the exception of a bookshop kept by a crypto-Communist, but the Sabbath had become profane for thousands of Jews employed in Government offices, banks and commercial firms. The dietary laws were largely observed in Jewish homes owing to the presence of older generations, but not in the fashionable Jewish clubs. Travel on the Sabbath was widespread, and among the wealthier classes the trend towards the adoption of outward forms of European life was displacing traditional customs and values very rapidly.

In brief, Baghdad between the two wars resembled the Jewish communities of Eastern Europe some 50 or 60 years ago but for the absence of zeal, both religious and irreligious. Baghdad was untouched by the equivalent of movements such as that of the Hassidim, which brought ecstasy into Jewish religious life, or that of the moralists, which invested it with a profound sense of inward earnestness: but it was also undisturbed by the anti-religious passion of European left-wing movements so that to superficial observers incapable of distinguishing conformity born of indifference from enthusiastic piety, Baghdad appeared to have remained a conservative community.

One of the merits of Lady Drower's book lies in the fact that she has succeeded in putting down on paper a painstaking account of the religious observances which she has seen with her own eyes during this period of decay. For the observances remained in force in the majority of households even though they were bereft of enthusiasm and tolerated rather than fulfilled by a large part of the younger generation. The synagogues were still frequented and the study of the Law was not entirely neglected even if its adherents appeared to adopt a defeatist attitude towards their own way of life or felt little confidence in their struggle to uphold it. I spent a considerable amount of time with them, and it is in the light of my personal knowledge of their studies and as a result of listening for many hours to the preachers and teachers of Baghdad that I should like to make a few remarks which may perhaps complete Lady Drower's picture of the religious life of this ancient community.

Most of the observances which she describes are observed in almost identical fashion throughout the traditional Jewish world: both in the

Middle East and Western Europe, and wherever the influence of the Kabbala extended, there was an extraordinarily happy fusion of mysticism with legal practice and theory as well as with the ethical ideas and moral teachings of the moralists and philosophers. In Baghdad, as elsewhere, stress was laid on the essential truth and unity of concrete and allegorical interpretations of Biblical narratives, laws and customs.

Let me give a few examples. The Passover ceremonial is to be taken literally as a memorial of the liberation of Israel from Egyptian slavery. But it also has a moral significance. It symbolizes the liberation of the spirit from the defilement of sin. The leaven forbidden during the feast represents the evil inclination which struggles for domination within all of us, the unleavened bread the victory of the pure aspirations of the soul over the appetites of the body. Again, ceremonies referring to the coming of the Messiah represent the eventual triumph of good over evil within individual human beings as well as physical liberation from oppression and violence. In general, the whole theological system of positive and negative commandments, which are intended to be obeyed as an expression of man's love and fear of God who gave them and as a means of drawing nearer to Him in every aspect of one's daily life by their meticulous observance, demands a greater degree of "inwardness" than is usually granted by those who see in customs and observances merely the workings of an ancient social traditional force.

I also had the privilege of participating on a number of occasions in the all-night vigils which were a feature of the religious life of the Jewish community of Baghdad. Even before my arrival I was naturally familiar with the universal Jewish custom of remaining awake in prayer and study throughout the night on the eve of Pentecost and on the eve of the Great *Hoshanah*. The purpose of these vigils is, of course, preservation from sexual impurity during the nights preceding the revelation of the Torah and the final seal on the Day of Judgment; but these vigils in the house of mourning at fixed dates during the year of mourning are unknown in European Jewish life. It was therefore with a certain eagerness that I accepted invitations to such gatherings.

I myself took part in the readings, and here again I was always impressed by the happy combination which had been brought about between the mystical ideas of the Zohar, such as the transmigration of souls, with the older Rabbinic ideas of the piety of children delivering their parents from purgatory. The whole ceremony was imbued with the fine moralistic conception inherent in Jewish thought of the divine test of the mourner who, in his affliction, refrains from showing resentment, and in the midst of an assembly of his relations and friends proclaims the praise of the Lord of life and death. Altogether the commandments of comforting the mourner and visiting the sick appealed to the heart of the Baghdadi Jew and were genuinely fulfilled even by those whose lives were not very much influenced by religious ideas. They really appeared to be convinced of the truth of the traditional belief that by their visits they were removing a part of the pain and affliction.

The community as we knew it is no longer there. Most of its members are in the Holy Land. Many of them have found suitable employment in government posts where their linguistic talents are required. Many others are living in discomfort, it may be true, and involved in the solution of various problems that seem insoluble, obsessed no doubt with the nostalgia which is the occupational disease of the refugee, but nevertheless more fortunate than their brothers in Central and Eastern Europe who would willingly have exchanged the gas chamber for the transit camp. This appears to be part of the tribute which the regions of the world exposed to nationalism have to pay for "independence" at the expense of their ancient minorities.

What of their future? What of the future of the customs and beliefs which Lady Drower has described? The younger and more adaptable elements among them will no doubt espouse the dominant secularist political creed to which they were attracted when they were in Baghdad in the hope of freedom from discrimination, of freer social intercourse between the sexes, of the abolition of the dowry system which makes the possession of marriageable daughters and sisters such an intolerable burden in many cases, of emancipation from the patriarchal household and other irksome social institutions. Among more conservative elements, a tendency towards the assimilation of members of the different Oriental Jewish communities with one another has been observed, so that within a few decades it is likely to be difficult to reconstruct a picture of the Jewish life of Baghdad. Lady Drower's scholarly observations provide such a picture painted by an unprejudiced observer with a wide experience of other faiths and customs. Her descriptions will not only provide material for future historians but a record and memorial of the religious atmosphere of the last years of a historical community.

(Written in 1953)

Prolegomena

The following sketches of Jewish custom and ritual were written after thirty years spent in Hither Asia. Some of my descriptions of local customs have appeared to people at home bizarre and contrary to all that they knew of Jewish law. I think that they believed me to have misunderstood these customs or to have failed to set them down with accuracy. I assured them, as I do now, that what I have written had been submitted to learned Jews of standing in Iraq and Jerusalem, persons quick to detect inaccuracies and to correct them. For such help and criticism I was indebted especially to Mr. Ezra Barzillay (now Haddad), at that time headmaster of one of the largest Jewish schools in Baghdad; to the then Chief rabbi of that city; and in Israel to several Jewish friends such as Dr. S. D. Goitein whose erudite studies on Yemenite Jews are well known. Mr. Haddad gave me much material, took me to Jewish houses and placed his scholarship, his time and his library most generously before me.

The mysticism of Jews in the Middle East, to those who know only the Jews of Europe, appears surprising, almost incredible. It is, nevertheless, very deeply rooted, and in Iraq Kabbalism and belief in the transmigration of souls, *gilgul neshamot*, is especially prevalent.

i. Domestic

Domestic ritual plays an important part in Jewish life all over the world. There is no record of the ritual drinking of wine and breaking of bread such as that which occurs on the eve and close of the Sabbath up to Exilic times, but they appear to have been practised regularly in the period which immediately preceded the Christian era.[3]

It is a pleasing and touching characteristic of Jewish ritual that every Jewish father is, as it were, a priest in his own house. In the synagogue only a Cohen may give the benediction, but in the sanctity of his home, at the head of the table prepared for the ritual, any Jewish father should on Friday night call his children to him and, laying his hands on their heads, should bless each in turn; the boys with the blessing of Jacob on the sons of Joseph ("God make thee as Ephraim and Manasseh," Gen. xlix, 20) and the girls with "God make thee as Rachel and as Leah," Ruth iv, 2). From their earliest years Jewish children associate home with the solemn kindling of the olive-oil lamp or candles by their mother on the Sabbath and with the simple rite wherewith their father drinks wine and breaks bread with them that evening and at the ceremony which ushers out the Day of Rest.

---

[3]"The Talmud records that it was a matter of dispute between the schools of Hillel and Shammai whether the Kiddush should come first and then the benediction over wine, or *vice versa*. Thus the custom was already a well-established one in pre-Christian times" (W. O. E. Oesterley and G. H. Box, *The Religion and Worship of the Synagogue*, London: Sir Isaac Pittman & Sons, 1907, p. 379f).

Evergreen Elijah

The Talmud gives high praise to the elaborately prepared meal of the Sabbath. A story is told about a Roman Emperor who asked the Jewish rabbi Joshua Ben Hananya, "How is it that the Sabbath food has so pleasant an odour?" to which the rabbi replied, "We possess a spice named 'Sabbath' which we place into it and which gives it fragrance." The Emperor asked for some of this spice, but was told, "It availeth him only who observeth the Sabbath." (Talmud, Shabb. 119a).

Of course, the blessing and ritual drinking of wine, and the benediction over bread and its ritual breaking and consumption are practised by Jews all over the world, but there are local differences. In case that Gentile readers are as ignorant as I was, I will tell them what I heard from Ezra and my friends in Baghdad and Jerusalem. In all Jewish households food for the Sabbath should be prepared and cooked on Friday because from sunset on Friday till sunset on Saturday no fire or light must be kindled. In Iraq it is customary to prepare at least one hot meal for Sabbath by leaving a stew or similar dish on hot embers (Heb. *hammīn*) so that it remains warm till noon on the Sabbath. The usual *hammīn* there was, until chicken became so dear, a dish of chicken and spiced rice called *tannūri*. In Kurdistan Jewish housewives set a pot of *haris* or *harīsa* upon four fire-bricks or stones over a *kanūn* (Arabic *moged*), a fire-hearth on the ground, this dish being a pottage of boiled wheat cooked with sheep's fat, meat and lentils. The heat is kept in by covering pot and hot ashes with a number of thick sacks or something of the kind. According to Brauer,[4] a similar dish or *kubanah* (a mess of durra or barley meal with sheep's fat and meat) is kept warm in the *tannūr*, a hollow earthen oven.

Strict Jews are expected to abstain from all work and business after midday on Friday, except from activities which prepare for the Sabbath such as shaving, bathing, cooking and so on. However wealthy a man may be, he should himself help with the household preparation for the Sabbath.[5] The taboo on striking a light after sunset on Friday is severe: no cigarette may be lit; no electric bell sounded, for this entails kindling a spark. Gentiles may be asked, however, to switch on a light or to make tea. In Baghdad Moslem boys parade the Jewish quarter carrying matches and crying, "Nār, nār!" (fire), who, for a trifle,

---

[4] E. Brauer, *Ethnologie der Jemenitischen Juden*, Heidelberg: Kulturgeschichtliche Bibliothek, 1. Reihe, 1904, p. 103.

[5] In the Talmud a story is told of rich rabbis who perform such service, one preparing a fish, another cutting wood or preparing tapers, a third (sitting on a golden chair!) helps to get the *ḥammīn* ready, and so on.

perform these or similar services.[6] This is frowned on by the very orthodox. As ordering *goyim* to do work on the Sabbath is in reality forbidden by the Law, pious Jews pay the boy beforehand; the very strict, however, refrain from tea brewed on the Sabbath.[7]

It is the duty of the mother to kindle the Sabbath lights before sunset on the eve, and these should be two, three, five, or seven. This is counted one of her three chief religious duties, the two others being ḥallah and ṭevīlah.[8] According to the Mishnah (Sabbath, II, 6) a woman who neglects any one of these three duties may die in childbirth. Before she kindles the Sabbath lights, the housewife should not only have completed all arrangements for the Sabbath and set out the table, but according to an old custom, should put aside a few coins to be given to the poor as *pidion nefesh* (soul-ransom) and so invoke Divine mercy for herself and her family. When kindling the candles or oil-lamps, she should shut her eyes and recite the prayer "Blessed art Thou, O Lord our God, King of the Universe, who hast sanctified us with His commandments and ordered us to light the Sabbath light." As the Sabbath is supposed to be kept from that moment, usually a little before sundown,[9] a pious Jewess in Baghdad

---

[6]In Europe such boys or men are called *shabbes goyim* (Shabbat Gentiles).

[7]Modern evasion of Sabbath prohibitions may be illustrated by a Jewish anecdote often told in Jerusalem. Travel by land of more than 2,000 cubits from the city boundary and riding in a conveyance are both forbidden. Travel by water is allowed, as a ship at sea cannot call into port every Sabbath. Two ladies sharing the back of a taxi with a Jew noticed on the way from Jerusalem that their neighbour sat uneasily. They discovered that he was sitting on a bottle of water, and he explained when they pressed him to put it elsewhere, that it was a way of turning the Sabbath journey into "travel on water."

[8]Ḥallah (according to my informant): when baking, she should throw a little dough into the oven as an offering to Yahweh. Ṭevīlah is the three-fold immersion after menstruation, childbirth etc. In Baghdad this is done in the house, either that in which she lives or a neighbour's. The older and larger houses in the Jewish quarter have a well in the cellar filled by seepage from the Tigris. In winter it is heated by putting into the water an iron tank (samovar) filled with burning wood. The tank has a chimney to carry off smoke. The well is called the *mikveh*.

[9]It should be about twenty minutes before sundown and the official end of the Sabbath is "when three stars appear." It is customary to add as much time as possible to the holy day. In Baghdad some pious women kindle the lights earlier than about twenty minutes (see Joseph Caro, *Talmud (Schulḥan 'aruch). Auszug enthaltend 100 heutzutage noch geltende, den Verkehr der Juden mit den Christen betreffenden Gesetze der Juden*, ed. E. Alfken, Dresden: A. Uhlig, 1936, I, par. 261, 2) provided that they will stay alight long enough. As a cloud sometimes makes it impossible to terminate the Sabbath by the appearance of three stars, a fixed time has been appointed in Baghdad as the official end, and that is twenty minutes after sunset.

before the benediction extinguishes the match or taper she used to kindle the lights because the Sabbath begins for her at the recital of the blessing, and the lights should go on burning until they go out of themselves. If lamps, they should contain enough vegetable oil to keep alight for three or four hours after dark. When she has recited the blessing, the woman opens her eyes and whispers a private prayer for husband, children and any sick member of the family. She should also move her hands towards the Sabbath light, then stroke her face with them so that the holy light may make her face to shine.[10]

The table is spread with a cloth, and has been carefully prepared for a meal. At the head of the table the housewife has put out the ritual breads, the salt and the goblet for the ritual wine, covering these with a smaller cloth, often embroidered with a Jewish emblem or inscription. The metal goblet is usually of silver and may be an heirloom. Amongst dishes prepared for the non-ritual part of the meal should be fish. Although fish is not considered by purists a ceremonial part of the Sabbath meal, it is customary and its appearance on the Sabbath table, together with that of garlic, is hallowed by ancient tradition.[11] The Rabbinic idea of a feast was fish or meat and fruit with four glasses of wine.

---

[10]This seems to be a purely local custom, and the pious gesture is not confined to Jews. Moslems make a similar movement, viz. of receiving in the palm, then smoothing the face and beard with the open hand after reciting the *Fātiḥah* which is said with palms upward). Similarly, when a Jacobite celebrant flutters his hands above the altar to symbolise the descent of the Holy Spirit, members of the congregation open their palms to receive light from heaven, and smooth their heads and faces with their opened hands.

[11]S. D. Goitein has pointed out to me that the first mention of fish as a Sabbath dish is Neh. xiii, 16, "There dwelt men of Tyre also therein, who brought fish and all manner of ware and sold them on the Sabbath unto the children of Judah and in Jerusalem." Fish and garlic are said by Jews to increase a man's power of procreation. Garlic increases seminal fluid, "...it fosters love and drives away enmity" (Talmud, Bab. K. 82a). The Talmud suggests that the Sabbath eve is an appropriate time for a pious Jew to approach his wife. (See also *Schulḥan 'aruch*, par. 280 and Talmud, Bab. 97b.)

The Qur'an refers to fish as a Sabbath dish, "Then their [the Jews'] fishes appearing on the surface of the water come to them on the day when they celebrate the Sabbath, but on a day wen they do not celebrate the Sabbath, fishes do not come to them" (Sura vii, 163). In Mesopotamia and on the Syrian coast fish were an ancient emblem of fertility, and as such they appear on images on the Nabataean goddess Derceto (Atergatis). According to I. Scheftelowitz, *Alt-Palästinischer Bauernglaube*, Hanover: Lafaire, 1925, p. 87, at a Jewish betrothal in Jerusalem women bring two fish bound together by a golden thread on a silver dish as a symbol of the future fertility of the young couple.

The number of ritual loaves in Baghdad should not be less than two; it is commonly two or four. Jewish mystics use twelve loaves which should be arranged to shape an *aleph*, one set of six lying above the other six. This arrangement symbolizes the mysterious name of God, which may be written but never pronounced. When performing his rite with these, the celebrant takes the middle two top loaves.

In Baghdad flat, round[12] flaps of household bread *(raghīf khubz)* are used, and sometimes a smaller round loaf about four inches thick called *ba'aba* is provided as well. Kurdish Jews prefer *raqīq*, a paper-thin disc of bread like the *marqūq* of the Lebanon. In Jerusalem the number of ritual loaves set on the table is generally two.

Two bunches of myrtle should be placed on the table-cover, "one for *zakor* and one for *shamor*," referring to the two versions of the commandments concerning the Sabbath: – "Remember *(zakor)* the Sabbath day" (Ex. xx, 8) and "Keep" *(shamor)* the Sabbath day to sanctify it" (Deut. v, 12).

Whilst preparations go on at home, the men and boys – for women seldom accompany men to the synagogue[13] – have been to the synagogue or have been engaged in "welcoming the Sabbath bride" in pious fashion with their friends.[14]

Jewish Kabbalists give as their reason for eating fish on Sabbath eve, that the souls of pious people pass into fish after death and that the benedictions help their progress, that is, the *tikkun* of their souls (see R. Abraham ben Raphael Halfon, *Hayyē Abraham*, Livorno, 1857, p. 37).

[12]The fashion in which women throughout the East flatten out a round ball of dough results naturally in a round loaf.

[13]In Oriental countries little is expected by Jews of their women in the way of public worship: their religious duties are chiefly at home. This is a traditional attitude towards the sex, nor is it peculiar to Jews. Moslems, Mandaeans and Zoroastrians in the Middle East tend to regard women as the "weaker vessel," also as a possible cause of pollution. In the Temple there was a women's Court where the women sat in a gallery, and in the Jewish synagogues women generally sit in the gallery. In the Mishnah, Berakhot iii, 3 we find, "Women, slaves and children are released from reading the *Shema'* and from the *Tefillin*, but are bound to the *Tefilla* (Eighteen Benedictions), to the *mezuzah* and the grace at the table." In Talmud, Hagiga i,1, the context is less flattering to the sex, "Every one is bound to appear in the temple at the chief feasts, except the deaf, idiots, children, persons of doubtful sex, hermaphrodites, women, unemancipated slaves, the lame, blind, sick, infirm and generally those unable to walk."

[14]In Baghdad, as elsewhere, Jewish mystics under the influence of the Safed Kabbalists of the 16th century (see I. Elbogen, *Der jüdische Gottesdienst in seiner geschichtlichen Entwicklung*, Frankfurt am Main: J. Kauffmann, 1931, p. 108 and G. Scholem, *Major Trends in Jewish Mysticism*, Jerusalem: Schocken, 1941, 7th lecture) perform the ceremony of "welcoming the Sabbath Bride" or "Queen Sabbath." This may be performed by any number of men. It begins at

When the master of the house re-enters, he should go directly to the spot where the Ķiddush is to be celebrated. The family stands grouped round the table whilst the father greets all present with *"Shabbath shalom"!* Some take a turn round the table holding the two bunches of myrtle in his right hand, and when again at the head of the table, he joins the two bunches together with the words *"zakor"* and *"shamor"* (see above) "said as one." Kabbalists maintain that this union is symbolic of the holy union of "Father and Mother," i.e. of the positive and negative aspects of developing creation, the expression into Being of non-Being.

He recites a prayer of welcome to the angels supposed to be gathering round the table, and then Prov. xxxi, 10-31.[15] He and all males present must wear a cap or other head-covering: women need not be covered. It is the duty of the housewife, or her representative, to fill the ritual goblet: the son should lift it from the table and hand it respectfully to his father with the greeting *"Kavod,"* or, sometimes *"Shabbath Shalom."*

The wine is usually either commercial wine, or some water in which raisins or grapes have been previously placed and squeezed (see Talmud, Baba B 97 b), at least this is so in old-fashioned Jewish houses in Iraq. There is, however, increasing use of locally made fermented wine, especially in Europeanized circles. The custom of adding a little water to the ritual wine has lapsed in Iraq but if the wine is commercially procured, the housewife generally dilutes it beforehand with water. Dilution was practised in Palestine at the time of Christ and is referred to in the Mishnah (see Berakoth vii, 5 and viii, 2).[16]

---

home an hour or so before sunset by chanting the Song of Songs in praise of the Bride. They then go to the open country and, as the sun sinks, stand facing the west with arms folded across the breast and eyes closed and recite Ps. xxix, *piūṭim* and the hymn of the Kabbalist R. Solomon al-Kabeṣ Halevi, "Come, my beloved, to greet the Bride and receive the presence of the Sabbath," which ends, "Come, O Thou Bride" (twice), "Queen Sabbath." When reciting the last verse each man turns his face left and right, ending with a bow forward. (See E. Joseph Haim, *Ben Ish Hai*, 2nd year, p. 13, a book on Jewish ritual in which many customs and rites peculiar to Iraq are described. Haim died in 1907.)

[15]The twenty-two verses of this hymn, according to the Zohar, represent twenty-two sources of grace and wealth.

[16]In Jerusalem I saw it twice performed at Ķiddush. Brauer makes no mention of adding water to the wine in his book about Yemenite Jews (see note 4, above), perhaps because they squeeze raisins or grapes into water just before the ceremony, like the Baghdadi Jews. When I attended Yemeni New Year's Eve, however, commixture was performed and they told me that it was a Sabbath custom with Yemenites. Kurdish Jews do so during the ritual only at Passover.

The *Kiddush* starts with the recital of Ps. xxiii ("The Lord is my shepherd"), then the first three verses of Gen. ii, "Thus the heavens and the earth were finished." The Grace comes next,

> Blessed art Thou, O Lord, our God, King of the Universe, who hast sanctified us by His commandments and chose us from amongst all nations and gave us with loving kindness the Sabbath as the head of all festivals in remembrance of the Creation and the exodus from Egypt....Blessed art Thou, O Lord, who sanctified the Sabbath.

The celebrant sips from the goblet, then passes it on to all present, women included, each sipping from it before handing it to the next person at the table. On receiving the *Kiddush*-cup[17] the recipient should kiss the hand of the giver. After the wine has passed round, the celebrant washes his hands, pouring water over each hand alternately thrice and beginning with the right. Next he lifts up two loaves, placing them oven-side to oven-side. In Jerusalem and in the Yemen[18] they are held vertically, in Iraq horizontally. The celebrant places one on each hand and repeats the blessing, "Blessed art Thou, o Lord, our God, King of the Universe, who bringeth forth bread from the earth."

He replaces them so that the loaf which had been uppermost is beneath, in preparation for the breaking. Old-fashioned Oriental Jews view with horror any use of a knife for the division, and explain that the table that night is an altar and since no cutting instrument should come near an altar (Ex. xx, 25), bread should be broken by hand. The celebrant dips the small piece which he has broken off thrice into the salt and eats it, then breaks off pieces for those at the table, dipping each into salt.[19] The bread is distributed in order of age and

---

[17] It is only on Passover eve that each member of the family has his or her own cup. At a Sabbath eve ceremony in Jerusalem at which I was present, the ritual wine was poured into small cups round the table, a Western innovation for the sake of hygiene.

[18] "He takes two flat loaves, puts them together and holds them between the spread fingers of both hands" (Brauer, p. 310).

[19] The Talmud, likening the table to an altar and the food to the meat-offering, quotes Lev. ii,13 as the reason for ritual salt, "Neither shalt thou suffer the salt of the covenant of thy God to be lacking from thy meat-offering: with all thine offerings thou shalt offer salt." Babylonians believed that the god Enlil ordained salt (*ṭabtu*) for food-offerings. Salt was an ingredient of Babylonian ritual bread, as it is of the Mandaean *pihta*, and salt is placed on the Mandaean *ṭariana* for the Blessed Oblation and other ritual meals. Salt is both strewn and melted during exorcism of evil spirits by Mandaeans, Moslems and Jews. A person thought to possess the "evil eye" is called "salt-eyed" by Iraqi Jews as a protective formula, and to protect a child or an object from baleful glances, salt is carried round the head of the child or round the object which

importance. When all have eaten, the secular part of the meal begins. It should include at least two different courses.

'Araq and other liquors are circulated, and special songs should be chanted to celebrate the advent of the *neshamah yetherah* (in Baghdad *neshamah yethīrah*) – the "Sabbath soul." A pious man should never discuss business during the Sabbath, nor should he say "next week I shall do such-and-such." Should such a remark escape him he should add instantly *"Bila qōl al-Shabbath!"*[20]

At the end of the meal grace is recited by the master of the house. Before he pronounces it, he must perform a ritual ablution, this time washing only the finger-tips. Care should be taken lest water thus used (*netilath yadayim*) fall to the ground, for this brings misfortune. It should be poured directly into a drain, not cast outside on the ground.

The benediction at the end of the Sabbath day is called the *Havdalah*. In Baghdad it has become customary to perform the ritual in the synagogue. When lighting the *Havdalah* torch, the *hazzan* obtains light from one of the oil-lamps kept perpetually alight in the synagogue in memory of some dead person. When kindling the wick, he holds a bunch of myrtle in his left hand. He recites benediction on the wine, and then, inhaling its fragrance, on the myrtle, and thirdly on the light. He must look at his finger-nails whilst pronouncing the blessing on God who separated light from darkness, the holy-day from week-days and Israel from Gentiles.[21] After the benedictions, he drinks a little of the wine and passes the cup to those nearest, who also drink. In Baghdad a *hazzan* does not consume all the wine in the goblet. When those near him have sipped wine, some of the remainder is dropped on the ground, whilst he recites "And I shall pour on you blessing without end."

---

invites envy. Salt is often put into the pocket of a new suit for this reason, and if it is not available, the word "salt" is introduced into conversation.

[20] Referring to Isa. lviii,13," If thou turn away thy foot from the Sabbath, from doing thy pleasure on my holy day..." (*Bila qōl al-Shabbath* is as much as to say apologetically, "Sabbath talk apart...").

[21] A *Pazend* prayer thanks God, amongst other favours acknowledged, "for having been born an *A'ir* (Iranian) and not a non-Iranian," for "having been born a male and not a female," for "having been born free and not a bondsman." The list of favours in the *Pazend* thanksgiving includes the blessing of light, creation, vegetation and so on. This is close to the Jewish prayer *Birkhoth Ha-Shahar* translated in S. Singer's Jewish prayerbook, *The Authorized Daily Prayer Book of the United Hebrew Congregations of the British Empire*, London: Eyre and Spottiswoode, 1944, "Blessed be the Eternal, our God, Master of the Universe, who has not caused me to be born an idolater...nor born a slave...nor born a woman."

A Jewish friend in Baghdad told me that when a boy, he used to run home from the synagogue as soon as the rite was over to tell his mother to kindle the household lights, while his elders followed soberly, arriving as the evening meal was ready. In most Oriental Jewish communities *Havdalah* is a family ritual. Yemenite Jews (Brauer, op. cit. p. 317) go home to kindle their own *Havdalah* light, obtaining the fire from still hot embers in the oven. The reason given for looking at the finger-nails as described above is that the light gleams on them as the curved fingers shade the palm, illustrating light and darkness. Benedictions over the *Havdalah* wine, myrtle[22] and light are performed as elsewhere, but a Yemeni celebrant pours a little wine over his right hand and wets his forehead with it. When he and his male children have drunk – for women do not partake of the *Havdalah* cup – he extinguishes the *Havdalah* light with the rest of the wine. This is done in Iraq also, but not in Kurdistan where it is blown out.

The restriction which deprives women from drinking *Havdalah* wine, is a punishment inflicted on women for the sin of Eve, who crushed some grapes from the forbidden tree, here supposed the vine, for Adam to drink; a sin which resulted in the curse of menstruation.[23] The passage is interesting in associating wine with the blood of the womb.[24]

The reason commonly given for inhalation by Jews is that the perfume strengthens a man for the departure of the Sabbath soul, or else that, when the Sabbath soul is fetched back to Heaven by welcoming angels, the perfume of myrtle serves to remove the taint of earth which clings to her after her earthly sojourn. The conflicting nature of these explanations suggests that the reason for inhalation is unknown. The *Zidqa brikha* ("Blessed Oblation") of the Mandaeans combine the ritual breaking of bread and drinking of *hamra* with inhalation and a meal, like the *Havdalah*, and during the myrtle ceremony, the myrtle is distributed to the priests taking part who place the sprigs in their turbans. Similarly, when Iraqi Jews return home from the synagogue after the *Havdalah* they bring with them sprigs of the myrtle over which the blessing was read and give them to the women of the

---

[22] In Europe a spice-box replaces the myrtle.
[23] *Shenē luḥoth ha-berith*, fol. 139b, Amsterdam, 1644.
[24] In the Oriental mass the cup is the symbol of the Virgin's womb; and the *hamra*-cup at the Mandaean *masiqta* is called "the womb of the Mother."

household, who place them in their headdresses and hair, whilst the men put myrtle in their hats for the rest of the evening.[25]

The Jewish close of the Sabbath is dedicated to Elijah. A long hymn in honor of this prophet is chanted before the *Havdalah* ritual begins. During the evening meal songs and poems relating to the feats of Elijah are sung in Hebrew and Arabic, and it is commonly believed in Iraq that this "ever-living one" visits every Jewish home that night to bless it with a benediction known as *birkat Eliahu ha-nabi*, "the Blessing of the prophet Elijah."[26] As it is believed that the dead undergoing punishment are granted respite from torment during the Sabbath, *Havdalah* is postponed as late as possible by some compassionate Jews. Elijah is looked on as a mediator for and helper of the dead.

A curious tradition about the meal may be mentioned for, though found only in a late source, the Zohar, it may be founded, like much else in that book, on popular belief. The supper is supposedly graced by the "Sabbath soul" who lingers till the last crumb is eaten before taking to flight.

Lastly, the *Havdalah* meal is said to strengthen a certain bone at the base of the neck, called by Baghdad rabbis the *neskoi*,[27] which is only nourished by the weekly *Havdalah* food. When a man dies and his bones moulder, this bone resists decomposition and becomes the seed of a new body at the Resurrection.[28]

---

[25] Myrtle used at *Havdalah* should not be dropped or cast down. Its use in Iraq for this ceremony is obligatory; elsewhere some Oriental Jews use sweet-smelling spices, or fragrant fruit.

[26] Some Jews will not keep a dog, lest its barking unclean presence should keep the prophet away. If a Baghdad Jewess is running short of flour in her bin, she may reply hopefully, "*Barakhath Eliahu an-Nebi,*" meaning that her supply will last out. The reference here is to I Kg. xviii, 8ff.

[27] Also called the *lūz*. This belief is mentioned by R. Joseph Haim, *Ben Ish Hai*, vol. III, 1912, p. 24.

[28] The idea that bones, or certain bones, are the seed of a "resurrection body" is found also in ancient Persia. The Zoroastrian saviour, the Saoshyant, who is to bring about the resurrection, is called also *Astvatereta*, "He who causes bones to arise" (cf. Ezek. xxviii, 3, "Son of man, can these bones live?"). The Zoroastrians' practice of keeping bones in ossuaries arose from the belief (which is also a Hebrew tradition) that revivification of the physical body after death depended on the preservation of bones, although the custom is now obsolete. It seems that in early times the Persians, after exposing corpses to birds of prey and wild beasts, collected the bones and kept them in *astodans*, ossuaries, believing them the seed of new bodies. This conception, filtering through Judaism to Christianity, led to materialistic theories of the early Church concerning the resurrection of the body. St. Paul (Rm. viii, 11) is at pains to explain that the resurrection body is a spiritual body. In this passage

ii. New Year: *Rosh Hashana*

By a fortunate chance I found myself in Jerusalem at the Jewish New Year, September 1943. Jewish acquaintances in the city exerted themselves to enable me to witness as many as possible of the ceremonies and customs of various immigrant Jewish communities representative of surrounding countries. To ask to see a Jewish domestic rite is, in effect, to seek an invitation to dinner, and this was a time when food was rationed and dear. I need have felt no embarrassment, for Jewish hospitality is traditionally generous to the "stranger that is within thy gates."

On New Year's Eve, that is to say on the eve of the first of Tishri,[29] I was taken to a synagogue belonging to Jews of Bokhara during evening prayer. As a woman, I sat in the screened-off partition at the back, where two white-clad Bokharan Jewesses sat cross-legged on wide benches, rocking themselves and reading from their Hebrew prayer-books. Through the lattice we could see the men beyond the partition, who were also chanting and swaying to and fro. They wore white, for many devout Jews wear their shrouds at this season and on the Day of Atonement. The young men wore hats: their elders looked more dignified in turbans.

From this place we went directly to the house of the chief rabbi of the Sephardic community, who was also robed in his shroud. He received us with kindly courtesy and explained that I was to be his guest only for the ritual part of the New Year's Eve meal, and that we had been specially invited that evening to the house of a Yemenite Jew,

---

(vs. 37 and elsewhere) his metaphor comparing burial to grain down in the ground is suggestive. Nevertheless, as is seen in the writings of some early fathers of the Church, "the resurrection of the flesh" remained a very literal belief, indeed it still survives.

[29]Whilst the Jewish calendar lists the months from Nisan (about April), the secular year begins on the first of Tishri, the seventh month, opening with a "memorial of blowing of trumpets" (Lev. xxiii, 24). Under Assyrian influence the beginning of the year came to be reckoned in spring. In the 6th century a celebration of the New Year, associated with the Day of Judgment, was regularly observed. Up to the development of the Diaspora in many lands the observance lasted one day; later it was extended to two. Orthodox Jews begin the preparation for the *yamim moraim* from the new moon of Elul, thirty days before *Rosh Hashanah* (New Year's day) by reciting the *seliḥoth* at dawn, these being prayers pleading for forgiveness and for the end of Israel's oppression. During the thirty days of Elul, Jewish mystics read a part of the Zohar called *Tikkunim* (restorations) for the benefit of souls in a state of transmigration (*gilgul neshamot*).

where we should participate in both ritual meal and the supper which follows it.

The ritual lights, two candles, had been kindled at sunset by his wife, and we joined in the usual benediction over wine. This was poured into a goblet, a little water was added, and the mixture was drunk by all round the table. The celebrant washed his hands, pronounced the blessing over two loaves held vertically between his hands, broke a piece from one, dipped it in salt, ate it and then distributed small pieces dipped in salt in the usual way.

Now began that which distinguished this meal from others. Small dishes containing the fruits to be eaten ritually stood on the table, and benediction was pronounced over each of these in turn, the celebrant eating his portion and the guests theirs before the next benediction was pronounced. First came a piece of apple dipped in honey, then pieces of pumpkin, a date and a piece of quince. The quince was a "new fruit," for at this festival it is obligatory to eat ritually of a fruit eaten for the first time that season. A fish's head lay on the platter: a "head" (of a fish or sheep) must figure at the secular meal.

Expressing our gratitude and leaving our hosts to enjoy their festal supper, we walked (for no other vehicle may be used on holy days) to a poor quarter of the new city. In the dark of the black-out we found a narrow street, a gutter running down its center, still wet and shining, for it and every house in it had been cleansed for the feast. Our host met us; he had come out to look for us as it was late. Like Joseph of Nazareth, our Yemenite host was a carpenter by trade, an intelligent and devout man who delighted in explaining every step in the ritual and expounding its meaning. Like those of his neighbors, his little house had been thoroughly scoured and cleaned, together with all the pots, pans and dishes. Metal cooking pots must be well-scalded and scrupulously cleansed at this season, also before Passover, and for a Jewish housewife this means that pots used for milky foods and those for meat are cleansed separately, for they must never come into contact.[30]

The ritual light gleamed from a glass bowl suspended from the ceiling: it contained olive-oil in which a long wick was laid. The table, upon which a white cloth was spread, was already furnished with the various ritual dishes and the two ritual breads were veiled by a small while cloth embroidered with religious emblems. Our host told us that

---

[30]Because of the injunction forbidding seething a kid in its mother's milk. This was a Canaanite rite and is described in a Ras Shamra text, "The Birth of the Beautiful and Gracious Gods" (see, Ch. Virolleaud, "La naissance des dieux gracieux et beaux," *Syria* 14, 1933).

in the Yemen it was customary to place greenery – myrtle or other foliage – round the table. Here I shall transcribe from notes taken at the time:

> The father took his place at the head of the table, pouring the ritual wine into a goblet, whilst his eldest boy, standing at his right, held a flask of water, a little of which was to be added to the wine. When the celebrant had drunk and the cup had been passed to all, all at the table rose and washed and dried their hands following the example of the master of the house.
>
> After our return to the table, the upper cloth was removed and the smaller veil, so that now the loaves were disclosed. The loaves, large, round and leavened, were in the centre, and our host told us that the roundness symbolised the perfection of the coming year. An auspicious meaning is attached to every ritual food eaten that evening, or to its name, e.g. the year is to be as sweet as the honey in which the apple is dipped. One of the company informed me that the apple represents the male principle of justice, honey the female principle which tempers justice with sweetness. Another quoted the Song of Solomon.[31]
>
> The breaking of bread followed, and in this household the salt into which every piece was dipped was mingled with sugar. Then came the apple dipped in honey, cooked leeks[32] and cooked spinach-beet (*silk*) and the proper benedictions for each was said before they were eaten. Our host said that in the Yemen on this occasion both these vegetables are eaten raw. Cooked *gara*, pumpkin mashed and flavoured with cinnamon, followed; next dates, each person eating a single date after the benediction, and then pomegranate seeds.

At the end of the ritual blessings and eating of the fruit and vegetables, secular food was brought in by the carpenter's wife, and no benediction was said over any part of this. Fish was the first course, then beans (*lūbia*) and the third course was chicken served with a spicy soup.

> Our host and his sons dipped into a saucer the famous Yemenite relish called *hilbah* compounded of many spices and condiments such as red pepper and cloves. Finally, a sheep's head, the traditional climax of the feast, was set on the table.
>
> Fruit was handed round as dessert after which plates were removed, leaving only the dishes of ritual food, re-covered with the upper cloth.

---

[31] There are references in the Song of Solomon to the apple (ii.3) and to honey (iv, 11): "As the apple-tree among the trees of the woods, so is my beloved" and "Thy lips, O my spouse, drop the honey-comb, honey and milk are under thy tongue." Quotations of verses to explain ritual does not imply that the customs originated in the verses, however.

[32] For instance, the leek is said to refer to the root KRT, "to cut," meaning: "our enemies shall be cut off."

After readings and hymns this too was removed, every person touching the cloth with reverent finger-tips which were carried to their lips. The wife, meanwhile, was washing plates and dishes. When she rejoined us and a hymn had been sung, one of the younger sons carefully collected the bread left on the table, kissed it and put it away. Lastly, the master of the house washed his hands again, and when a psalm had been recited, he said the grace.

The ritual on the second night of the feast is the same as that on the Eve. After the service in the synagogue, the day is spent in visiting friends and relatives. On the second night I was again invited, this time to the house of one of the Ashkenazi community. My host was a scholar of European reputation. Ashkenazim observe the usual rules concerning the ritual lights, but pour no water into the wine for Kiddush. The differences in the New Year ritual at table were small. Our host did not break, but cut the bread after holding two rounds together in the usual way, and when he ate his own piece and distributed pieces to those at table, he did not first dip the bread into salt or sugar. The eating and benediction of the various fruits and vegetables began with a date, and there was a fruit eaten for the first time in its season.[33] At the secular meal fish was eaten, and other dishes, and the repast concluded in the traditional way with the "head." Towards the end of the meal the father observed the charming ceremony of blessing his children, one by one, but I was told that this should have been performed before the Kiddush. Psalms and hymns were chanted, and when we rose from table the host washed his hands.

On the first day of the New Year I went with a friend to visit some of the synagogues in the Old City.[34] We went first to a tiny upper room used as a synagogue by Kabbalists. These form an exclusive group in the city and admit fresh adherents with reluctance. No women were allowed within, and so we looked in from windows on the flat terrace outside. Most of those present were aged and elderly and their white beards and reverend appearances lent dignity to the assembly. The room, which had windows on the east and west, was full of light and its interior was furnished simply. Low benches covered with carpets were ranged round the walls, and upon these some stood throughout, their slippers on the floor beside them. Most of them wore their white

---

[33] It is obligatory to eat a new fruit for the first time on the second night, but it has become customary with Sephardic and most Oriental Jews to eat it on the first night.

[34] These synagogues are now, of course, in the Arab quarter. My visit took place before the Mandate was ended.

shrouds, and handsome praying shawls[35] draped over the scarlet fezes and the turbans on their heads, fell down over their shoulders. These shawls, some of thick silk, were striped black and white with a blue patch at one corner.[36]

When we arrived, the *Tefilla* (*'Amidah*)[37] was being recited silently. At the beginning and end of certain blessings every man bowed. Not a sound was heard throughout and this sunlit silence, broken only by the ticking of the clock hung on a wall and the occasional voice or laughter of a child outside, was singularly impressive. The *ḥazzan* (the precentor) and his assistant stood in the middle of the room: upon the desk before them a scroll of the Law was displayed in a handsome folding case.

When the moment arrived for the blowing of the ram's horn, the *shofar*, it was the *ḥazzan* who sounded it. The *shofar* is blown in several prescribed variations, such as a single long blast, several notes repeated staccato, a low blast carried up glissando to a higher octave, and so on. These are called *teru'oth* or *teḥi'oth*. After each variation there was a pause for meditation whilst the worshippers rocked their bodies in silence. Mystics claim to discover deep inspiration in these uncouth sounds.[38] Hoarse and rusty, echoing as it were out of a vast and

---

[35]The *ṣiṣith* (pl. *ṣiṣioth*) were tassels or a fringe of hyacinth blue or white wool which every Israelite had to wear at the four corners of his upper garment (Num xv, 37 *et seq.* and Deut xxii,12.) (See E. Schürer, *A History of the Jewish People in the Time of Christ*, Edinburgh: T & T Clark, div. ii, vol. ii, p. 112.) The praying shawl (*ṭallith*) used in Iraq is usually of white silk striped with blue or black, with fringes at the four corners. A benediction is recited when putting it on. The large praying-shawl is worn at morning-prayer and placed over the head-dress; the other is a miniature, with the sacred thread attached at each corner. This "sacred thread," which is of pure linen, is always hidden, but worn over the shirt and not next to the skin. This Jewish "sacred thread" recalls that of the Parsis, which is, however, a thin woolen girdle worn beneath the clothes.

[36]The sky-blue patch on the praying shawl may represent "something blue," which in many lands invokes celestial protection. The English bride, the Arab mother who sews on a blue bead, the Mandaean scrap of blue, or blue garment placed over the initiation hut (see E. S. Drower, *The Mandaeans of Iraq and Iran*, Leiden: Brill 1937, p. 149-50) are examples of this very common way of protecting anything fair and enviable. A popular Jewish saying in Baghdad to describe a person without fault is, "he is all blue," which refers to the blue patch on the *ṭallith*.

[37]The *Tefillah* or *'Amidah* is also known as the "Prayer of Eighteen Benedictions" (see note 13, above). In fact, these are nineteen in number, and on festivals and Sabbaths seven. On New Year's Day they are nine.

[38]I was reminded on hearing the *shofar* of the Yazidi custom of sounding a shrill note on a pipe before a tomb at the spring festival. This is followed by a ritual dance (see E. S. Drower, *Peacock Angel*, London: John Murray, 1941, p.

distant past, they seem to speak of ancestors long mingled with the dust, who tended their flocks on Mesopotamian plains and Canaanite hills.

This Quakerish conventicle was very different from the synagogue which we visited next that morning. It was a large, grimy, untidy and somewhat dilapidated Ashkenazi building. Elder women in the gallery made no attempt to restrain the noise of the children or the chatter of younger Jewesses. They appeared devout, and, despite the din about them, bowed their grey heads to their books and often wept, apparently with little regard to what was being chanted below by the men.

On New Year's Eve in Iraq Jews put on white garments, but not shrouds, after they have bathed in the ritual pool (*miḳveh*); then they go to the synagogue for evening prayers whilst the housewife lights the New Year candles or lamps, as on Sabbath eve. I was never in Baghdad for the Jewish New Year, and was given a description of it by Mr. Ezra Haddad in the following words:

> On the day preceding *Rosh Hashanah* Jews, young and old, with a good proportion of women-folk, throng the synagogue for the *Seliḥoth pidion nefesh* (soul ransom) and morning prayers. Money is distributed lavishly to the poor and many families sacrifice a lamb before sunrise as ransom for their welfare in the New Year. After the morning service the *Hattarat Nedarim* (annulment of religious vows) is recited by three members of the congregation who form a temporary *Beth Din* (court of justice).
>
> Then thousands of Jews of every age crowd to the roads leading to the Jewish cemetery, where a special memorial service and the *Ḳaddish* are recited for the dead. All that day housewives prepare for the New Year's ritual feast. The men return to find the ritual lights kindled at sunset burning and all set for the meal. The house has been scrubbed; there are white seats round a ritual table on which the two ritual loaves are covered with a white cloth. Members of the family, their faces smiling, greet one another with *le shanah ṭovah* (for a good year). The *Ḳiddush* over the cup of wine is recited with special reference to the Day of Memorial and the Day of the Blowing of the Ram's Horn. Then come the ritual washing of hands and the breaking of bread. Great care is taken lest any sour food be eaten at this season: the morsels of ritual bread usually dipped in salt should at this meal be dipped in sugar, for sweet things are of good augury. The ritual dishes should include special dishes: fresh dates, *lūbia* (beans), leek, boiled *silḳ* (spinach beet), pomegranate, apples sweetened with honey, medlar and cooked ram's head.

---

130). Simple Jews believe that the horn is blown to attract the attention of the Almighty. The Talmud gives another explanation.

I was told also that on New Year's Day Baghdadi Jews attend the synagogue two hours before the morning service to recite the *Aḳedhah* (Sacrifice of Isaac), a composition in prose and verse relating the Bible story and the Haggadah (legend woven around it), the recitation being both in Hebrew and in colloquial Jewish Arabic. The use of the ram's horn at New Year is traditionally related to the sacrifice of Isaac. It is blown at the morning service after the reading from the Scriptures. The first three blasts are listened to seated, the others are blown during the 'Amidah. The service is concluded by the "great blast" (*teru'ah gedolah*). The rest of the day is devoted to reading the Torah and to penitence.

After the morning *Ḳiddush* and breakfast, men gather in groups of ten or more and recite the Psalms. When the reading is complete, three kinds of food, bread, fruit and vegetables, are distributed to the company, benedictions are said over them and a *Hashkavah*[39] for the dead is recited. After midday service (*Minḥah*) it is customary to perform the *tashlikh* ("casting off") of sin, a rite representing "Thou wilt cast all their sins into the depth of the sea" (Micah vii, 19). It is performed in the synagogue beside a pool containing seepage from the Tigris. Whilst reading appropriate verses and penitential psalms, each man shakes the end of his garments at the edge of the pool as if casting away his sins. The custom, once practised also in Europe,[40] is of uncertain origin, but is first mentioned by Jacop Halevi Mölln in the 15th century.

The second day of the New Year, except for the *tashlikh*, is observed in a manner similar to the first. The first ten days of the first month of the year are called the Ten Days of Repentance. The third of Tishri commemorates the assassinated governor of Judah, Gedaliah, son of Aḥikam, and is a fast.[41] During the ten days religious Jews abstain from indulgence in food, drink and other bodily pleasures. Appropriate psalms and *Abhinu Malkenu* (Our Father the King), an eleventh-century liturgy, are added to the daily service and the *Seliḥoth*[42] are recited at dawn.

---

[39] A service and prayer of requiem (see section iii, below).
[40] According to the *Jewish Encyclopaedia*, strictly orthodox Jews throw crumbs of bread into rivers and streams. The *tashlikh* is mentioned in the Zohar, Lev. 101, a-b.
[41] Five fasts in the Jewish calendar commemorate national calamities.
[42] See note 29, above.

iii. The Day of Atonement *(Yom Kippur)* and the Feast of Tabernacles

Preparation for the Day of Atonement, which is the culmination of these first ten days of solemnity in the New Year, starts on the eve. On the morning of the eve the Jews of Iraq, Kurdistan and other countries should sacrifice a white cock for every male, and a white hen for every female in the house. Up to a time when the market prices became so high that the very poor could not afford the sacrifice,[43] this was always performed in Iraq. For a pregnant woman two hens and a cock were sacrificed, since her children might be of either sex. Scores of Jewish slaughterers used to go round the Jewish quarter in Baghdad, collecting birds for slaughter. In most simple homes it was believed that the sins of the family were transferred to the birds. The family ate the sacrificed fowls, for a Jew should fortify himself before fasting by eating seven times. In Iraq it was the custom that a young boy or girl should present the fowl killed in his or her name to the woman who had nursed him or her when an infant.[44] Europeanised Jews sometimes presented the fowls to the poor.

After the fowls had been sacrificed, people hurried to the synagogue for the *Seliḥoth*, morning service and *Ḥattarath Nedarim*, and thence a stream of mourners went to the Jewish cemetery where, as on New Year's Eve, they prayed for departed members of the family.

At noon all business activities ceased: shutters were up in Jewish shops, and every Jew prepared himself solemnly for the Great Fast. Women remained at home. The *Minḥah* service in the synagogue began about 3 p.m., and it finished with the *malkuth* (flagellation), a practice which has, apparently, died out in more Europeanised Middle Eastern circles, such as Egypt. About two hours before sunset, pious Jews at the synagogue stripped themselves to the waist and presented themselves to the *ḥazzans*. This official stood near a wooden pole or whipping post attached to the wall of the synagogues. The penitent, who faced north or south but never east or west, leant on the post and covered his head with his arms, whilst the *ḥazzan*'s assistant, standing by, bid him, "Remember, the right over the left!"[45]

The *ḥazzan* used a curious whip for the flagellation: it was a flat scourge of sheep-skin sewn together with donkey-skin thongs and mounted in a wooden handle. It was surmounted by two narrow flaps of

---

[43] Money may now be substituted.
[44] If the nurse lives with the family, on a Seder night her nurslings give her eggs.
[45] Zoroastrians and Mandaeans associate the right with spirit and the left with matter, also, respectively, with the male and female principle of creation. The identification is found in Gnostic literature.

bull-skin and ass-skin.[46] The *ḥazzan* administered thirty-nine (thrice thirteen) strokes,[47] first on the left shoulder, then on the right and finally on the middle of the back. Whilst these were applied, the penitent confessed his sins in a low voice and the *ḥazzan* recited three times Psalm lxxviii, 38, the number of Hebrew words being thirteen. As each man's ordeal was over, he returned to his house, washed and then immersed himself in a well of "flowing" water, the ritual bath or *miḳveh*. Kurdish Jews plunge beneath the surface of a river or stream.

Before sitting down to the solid meal which follows their bath in the *miḳveh*, the men put on snow-white garments. On the eve of Yom Kippur it is an old custom to visit as many friends as possible and especially those with whom there has been disagreement, and to ask forgiveness for any injury which may have been done, whether wittingly or unwittingly, since unforgiven hurt of others hinders the forgiveness of God.[48] Before evening service[49] the *ḥazzan* cries out in the synagogue, "My masters, have ye forgiven one another?" and the congregation answer as one man, "We have forgiven."

---

[46] A rabbi in Baghdad objected to this description, saying that the scourge should be of bull's skin with flaps of ass-skin, so as to agree with Isa. i,3," The ox knoweth his owner and the ass his master's crib." The scourge was described and sketched for me by one whose accuracy I found usually unimpeachable. The bull, ass and sheep-skin suggest a fertility-rite, for the three represent a humble farmer's stock-in-trade. Flagellation is a well-known form of fertility magic. On the eve of Passover, Baghdadi Jews used to strike the *ḥazzan* lightly with a leek, green vegetable or herb, saying, *"Shena khadhera"* (A green year). Kurdish Jews did the same at Tabernacles. At the latter feast the ground is beaten with willow-twigs.

[47] It is customary to stop short of the forty strokes allowed by Mosaic law even in the Talmudic period.

[48] Moslems believe that a man cannot die without the forgiveness of those he has injured.

[49] The service begins with *Kol Nidre* (All vows) recited in Aramaic, and during the recitation seven scrolls of the Law are carried by seven members of the congregation, one of whom recites the *Sheheḥeyanu* benediction,"Blessed art Thou, O Lord, King of the Universe, who hast preserved us and kept us unto this day." The *ḥazzan* recites a prayer for the reigning rule, the scrolls are replaced and the evening prayer proceed. (The *Kol Nidre* annuls any vows between man and God which because of human frailty may not have been possible to carry out, but commitments to fellow-men are kept. Its origin, according to S. Krauss, *Das Problem Kol Nidre*, Frankfurt am Main: Buchdr. D. Droller, 1928, seems to lie in the ceremonial used in a lawcourt in connection with vows.)

In Kurdistan the large *Havdalah* candle used in synagogues from Yom Kippur to Purim is made of candle ends melted down by the *shammash* and moulded into a single candle. Candles used at Purim are collected to form another tall *Havdalah* candle.

There are five services on the Day of Atonement including that of the eve: the morning service starts at dawn. The final service is the *Neilah (Neilath She'arim)*, the "closing of the gates," at which the *shofar* is blown to signal the end of the feast. The *Havdalah* ceremony is performed in the synagogue before the men return to their homes where the table is set, as on the eve of the Sabbath, with ritual wine, bread and myrtle.

The Feast of Tabernacles is celebrated on the fifth day after the Day of Atonement and usually falls in the last week of September or during the first fortnight of October. The calendar is regulated so that Yom Kippur cannot occur on a Friday or a Sunday: nor can the first day of Tabernacles fall on a Friday. It is the last of three great festivals called Festivals of Pilgrimage: these are Passover, which according to rabbinical teaching commemorates Exodus; Pentecost – the giving of the Law; and Tabernacles – the sojourn in the wilderness.

In Canaan the feast coincided with the local vintage festival. The booth of tabernacle *(sukkah)* gives its name of Sukkoth to the feast. According to Jewish tradition it is the *lulab* used at the feast which is described in Lev. xxiii, 40 as made of "palm-trees, boughs of thick trees and willows of the brook," but the description suits better the Oriental version of the booth itself. The chief feature of Tabernacles is the construction of and camping out in the *sukkah*. Its building is carefully described in the Mishnah, Tosefta and the two Talmuds (Jerusalem and Babylonian). It may not be a lean-to structure and must be a lightly constructed wooden building with a trellis roof leaving the sky visible within. In such countries as Palestine and Iraq living and sleeping in the *sukkah* entail small discomfort, for the festival comes before the first autumn rains, although an early shower may sometimes fall.

The second day of Tabernacles was anciently known as the "Feast of Water-Drawing" (Mishnah, Sukkah, iv, 9, 10) because on that day the priest poured his libation of water and wine on the altar at the Temple, a rite intended probably to bring down rain and a good season.[50] A popular saying in Baghdad runs: "The first shower of rain always falls during the feast of the Jews." On the seventh day a prayer for rain is recited in the synagogues. Arabs in Iraq call the *sukkah* an *'arzulah*[51] and the feast *'Id-ul-'Arāzīl*, and believe that the Jews build them to

---

[50] See S. H. Hooke, ed., *Myth and ritual; essays on the myth and ritual of the Hebrews in relation to the culture pattern of the ancient East*, Oxford: Oxford University Press, 1933, p. 138.

[51]In Syria and Palestine the small hut of boughs raised on a platform or built in a tree in which the owner of a fruit-garden or vineyard – or his watch-man – sleeps at night when the picking season is on, is called an *'arzal*. From this hut the watcher is able to keep a look-out for marauders.

draw down rain and that they may not be removed until they have been wetted by raindrops. The light shower which occasionally falls during the festival may have caused this belief.

In Iraq the feast was celebrated with much ceremony. During the four preceding days, thousands of palm-branches were sold in Jewish quarters and boys could be seen bearing home armfuls of greenery with great glee. Activity increased on the eve of the festival and the little shops and bazaars were busy.

Great care is taken to make the booth conform to the rules. It may be built in the open courtyard or on the flat roof. The green decoration in Baghdad was usually of palm-leaves: sometimes curtains were hung round it and, to the delight of the children, pomegranates and lemons suspended from the latticed roof. Colored pictures of patriarchs or of Scriptural scenes were occasionally added as an extra adornment. During the seven days of the feast a pious Jew should not eat, sleep or receive guests outside the *sukkah*, but children and women are excepted.

Each of the seven nights of the feast is dedicated to one of the seven great patriarchs of Israel: Abraham, Isaac, Jacob, Moses, Aaron, Joseph and David. These are called the *ushpizin* (guests)[52] and the patriarch who is the guest of the evening is believed to be present in spirit in the *sukkah*.[53] A special lamp is lit in his honor and his share of the evening meal goes to the poor.

One honored guest, however, is supposed to grace the hut every night, namely the *'al-Khidr*, "the green one," i.e. Elijah, for whom a chair is set out. At a meal in the *sukkah* of some Baghdad friends to which I was invited, a handsome white silk veil embroidered with silver was draped over Elijah's chair and a copy of the Torah lay on the seat. It was the first night of the feast, and my hosts were well-to-do and Europeanised. As the *sukkah* was not large enough to contain the large number of guests, the Chief Rabbi, the master of the house and a

---

[52] A Talmudic loan-word from the Persian. This Jewish entertainment of ancestral spirits and belief that they enjoy by proxy food provided for them, is significant. The *fravashis* of the Zoroastrians and the ancestor spirits of the Mandaeans are also supposed to sit at the ritual table and partake of food put aside for them at certain festivals.

[53] Should a man bearing the name of the patriarch to be commemorated be present, the honour of reciting the prayer in his honour falls to his share. If, as happens in a large assembly, there are several of that name, recital is sold by auction to the Josephs or Jacobs and so on who claim the right, and the money is given either to the synagogue or to the poor. (See below, note 60, [Editor's Note].)

few guests including myself sat in the booth for the ritual part of the meal: for the secular part we adjourned to the dining room.[54]

For the ritual meal a table covered with a white cloth was brought into the *sukkah*. Upon it was a heap of freshly plucked myrtle and, beneath an embroidered white cover, two pairs of round, flat leavened loaves of bread and a salt-cellar. The *Kiddush* prescribed for the festival was performed as on a Sabbath eve and, according to local custom, no water was added to the wine. After the rabbi had washed his hands the cover over the bread was removed and he selected to loaves, held them up together with the oven sides touching, then, taking the undermost and placing it above the uppermost, he lifted it, pronounced the benediction, dipped it in salt thrice, ate it, and handed out fragments dipped in salt to all in the *sukkah*. We then rejoined those in the dining room.

The simple ritual described is the prelude to the evening meal in the *sukkah* on the two remaining nights of the feast. The next day I attended one of the largest synagogues. There I saw the culminating ritual of the festival, in which *lulab* and *ethrog*, play leading parts. The former is a neatly woven wand composed of green palm-leaf,[55] fresh myrtle and willow: the *ethrog*, called in Arabic a *trunj*,[56] is a citron especially chosen for its species and shape. On our arrival, we were offered both by an attendant standing by the door. I was warned to remove my rings before taking them, for no jewelery of any kind must be worn on hand or arm. The citron was received into the left hand and the *lulab* into the right,[57] and I saw that each recipient before handing them back to the attendant moved them in the direction of the cardinal points and lifted them up and down in a vertical movement.

During the service within there was a ceremony which brought to mind an Orthodox rite I had seen in early autumn, again about the season of early rains, namely the Feast of the Cross.[58] It was when the

---

[54]This would have displeased the strictly orthodox.
[55]See p. 31, above.
[56]The *ethrog* or *trunj*, a citrous fruit like a large lemon, is credited by Arabs with power to fertilise the womb. I was told a tale in which a man who ate one gave birth after nine months to a child. Eastern Jews believe that it has magic powers. A friend in Jerusalem was kind enough to consult Mr. Molho, who has studied the folklore of Sephardic Jews in Salonika, and Mr. Almaliah, an authority on Oriental Judaism upon the subject. Moorish Jews take an *ethrog* with them travelling by sea and cast it into the waves if there is a storm.
[57]Caro, *Schulhan 'aruch* I, par. 561.
[58]This took place in the Holy Sepulchre. The relic of the cross and other crosses are carried in procession with nosegays of flowers and greenery, especially sweet-smelling herbs such as basil and mint. A tray of flowers and greenery is carried after the relic into the chapel of Golgotha. Here prayers for the

ḥazzan and his assistant walked round the *tevah* (reading platform), each carrying his *lulab* and *ethrog*. During the recital of the *Hallel* (hymns of praise), they paused and faced west (roughly towards Jerusalem), extended their arms before them, and then brought the *lulabs* and *ethrogs* sharply back to their bodies, so that their hands touched the waist. This was done thrice. Next, they thrice lifted and lowered them. Then, again three times, they made a scooping movement towards the ground, returning their hands after each movement to waist level. Turning to face the east, they repeated the whole operation, and again when facing the south and the north. Thus three symbolical movements, developed from a pattern of four plus two movements are repeated facing the cardinal points of the compass.[59]

This circumambulation of the *tevah* is repeated daily during the seven days of the feast, and the *Hallel* are added to morning service. On the first day of the feast, it is customary to pay visits to friends and relatives, indeed the whole week is a time of gay happiness in contrast to the gloom of the first ten days of the year.

The eve of the seventh day is called *Hosha'na Rabba* – the "Great Hosanna." In the house of any family which has suffered bereavement, a *Hashkavah* ceremony is performed, and it becomes necessary to describe what form a *Hashkavah* takes in Iraq. The word means "causing to lie down," its equivalent is "requiem." I will quote from my notes,

> In Baghdad it is celebrated on certain days of solemnity and at stated intervals after death. The main feature of the ceremony are a ritual meal, a vigil, the recital of Psalms and passages from holy books, and of the *Ḳaddish* and *Hashkavah* prayers.
>
> The deceased is mentioned by name: if a man, "N. son of N." (his father); if a woman, "N. daughter of N." (her mother).
>
> On the eve of *Hosha'na Rabba* I was invited to the house of a man who had lost his wife to assist at the *Hashkavah* recited in commemoration of the dead woman. Any family which has suffered bereavement keeps vigil on this night, and it is the duty of any pious Jew, bereaved or not, to spend hours of vigil in prayer for, according to the Kabbalists, a man's fate is finally sealed that night and redemption may be gained by participating in such a service as the *Hashkavah*.
>
> At least ten men over thirteen years of age should be present, able to share the reading if possible; if not, the services of professional

---

community were said by the patriarch at each of the four quarters of the chapel, and facing each in turn, the patriarch and the deacon who carried the tray thrice lowered their burden to the ground. This recalled to me the Jewish handling of *lulab* and *ethrog*.

[59] The movements are called *Ni'anu'a*, "shaking."

readers are hired. On this occasion one professional reader had been engaged, a blind man, *ḥazzan* at a neighbouring synagogue and teacher at a school for the blind. He was dependent on a prodigious memory and was famous for his melodious chanting. The readings to be got through before dawn were the *Parasha* (from the five books of Moses), the *Peṭirah* (the story of the death of Moses from the Midrash), the *Idhra Zuta* ("little assembly") in Aramaic from the Zohar; the *Tehelʿim* (psalms of David divided into parts); the *Berakha* (blessing); and, lastly, the *Hashkavah* which lent its name to the whole.

Though electric light shone overhead a number of lighted candles stood on a tray upon the table. Lighted candles are a necessary part of the ritual, known as the *Ḥathimah* ("sealing"). After the reading of the seven parts of the psalms a prayer was said in honour of the *ushpizin* (guests), that is the seven patriarchs Abraham, Isaac, Jacob, Joseph, Aaron, Moses and David. These are supposed to be present successively each night of the seven days of the festival...[60]

After the *Parshar*, *Idhra* and *Tehelim*, not only the bereaved husband, but others who had lost relatives during the year rose and recited the *Kaddish* for their dead, facing Jerusalem. For the *Hashkavah* a tray was brought in upon which were set out four round loaves of household bread, some salt, dates, melon, oranges and other fruit. The tray should have been brought in by the mistress of the house, but on this melancholy occasion it was she herself whom we were

---

[60](See p. 32, above.) The omitted part is mentioned in Drower's *Water into Wine* (see Editor's Introduction, p. 4) and connects with Drower's footnote 53 here in section iii, regarding auctionings. Such acts incensed Drower's European Jewish readers, but auctionings are attested in Drower's account of a regular Sabbath service in an Iraqi synagogue. On p. 20-21 of *Water into Wine* she gives this description,

There should be eight readings from the Torah....In most synagogues in the Near and Middle East the "reading" is nominal; the man summoned to the platform stands to the right of the *hazan*, who reads as his proxy. The privilege of reading the sixth, seventh and eighth passages is auctioned, and this singular practice is extended on days of high festival to all the readings. The first reader must be a cohen [priest]. I was present on such an occasion in Iraq. The synagogue servant, the *shammash*, walked round the synagogue like an auctioneer, calling for bids. As few cohens were present, bidding was slack. At length the *shammash* declared the result: a boy aged about thirteen had won the honour for about two shillings. The child mounted the platform, repeated the prefatory prayer in a low voice and then the *hazan* chanted the passage for him. The next reader had to be a *lewi* (Levite) and, after a similar auction, an old man obtained the privilege for a small sum....His successor was, by rule, an 'Israelite' and competition was sharper. A comfortably-built tradesman wearing a morning-coat capped the bids with a sum equivalent to twelve shillings. Had the congregation been larger, bidding would have run higher. This auctioning, I was informed, could be traced back to a similar practice in the Temple of Jerusalem. [Editor's note]

commemorating. I was told that both "tree fruit" and "fruit of the earth" must be represented (i.e. dates and grapes for the former and melon and pumpkins for the latter).

After washing his hands ritually (i.e. pouring water thrice over each hand), the master of the house broke the bread, dipped a fragment of it in salt, ate it, and then distributed small pieces dipped in salt to all present.[61]

Next, he recited the proper benedictions over the fruit and these too were handed round and eaten. Benedictions and ritual consumption of the fruits of the earth followed in due succession.

I did not stay till dawn, with the others, but was told that at the conclusion of the ceremony, all walked to the synagogue for the morning service.

Brauer[62] recounts that Yemenite Jews, in the common belief that a man's fate is settled on the eve of *Hosha'na Rabba* — for one who fails to see his shadow on the wall that night will die within the twelve-month — also believe that a person's destiny can be foretold from the form of his shadow.

After dawn on the seventh day, however, all gloomy thoughts should disappear. It is the "Great Hosanna," the last day of the feast. Early in the morning the synagogues are crowded for the *lulab* and *ethrog* ceremonies described above. Men bring five, and sometimes three, twigs of fresh green willow bound with a strip of palm and strike the ground five times, at least this is so in Iraq; in Jerusalem I was told that they strike the ground repeatedly, "as often as possible." Kurdish Jews strike the *ḥazzan* playfully with the twigs.[63]

The eighth day (Tishri 22) is a separate feast called *Shemini Aṣereth*, the Feast of Solemn Assembly.[64] Memorial prayers for the dead are recited and prayers for rain.

The ninth day (Tishri 23) is called *Simhat Torah*, Rejoicing over the Law. Its motive is joy over completing a cycle of Scripture readings, and when the last lines of Deuteronomy have been read at the noonday service, the end of the Pentateuch is followed immediately by the first

---

[61]This household bread is not to be confused with the *ka'ak* also distributed at *Hashkavah* feasts. These are rings of bread made of flour mingled with crushed terebinth berries *(habbah helwa)*. They are not dipped in salt when handed round and the blessing said for them is, "Blessed be Thou...who didst create different kinds of food," i.e. *mezonoth* (not *ha-moṣi* as for ordinary bread, "Blessed be Thou...who bringeth forth bread from the earth").
[62]Brauer, p. 324.
[63]See note 46, above.
[64]The Yazidis have a Feast of Assembly about this season, most probably connected with the autumn rains. It includes the ritual chase and slaughter of a bull, and a dance.

chapter of Genesis. Each man is prepared to be called on to read his portion. The reading is accompanied by great pomp and rejoicing, and those invited to read the last and begin the first chapters of the Pentateuch are called "bridegrooms." The scrolls are carried in procession, followed by men and children singing the Hosannah and clapping their hands, whilst the women onlookers utter their shrill *helahil* (joy-cries).

I visited a Baghdad synagogue on this day and watched men earnestly walking round and round the *tevah* reading from their books, whilst those who entered went to the ledge which surrounded the walls of the synagogue to salute the scrolls exhibited on it. These scrolls, some in silver cases of great age, were reverently kissed one by one, usually just by touching with the finger-tips which were then carried to the mouth. In my time, these ceremonies were sober, but I was told that, within the memory of many, the Great Synagogue in Baghdad was crowded all day by a boisterously happy crowd which sang and danced until the late hours, for this day marks the end of one of the two happiest seasons of the Jewish calendar. Brauer[65] describes the dance of Yemenite Jews around the reading desk on this day of days, every dancer clasping a roll to his breast. Since the exodus of 1952-53 many of these synagogues are empty, and the scrolls carried away by those who fled to Israel, a promised land which is nevertheless, to many, a foreign land full of things unfamiliar.

To end this chapter I quote from Israel Zangwill's translation into English verse of a hymn for rain chanted on the eighth day of the Feast of Tabernacles. It was written presumably in the sixth century by the famous hymn-writer, Eleazar Ḳalīr.[66] I was told by a credible authority that the same hymn is chanted at Passover, substituting the word "dew" for "rain." I ventured therefore to give the version as for the former feast, changing by a single word Zangwill's translation. The first and last verses run,

> Rain, precious rain, unto Thy land forlorn
> Pour out Thy blessings in Thy exultation
> To strengthen us with ample wine and corn
> And give Thy chosen city safe foundation
> > In rain.
>
> ....
>
> Dear precious rain, that we our harvests reap

---

[65]Brauer, p. 324-25.
[66]Ḳalīr was the most famous of all the early *paiṭanim*. See Elbogen, p. 310-21.

And guard our fatted flocks and herds from leanness: Behold, our people follow Thee like sheep,
And look to Thee to give the earth her greenness
   With rain.[67]

iv. The Feast for the Blossoming of Trees

The Feast for the Blossoming of the Trees falls about six weeks after Hanukkah. Its name in the vernacular is *Tefkī'a ash-Shejer* ("The Bursting into Leaf) of Trees", rabbinically known as *Rosh Hashana la-Ilanoth* ("The New Year for Trees"). The date is Shebhat 15th, the season in the part of Iraq which was once Babylonia in early spring when twigs redden with sap in the fruit gardens, buds swell and early almond-blossom blushes against a pale blue sky.

Jewish friends arranged a visit to a house where rites proper to the occasion were to be celebrated. My hosts were two young men who had lost their father five months before, and the ritual feast was to benefit his soul. The men sat on benches spread with carpets round the open courtyard, a space no bigger than a room. The walls were hung with more carpets, the colors of which, illumined by lamps suspended near them, glowed warmly and gave to the gathering an almost festive air. A gallery which ran round the courtyard above was crowded with hooded women whose presence was felt rather than seen, for above it was dark, and the light below dimmed the stars which pricked the patch of the night-sky above us. Upon a table near the center of the yard were set dishes piled with oranges and other fruits and vegetables, a generous and colorful display.

The company had the sober happiness of knowing that they were gathered together to perform a meritorious rite. It would not only solace the soul of the dead man, but might perchance work the salvation of other souls pent, so Kabbalists believe, in the physical form of apple, pear or pumpkin for sins committed on earth. The Law is exacting, even the best may sin unknowingly. There must be purification, expiation. After death, souls of the careless or impious may find themselves imprisoned in non-human shape, unable to communicate with the living save in dream. We spoke quietly of such matters as we sat. The strong-featured rabbi wearing a red fez, turban and robes dominated the assembly: the others wore drab European suits and the *sidara*, a black forage-cap adopted as a badge of modern progress. I ventured to ask him which was the lighter sentence for a soul doomed to suffer *gilgul*

---

[67]From I. Zangwill, *The Voice of Jerusalem*, London: W. Heinemann, 1920, p. 155.

neshamoth. Was it to pass at death into an animal or into a tree? A circle of intelligent faces turned to hear his reply.

"Best it is for an erring soul to be reborn as a man *(admi).* Next it is better for a sinful one to be reborn as an animal fit for food than to pass into a tree or fruit. Only the very evil pass into unclean animals or into reptiles."

The book before the rabbi was the *Peri 'eṣ Hadar,*[68] a Baghdadi version of the liturgical office for the night. This is based on the *Sefer Hemdath Ha-Yamin* which was ascribed to a famous seventeenth-century Kabbalist, Nathan of Gaza.[69] Kabbalists, and a large proportion of Iraqi Jews are fervent believers in Kabbalism, hold that souls imprisoned in ritually clean animals or in fruit or vegetables lawful as food, can be released and redeemed if these are eaten ritually by pious persons. To illustrate this, Rabbi Joseph told us the following tale, a version of which was given to me afterwards by Mr. Ezra Haddad. He told me that the story was often quoted in Iraq synagogues.

> Ninety years ago, traders in sheep and cattle had their market in the outskirts of the city of Baghdad, and butchers of the town went there daily to buy sheep for the slaughter-house.
>
> Now a certain Jewish butcher, a poor man, was accustomed to come there every day to purchase a sheep or two with what little money he could get together. As a rule, he could only buy thinner stock passed over by richer butchers. One day, at the closing of the market, he was preparing to return to town almost empty-handed when he saw an Arab driving a sheep which came running towards him. As most butchers had already left, the Arab offered him the sheep at a comparatively low price considering that the creature was big and fat. When he hesitated, the Arab reduced his price further. Finally, for an unusually small sum, the sheep became his.
>
> He drove the sheep before him into the town but, to his surprise, the animal needed no urging and ran ahead of him as if it knew the road. They reached the butcher's house, and, realising what a good bargain he had made, the good man decided to postpone its slaughter till Friday morning, when Jews buy choice meat for the day of rest.

---

[68] The version used in Baghdad was enlarged by additional songs and prayers by a modern Kabbalist, Rabbi Joseph Haim of Baghdad. The first edition of his book *Ben Ish Hai* was printed in Jerusalem; the third edition in Baghdad, 1912. Haim was an authority on Jewish ritual, a noted mystic and preacher and highly esteemed in Baghdad. (See note 14, above.)

[69] He was a follower of the notorious pseudo-Messiah Sabbatai Zevi (1625-1676 A.D.). For the story of the latter, an extraordinary personality and his school, see Scholem, pp. 183-320. (Scholem's *Sabbatai Sevi. The Mystical Messiah 1626-1676,* London: Routledge and Kegan Paul, 1973, was first published after Drower's death. [Editor's note].) *Peri 'eṣ-Hadar* was however written in Jerusalem at the end of the 17th century.

That night, as the butcher slept, he was roused by a beating at the door. He opened it, and saw the servant of the Grand Rabbi of Baghdad, who bade him attend his master instantly, on an urgent matter.

The butcher, not strictly a religious man, refused to leave his house at that time of night and returned to his bed. No sooner had he fallen asleep, than in a dream he saw an old man with a long white beard, wearing a mantle and an angelic appearance, who ordered him sternly to obey the Rabbi and to go to him, as the matter was of utmost importance.

Mystified, the poor man awoke, and as he was pondering whether his dream was sent from Heaven, a second knock was heard at his door. It was a second summons to the Rabbi's house. This time the butcher, his dream fresh in his mind, accompanied the messenger immediately.

The Grand Rabbi asked the butcher if he had bought a sheep the previous day and whether he meant to slay it the next morning. The butcher assented, adding that he intended to kill the beast on Friday morning. But how, he asked, did the Master know about the animal, and why did he trouble about it in the middle of the night?

The Master replied, "My son, whilst asleep in my bed tonight, I beheld a vision. A white-bearded man wrapped in a white mantle, whose appearance was that of an angel of God, stood beside me. With him was a strange ghost which gazed at me mournfully and was mute. The angelic visitor said to me solemnly, 'Know, O my son, that this ghost is the spirit of a well-known member of your community who died some years ago. As in his lifetime he was sinful, his soul passed after death into several plants and animals, so that he might thus be purified and restored. He now inhabits the body of a sheep sold yesterday to a Jewish butcher. If this animal is slaughtered ritually according to the Law of God, and its flesh is eaten ritually by some pious poor people with the customary grace, this wandering soul will be restored and its sufferings ended. If not, it will resume its arduous journeyings in the world of sinful spirits.' The old man gave your name and then he and his silent companion disappeared."

The butcher listened to this with a throbbing heart, remembering his own dream. He immediately agreed to hand over the sheep to the Master, that he might do as seemed to him best. Next morning, accordingly, the fat animal was led to the Rabbi's house, where a *shohet* (ritual slaughterer) waited with his ritually cleansed knife. After a short prayer, he slew the sheep, which had been pronounced *kosher* (fit for lawful food).

The flesh was washed and salted according to Jewish law, and cooked carefully. The Rabbi invited ten poor, God-fearing folk to dine. Psalms were recited and the meal served and eaten according to Jewish custom. When all had finished, the Master delivered a discourse about the mysterious wandering of souls in the great realm of spirits, the transmigration of sinful souls and the importance of their restoration. When his sermon was ended, the Ḳaddish and the Hashkavah were solemnly recited and the congregation dismissed.

That night, whilst the reverend Master slept, the angelic old man reappeared to him in dream. He was accompanied by the same ghostly spirit of the previous night, but this time the latter was clad in a multi-coloured shroud of celestial light, and its face glowed with happiness. The angelic visitant thanked the Master for his care and zeal, whereby a wandering soul had been redeemed and translated to Paradise.

It appears that the "New Year for Trees" originally marked the day appointed for the settlement of dues and tithes on fruit. It was also observed by some as an "Arbour Day," and in modern Israel it has been especially selected for the replanting of trees in a country that has been shockingly denuded of its once luxuriant forests. In Jerusalem long ago it was the custom to plant a cedar for every new-born male and a cypress for every female, possibly an attempt at reforestation, for the reckless hacking down of trees for firewood and the onslaughts of the goats which are "poor man's cows" are no recent phenomenon. However, when a marriage had been arranged for a girl or youth, his or her tree was cut down and used for door-posts for the nuptial canopy (ḥuppah).[70]

In Iraq there is no planting of trees, and observance is confined to the ritual eating of fruit.[71] As indicated above, the custom is Kabbalistic and in Palestine dates back to the settlement of Kabbalists there in the sixteenth century. The origin of the feast is almost certainly ancient, and marks a natural turning-point in the seasons, the time of bursting buds, the first signs of the Oriental spring. Shevaṭ is the eleventh month of the Jewish religious year and the fifth month of the lay year; nevertheless, this feast ranks as one of the "New Years."

---

[70]Talmud, Gitt. 57a.

[71]This ritual resembles so nearly Parsi ritual eating of fruits and vegetables for the benefit of the dead that it is extremely probable that Kabbalists attached their own interpretation to ceremonies traditional in Iran and Babylonia under the Persians and still persisting in these countries in various forms, religious and otherwise. Just as Kabbalists found tortuous esoteric meanings in the Halakhah and hidden significance in every word, so did they twist traditional customs to fit their own conceptions of the soul's destiny. Scholem (p. 31) says,

> By interpreting every religious act as a mystery, even where its meaning was clear for all to see or was expressly mentioned in the written or oral Law, a strong link was forged between Kabbalah and Halakhah which appears to me to have been, in large part, responsible for the influences of Kabbalistic thought over the minds and hearts of successive generations.

In so doing, Kabbalists repeated a process already practised by early Israelites, who bent traditional magic and pagan custom into a formal shape intended to remind the Jew of his history and destiny as the chosen people.

The digression and tale have led us away from the small courtyard in the Jewish quarter of Baghdad where its celebration was taking place.

The first reading of the evening was from the first chapter of Genesis which describes the Creation.[72] Then came a reading from Deuteronomy about the fruits and produce of Palestine, passages from the prophets (Ezek. xvii, xxxiv, and xlvii and Joel ii), from Psalms 72, 147, 148, 85 and 126), and excerpts from the Zohar giving a mystical interpretation of Genesis (33a); Leviticus (18) and Deuteronomy (Ekeb).

Next the rabbi recited a prayer for the "coming out" of trees and for the restoration (*tikkun*) of any soul incarnate in fruit or fruit-trees.

The ritual meal began with a reading from the Zohar about wheat; and leavened and ring-shaped loaves baked in the kitchen of our hosts were handed round to the company and each person recited the grace for fruit of the earth before eating the bread. A dish of olives was passed next, and we all took and ate an olive after a reading from the Midrash concerning olives.[73] The consumption of a date after a reading from the same book followed and the appropriate blessings were spoken over both fruits. Then a non-ritual dish was introduced, a dish of fish, from which we speared small pieces as the dish went round. On this night all animal food is forbidden.

The ritual meal was resumed: next came "product of the Vine," raisins and sultanas, black and white, and as they were eaten one of the company recited the appropriate blessing for them. Various kinds of wine were brought in, non-fermented and made from black and white sultanas and other sorts of dried grapes. We took and drank a ritual glass of each, blessing being recited over every glassful.[74] An extract from the tractate *Ma'sroth* (tithes) in the Mishnah was read before we ate the dried figs handed out to us. Appropriate passages from the Zohar or Mishnah were read before the ritual consumption of the following: apple, pomegranate, beans, beetroot, raw cabbage, lettuce, raw carrot and cooked turnip, and a blessing for "fruits of the earth" was recited over each.

All then sang a hymn of thanks and a hymn for the blossoming of trees. Sections of orange, apple and dried apricots were offered round and eaten, and an *ethrog* was passed from hand to hand and its

---

[72]Note that the Creation is commemorated at each New Year rite.

[73]This passage offers a bleak prospect to Jewry, since it asserts that Israel gives its best to the world when oppressed, just as the olive exudes its precious oil when crushed. The meaning of course is that the best in a community is called out by concentrated effort.

[74]This is not a *Kiddush*.

Evergreen Elijah

fragrance inhaled,[75] but it was not eaten like other fruit. Nuts, prunes, melon and other kinds of fruit were distributed to us all, but appropriate readings accompanied only the walnuts, almonds, carobs, prunes, lemons and hazel-nuts. Wealthy Jews pride themselves on being able to place upon the ritual table as many kinds of fruit and vegetable, fresh, dried and preserved as it is possible to obtain.[76]

I have omitted to mention that all who attended the ceremony were offered tea on arrival, coffee later on in the evening and fruit squash of various kinds at intervals. These were, however, not ritual drinks.

Finally, our two young hosts stood up, faced Jerusalem, and said the *Kaddish*, rising on their toes at the words "May He who granteth peace in His heaven, in His mercy bestow peace upon us and upon all the people of Israel." All the men joined in the final lines of this traditional prayer for the dead, and recited with the brothers the *Hashkavah* prayer for the soul of the deceased head of the house.

v. Purim

Purim[77] falls on the 14th of Adar, that is about our March, and is a celebration of the story told in the Book of Esther. I was taken on Purim to a synagogue in the heart of the city of Baghdad. Like the ancient synagogue excavated by the archaeologists in Dura Europos, it was once

---

[75]Inhalation is a characteristic Parsi and Mandaean rite; the *barsom* of the former and the inhalation of the latter at *Zidqa Brikha* (Blessed Oblation) are accompanied by the proper prayers. I was told, when I saw inhalation of the fragrance of the *ethrog* during the Feast of Tabernacles, that this was not an orthodox act. It may be inhaled at *Havdalah (Anglicé Habhdalah)*.

[76]Mandaeans enumerate amongst the fruits to be eaten at *Lofani* (a meal of commemoration for the dead), wheat (bread), dates, cocoanut, almonds, walnuts, pomegranates (or their seeds), quince (fresh or dried), onion, and as much fruit and as many vegetables in season as possible. Raisins or fresh grapes must always be on the ritual table. The same holds for a Zidqa Brikha, also for the benefit of the dead.

Jewish mystics specify thirty kinds of fruit divided into three groups of ten representing the ten *sefiroth*. The first group includes fruits with soft skins and small pips, such as grapes. The second group includes fruits with soft skins and hard stones, such as olives, dates and apricots. The third group is of "fruits" with hard shells and hard kernels, i.e. nuts of all kinds. Mystics explain ritual eating of fruit as a form of expiation of Adam's original sin of eating from the Tree of Knowledge. With European Jews it was the custom formerly to eat fifteen different kinds of fruit.

[77]Drower had put the Purim material *after* the Passover section, but I have placed it here in order to adhere to the Jewish festal cycle. [Editor's note]

a private house, bequeathed to the Jewish community by its former owner.

A crowd of beggars mobbed the door, shaking their boxes and plucking at our sleeves, for it is the duty of every Israelite to bestow alms at least twice on the day which marks the deliverance of his nation from mortal danger. Those who escaped the beggars were confronted by the box marked *Pidion Nefesh*[78] just within the door. In the archway there was the usual small tank of flowing water placed there to enable everyone entering to perform his ritual ablution.

The house was of the old Baghdadi type. A projecting wooden gallery supported by painted wooden columns ran round the upper storey overlooking a large open courtyard. This courtyard was crowded with women, most of them wearing sober black *abas* (wimple-cloaks). A few matrons of the older generation wore the voluminous, sumptuous *izār*,[79] its stiff silken folds brocaded with gold or silver thread. This, worn over the head and drawn in at the waist, reached the ankles. Their faces were masked by a square black blinker of goat's hair edged by silver, the *khilīyah*. The lower storey, the rooms leading off the courtyard, consisted of *saradīb*, that is to say rooms built half underground for coolness in the heat of summer, and reached by a few steps. On the outer walls of these hung framed and glazed inscriptions in Hebrew. When passing these, many touched the holy words and then brought their fingers devoutly to their lips. Whilst the women crowded the courtyard, the men all went to the gallery and the rooms which led off it.

The *ḥazzan* had his platform on the side of the gallery facing Jerusalem. The sun had already set in a golden cloud and the sky above the courtyard was darkening to the tranquil indigo of night. The evening service was not yet concluded; the solemn reading of the Book of Esther, the *Megillah*,[80] was to follow it. The reading should begin twenty minutes after the sun has disappeared.

My companion and I went upstairs. The Eighteen Benedictions were being silently recited, and as mourners ended the *Ḳaddish* said aloud

---

[78]I.e. "soul-ransom." A sum expended in charity is a virtuous deed which averts Divine displeasure and protects the giver from misfortune. It replaces sacrifice.

[79]These handsome examples of the weaver's art are often presented to a synagogue at the death of their owners with an inscription commemorating the deceased. Both *izār* and inscription are hung on the walls of the synagogue.

[80]Women are not exempted from reading the *Megillah*, but if household duties prevent their attendance at the synagogue, the scroll is read for them at home, with the customary blessings before and after.

by them alone for their dead, they took three steps backwards, as is the custom.

Many present had come provided with scrolls of the Book of Esther, and these were mostly hand-written. When the time arrived, my friend produced a small scroll on a wooden roller: it was beautifully copied on gazelle-skin. In the interval between evening service and the reading, a long hymn was sung by the congregation; this dealt with the epic of Esther: its author was a Baghdadi and the music, Oriental in character, was composed in Baghdad.

When the time came for the reading, a perceptible excitement stirred the people. The ḥazzan on his tribune read the scroll standing, the hard artificial light throwing into relief his pale, heavy features, his dark hair and his red fez. He chanted throughout, and the congregation, pressed together in gallery and courtyard, chanted certain passages with him, reciting them in one breath. Sometimes his voice rose, and the note of the chant with it, as if in exultation, as the story of fear, triumph and revenge unfolded. Whenever Haman's name was mentioned there was a mighty clattering: every person stamped the right foot hard on the ground as if to crush down the hated foe forever. My neighbor showed me in his roll the names of the ten sons of Haman listed column-wise, for tradition has it that they were hanged on a tall gallows, the one above the other. Thus the copyist hanged them in effigy afresh.

A flowing tide of emotion stirred the closely-packed crowd of listeners, and when the last verse was done there was a great clamor in which the hate of generations spoke,

Cursed be Haman!
Blessed be Mordecai!

Before the first World War, the feast was looked for eagerly by Jewish children, for small boys used to carry round from house to house an effigy of the execrated *goy*, begging small coins for the fireworks to be let off during the burning of the figure that evening in a bonfire. According to Brauer, this was the custom too in the Yemen. He says that it is the duty of a Yemenite father to read the Megillah to his family both in the original and in Arabic.[81] In Aden the honor of reading it in the synagogue is auctioned, usually between bridegrooms, the money being expended on oil for lamps or candles. In Aden ten candles are lighted on the eve and next morning, and these are called "the ten sons of Haman." This and Brauer's mention of presenting eggs dyed red on

---

[81]Brauer, p. 332ff. He wrote, of course, before the exodus of Yemenite Jews to Israel. I do not know how many Jews remain in the Yemen today.

the morning of Purim suggest a former spring-time ritual. In the year of the service I have described, "Haman" was most certainly identified by most of the congregation with Hitler, and he must have been a symbolic figure[82] throughout the ages, representative of any alien oppressor. It was formerly considered praiseworthy and meritorious to drink at Purim until it was no longer possible to distinguish the phrases which bless and curse the two figures, Gentile and Jew,[83] but this is rare nowadays. Al-Birūnī refers to the practice of beating and burning the effigy of Haman at Hanukkah,[84] but he may, of course, have mistaken the identity of the figure.

vi. Passover

The fourteenth of Nisan, the day before Passover, is observed by Jews as a fast for "first-born"[85] offspring. Every male "first-born"

---

[82] The historicity of the Book of Esther is disputed. For a brief analysis and discussion of this subject, see W. O. E. Oesterley and Th. E. Robinson, *An Introduction to the Books of the Old Testament*, New York: Macmillan, 1934, p. 139 *et seq*.

[83] The Hebrew letters composing the phrases "Cursed be Haman" and "Blessed be Mordecai" are numerically equivalent (Megillah, 7b).

[84] Al-Biruni, *The Chronology of Ancient Nations: an English Version of the Arabic text of Athar ul-Bakiya of Al-Biruni*. Translated, edited, with notes and index by C. E. Sachau, London: W. H. Allen, Publ. for the Oriental Translation Fund of Great Britain and Ireland, 1879, p. 274.

[85] See Ex. xiii, 2; Num. iii, 12 and 13 and ibid. xviii, 15. On the thirtieth day after the birth of a first-born son every Israelite (Cohens and Levites excepted) must redeem the child by a sum equivalent to five shekels, provided that no abortion or female child preceded him. In Iraq the "redemption" took place with pomp and ceremony. Friends and relatives were asked to attend. The time was usually 10 a.m., and a Cohen (preferably a pious person) officiated.

The ceremony began with the singing of psalms and hymns to the accompaniment of a brass band or other music. The father lifted the child in his arms and offered him to the Cohen. The latter questioned the parents to ascertain for certain that the child is their own and indeed "he that opened the matrix." When affirmative answers were given, the Cohen took the child in his arms and declared that it was his by the law of God. The mother had then to expostulate. The Cohen then explained the law to her, but added that she may ask her husband to redeem the child. The father then produced a gift, often a silver goblet; the value of the offering was not supposed to be less than five dirhems, but was of course more in the case of the wealthy. The Cohen accepted it, and whilst the grace for redemption and the *Sheheheyanu* was recited, the father took the boy from the Cohen and handed him to his mother.

This was the signal for shrill joy-cries from the women and blasts from the band (seldom in tune). The joyful day was the occasion of a lavish family feast. Sweets were distributed, food and money given to the poor and generous hospitality offered to all. Few Jews in Iraq kept cattle, so that a redemption of

should fast from daybreak to dusk. Jews in Iraq and Kurdistan make it an eldest child irrespective of sex, and if the child is weak, small or unwilling to fast, the father or mother fasts in its stead. In these countries the fasting "first-born" should in theory be invited to break his fast by one whose son has been circumcised that day, or he may eat his first meal with a bridegroom. This custom prevails elsewhere also, but as any religious meal will serve, it is often arranged that the fast shall be broken at the ritual repast that takes place at the completion of study of a tractate, this being arranged to coincide.

Preparations for Passover begin from the new moon of Nisan, that is, nearly two weeks before the festival itself. Fifty years back or more, wealthy orthodox Jews in Iraq used to go out to the harvest-fields to gather good corn for the next Passover, and this wheat, called *shemūrah* (guarded) was carefully stored where it could not ferment. Brauer describes a similar custom in the Yemen.[86] Preparations for Passover bread, according to him, began there soon after Purim; the wheat was threshed with sticks, sifted and placed in great jars. Later it was put between green plants in layers, covered and left twice for twenty-four hours. It swells, and the process results in whitening the grain before it is milled. Whitening by fruit-juice is also allowed, and such a process is not considered ritually illegal.

Such methods of whitening the flour are unknown in Iraq, and the wheat was usually bought in the market, but was minutely examined to see that no barley or foreign matter was mingled with it. Similar care is taken about rice eaten during the festival; the women put it on a big tray and examine it grain by grain. Only ritually clean utensils are used for the feast: well-to-do families keep certain vessels, pots and crockery especially for Passover, others content themselves with cleansing those that they have by immersing them in boiling water. This ritual cleansing is called *Ḥag'alah*. In Baghdad, in addition to the ritual bread, (*maṣṣoth*, Arabic *faṭīr*) women prepare specially-made loaves of unleavened household bread; this is saltless, round, thin, large and very brittle. This bread (Arabic *khubz rqaq*, Jewish *jeradīq*) will keep indefinitely and is thought to bring blessing. When eaten, it is dipped into salted water to soften it. To quote from notes about the ritual bread,

---

the "first-born" with an ass or lamb rarely took place. I was told by a Jewish friend that he remembered as a boy meeting an ass-foal richly caparisoned and decorated passing through the narrow streets on its way to be "ransom," and that it attracted much notice from Jewish passers-by, whom Moslem onlookers scornfully accused of "worshipping unclean beasts."

[86] P. 338.

In Kurdistan, not only must men draw the water for the mixing on Nisan 13th – a task at other times allotted to women – but only men may mix the dough, shape the loaves (*maṣṣoth*) and put them in the oven. Thirty or forty years ago, throughout Iraq, hundreds of Jews were to be seen on Passover eve on their way to the river Tigris, there to fill their jars with ritually-drawn water, whilst they recited a special blessing. Now the rule which forbade women to touch the dough to be made for the *maṣṣoth* has been relaxed, but no woman who is menstruant or not purified after menstruation or childbirth take part in its preparation.

The search for leaven takes place on the eve of Nisan 14th in every Jewish house, usually just after the evening service. Housewives prudently stint the ordinary household bread the day before, so that little shall be wasted when the collected leaven is burnt by the master of the house. The ritual burning should take place during the first third of the day, before noon.

I was privileged several times to assist at the *seder* meal, the ritual repast eaten on the eve of the feast. As celebrated in Baghdad whilst we lived there a striking feature of the meal was the cheerful, not to say hilarious, spirit in which it was celebrated. The homes of better-class Jews seemed to lack the carefree joviality which pervaded the poorer quarters on this all-important night; but even so there was less solemnity about the eating of the *seder* meal than in Europe.

One year I was the guest of a humble family who welcomed me, a complete stranger and not of their faith, with a cordiality which showed no sign of being forced. The Talmud exhorts householders to leave the door open and to welcome any guest who cares to enter, and the spirit of this hospitable injunction is alive today in every Oriental Jewish home. In Kurdistan and the Yemen the rule is literally observed and the house-door left ajar. Iraqi and Yemeni Jews set an extra cup on the table, said to be provided for any chance guest, and a wish for such a visitor is expressed in the first chapter of the Haggadah[87], "He who is hungry, let him come and partake; he who is needy, let him come and celebrate the Passover."

In the house to which I had come – that of an artisan – a spirit of gladness reigned throughout. The words to be recited, the Haggadah, were chanted either by single members of the family or by all together, the chief role falling to the master of the house, and the chant was often interrupted by happy laughter and portions of the reading

---

[87] The name given to the service-book intended for home use at the ritual meal and feast. This is recited in both Hebrew and Arabic. The word *haggadah* means "telling," "recital."

Evergreen Elijah

accompanied by a rhythmic clapping of hands and by the occasional high, trilling joy-cries *(helahil)* of the women.

By the time of my arrival a little after sunset, the table was set and all was ready for the feast. It was common to use a tray for the *seder* (arrangement of the ritual foods), but as my hosts had lost theirs during the riots and looting of 1941, their table had to serve for both the ritual and the non-ritual parts of the meal. The shape of the tray is not specified: it is generally round, but the book of ritual (Haggadah) published in Baghdad, illustrates it as an oblong. I give here a rough sketch of the *seder* as shown in this book.

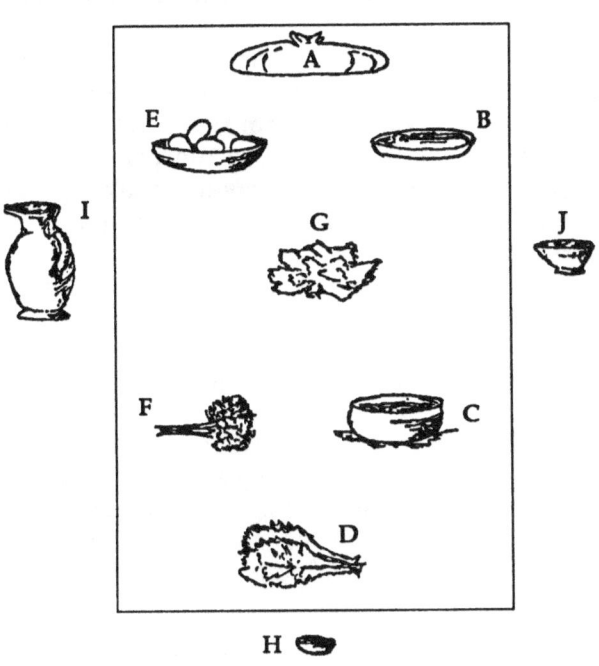

- A. The *maṣṣoth*
- B. The shankbone
- C. *Ḥaroseth*
- D. Lettuce
- E. Eggs
- F. Parsley
- G. Endive
- H. Salt
- I. Wine
- J. Lemon-juice

My host sat facing the *maṣṣoth* with the other ritual foods between them and himself. As it happened to be also the eve of the Sabbath, we began with the welcoming of the angels and the Ḵiddush. Whilst the blessing for the wine was recited, we all stood. At Passover, however, no ritual cup is handed round as everyone at table is provided with a separate cup. It was raisin wine. Each of the four cups to be emptied during the evening must be drunk sitting and leaning to the left, a posture said to symbolize ease.

When the first cup had been drunk, every person round the table took his neighbor's right hand in his own, and then carried his fingertips to his lips.[88]

The word *seder* means order, or arrangement, and applies to the evening's programme or ritual. The head of the family is told to memorize the fifteen chief items of that ritual, lest he omit a part.

After the Ḵaddesh as it is called in the list of items, comes the ablution *u-reḥaṣ*, so that when the ceremony of taking hands was over, the wife brought in a basin of water and towels, and all washed their hands in the ritual manner.

Next on the list came *Karpas* (parsley), i.e. the ceremony of dipping the parsley into the lemon-juice. The celebrant dipped a piece, ate it, and then dipped in other sprigs which were passed round and eaten. *Yaḥaṣ* followed, that is to say "the dividing." He unwrapped the three, round unleavened loaves[89] and, selecting the middle loaf, held it up with his left hand and traced on it with his right forefinger Hebrew characters representing the word Yahweh[90] before he broke it into two halves. One half he wrapped in a large silk handkerchief which he tied to the shoulder of his young son beside him amidst the joy-cries of the women.[91] The bundle was said by my companion to

---

[88]Cf. the Mandaean *kushṭa* a ritual handshake performed in just this manner. The *kushṭa* usually marks the close of a part of a rite: it is also performed when making a pact or promise.

[89]The loaves had been marked in six places by a pointed instrument before baking; this, I was told, was to prevent rising. Nine similar marks on the Parsi *darun* called "the named" represent "good thoughts, good words, good deeds." "Unnamed" *daruns* are pricked four times only. Four marks appear on the sacramental loaf of Orthodox Christians, but to these no meaning is attached.

[90]A Kabbalistic practice.

[91]This ritual was performed differently in the Chief Rabbi's house when I dined with him one Passover. When the rabbi halved the loaf, he wrapped half in a white cloth and handed it to his neighbour on the right who took it, kissed the rabbi's hand and passed it on to his right-hand neighbour. The bread went thus round the table, each recipient kissing the hand from which he received it. The *afikoman* was placed under the armpit of the youngest boy present.

represent the bread carried away by the Israelites fleeing from Egypt. The second half he held out so that all round the table could grasp or touch it with the right hand whilst they repeated, "Lo, this is the bread of affliction." The bread was lifted up high for the rest of the recitation.

The *Maggid*, the recital of the narration *(haggadah)* was preceded by a gay and pretty piece of playacting, popular throughout Iraq. A group of young people left the room which opened on to a balcony overhanging the courtyard. Much giggling was heard outside, and when my host asked in Arabic, "Whence came ye?", the answer came from without, "From Egypt." Then, "*Wain raiḥīn?* (Whither going?)" and the answer, "*Li Yerushalāim* (To Jerusalem),*"* and in they scrambled, laughing, to reseat themselves again at the table. Our head servant for many years, a Kurdish Jew, told me that in Kurdistan one of the company when performing this byplay usually dresses himself as a figure of fun, swathed in cloth to conceal a huge false belly and wearing an exaggeratedly big turban as the traveller from Egypt. Buffoonery like this, he said, was prolonged, so that the *seder* often lasted till midnight.[92]

The youngest present, in this case the little son, asked with no prompting, "Wherefore is this night distinguished above all other nights?" He had four such questions to ask; these serving to introduce the narration with its commentary. The recital embraces the principal events of national history: the covenant between the Lord and Abraham, the story of the children of Egypt, their oppression, the leadership of Moses, the plagues of Egypt and so on. During the recitation several ritual acts took place, for instance a cup of wine, filled after "the bread of affliction," was lifted up by our host and set down again. After the second chapter of the Haggadah, eggs[93] were

---

[92] It must be remembered that many families in Iraq must be the descendants of Jewish exiles who refused to return to Judea in the days of Ezra – only a minority went back. They were, after all, in the land of their father Abraham. Whilst they lived at peace with Arab neighbours, "This year we are as slaves; next year we shall be as freemen in the land of Israel" had little point for them. The events of 1951 gave the words a new and poignant meaning, and tragic uprooting was at hand for most of those who had once recited them unthinkingly and light-heartedly.

[93] Eggs are universally connected with ceremonies symbolic of life renewed. In the *Riman* ceremony of the Parsis which symbolises regeneration, the sacramental drink is brought in an egg-shell and at the *Bāj* ceremony for the dead eggs are placed with the bread, fruit and cheese for three nights after death (*Shayist-nē-Shayist; a Pahlavi text on religious customs*. Edited, transliterated and translated with introduction and notes by Jehangir C. Tavadia, Alt- und neu- Indische Studien 3, Hamburg: Friedrichsen, de Gruyter,

distributed, blessing was said over them and each person dipped his egg into the salt and ate it. At the words "with this bone," the son of the house lifted the meatless shankbone.[94]

Whilst the relation of the sorrows of Israel in Egypt was read the mother slipped out and brought in an earthenware bowl partly filled with water. This she set before her husband and during the enumeration of the ten plagues he dropped wine into it; first three times, and then each time that one of the ten plagues was mentioned until at a final three droppings into the bowl the wine-cup was empty. The reddened water, now known as "blood," was then taken outside by one of the women and poured outside the street-door on the ground by the threshold. This is a purely Iraqi custom.

The second cup of wine was drunk at the end of the narrative after the first part of the *Hallel*. [95] The ritual eating of bread, the *moṣi*, was the next step. The master of the house washed his hands, broke a piece from the upper loaf and another from the half-loaf previously left in its place between the upper and lower loaves, and, holding both together, dipped the bread in the salt three times whilst reciting the grace for the bread. All those round the table washed their hands again, then ate a fragment of bread, dipping it in salt and repeating the benediction.

Maror (bitter herb) was the next ritual food. It was represented on the table by endive (succory is sometimes used as *maror* in Iraq). The father picked up lettuce and endive from the table, held them together, dipped them in *ḥaroseth* and ate it, and his example with the proper formula was followed by the company. In Iraq *ḥaroseth* – locally *ḥalaīk* – consists of walnuts pounded and mixed with *dibis* (inspissated dates). To eat a mixture of pounded nuts and some sweet or syrupy fluid such as honey or date-syrup is a common feature of a number of "New Year" feasts.[96] The Mishnah (Pesahim 10, 3) says that

---

1930, xvii, 1-3). At *Nau Roz*, the spring festival, Shi'a Moslems place eggs on the ritual table set out on the eve. At the same time of year, at their spring festival, Yazidis exchange coloured eggs, just as Christians do at Easter.

[94] He must also point at the bone at the words "the Paschal lamb which our ancestors ate." These are the two sole occasions on which the bone is referred to in the ritual.

[95] *Hallel* is the Talmudic name given to Ps. cxiii-cxviii recited at the new moon and other festivals.

[96] For instance, at the feast of *Khidhr Elias* celebrated in spring by Christians, the tray put out for him on the eve includes a mixture of nuts, spices and date-syrup, the nuts (symbol of resurgence) being pounded. The Parsi *haoma*, Mandaean *misha* and the Shi'a *samanu* are all ritually prepared by pounding, and nuts form a chief ingredient of the latter.

it was disputed whether ḥaroseth was a religious obligation. (Throughout this treatise, when referring to the cups the Mishnah speaks of a "mixed cup".)

The next item on the ritual programme was *Korekh* (the "rolling" or "furling"). A special hymn was recited for this part of the rite. The father took the third loaf, broke off a piece, placed a leaf of lettuce on it and then rolled the thin, soft bread like a scroll round the lettuce, dipped it into the ḥaroseth and ate it. He handed pieces of bread to the others, who did the same.[97] When the bread and lettuce had been eaten, all washed hands again and the mother brought in the secular dishes and set them on the table. This, in the programme, is the *Shulan 'Orekh*, the "preparing the table." It was a simple meal eaten as a single course, and the meat, naturally, was lamb.

When it was over, and grace had been recited, the third cup was filled and the half-loaf with had been given to the boy in the earlier part of the ceremony was removed from his shoulder, divided into portions and eaten. According to Iraqi tradition, this half-loaf, the *afikoman* (the word means perhaps things served after a meal, dessert) should be consumed before midnight. It is local custom to cut two rings of bread from it which serve as talismans throughout the year. Kept in a purse, they increase wealth and they avert the Evil Eye. Travellers carry them as protection against robbers: ground and mixed with water and administered to a woman in childbirth they ensure safe and speedy delivery. Some carry a lump of salt with the rings.

Traditionally, meat representing part of the festival sacrifice should be eaten at this stage of the proceedings, but on the occasion when I assisted at the *seder* meal in Baghdad this was not done; indeed in some families the bone was dry and had been used at other Passovers.[98]

The third cup of wine was drunk and after the recital of the second part of the *Hallel*, reading being sometimes in unison and sometimes chanted by a single member of the company, the evening was concluded by the *Nerṣa* (*nirṣa*: "accepted"), that is, the ending of the *seder* by drinking the fourth cup. Before it was emptied, however, oranges were

---

[97] At the Chief Rabbi's house the *korekh* was performed otherwise: he put some ḥaroseth with the lettuce before he rolled it with the bread and dipped it into the ḥaroseth bowl. The ritual of *korekh* is attributed to the famous Talmudist R. Hillel the Elder.

[98] I am told that Ashkenazim remove the dish containing the egg and shankbone which they put in one dish when the *afikoman* is first set aside, so that they can grasp the *seder* dish or tray; but, according to their *Haggadah*, they apparently leave them on the table, since the rubric orders that they shall point at them when reciting "the Paschal lamb..." (see note 94, just above).

brought in, and eaten after a benediction, for my host, a Kabbalist, had been taught that by eating "fruit of the tree" with the proper grace on this sacred night a soul suffering *gilgul neshamoth* in the shape of the fruit might perchance be liberated.

Before the gathering broke up, Ḥad Gadia ("One Goat") was chanted; all joining gleefully in a well-known air. This ditty in Aramaic is kin to the nursery rhyme of "The Old Woman and her Pig" and has an Iraqi counterpart in "The Old Woman and her Goat" in which a goat bargains in order not to go to the well "in this rain."[99] There must be versions in other lands. Rabbinical commentators, disdainful of folk-song, have attributed to it an allegorical significance.[100] Is there not a possibility, however, that the gay little song was intended as a kindly relaxation, a concession to little Jewish sleepy heads tired out after a long and exciting evening?

It will be seen that even within the boundaries of one city there are variations of the manner in which the *seder* rites are celebrated. As for the Haggadah itself, not only does the Iraqi text differ from that used in Jerusalem, but it takes twice as long, because every passage is repeated in Arabic. In Jerusalem the Ashkenazim – the Iraqi Jews would class themselves as Sephardim – make ḥaroseth of apple, almonds, raisin and cinnamon chopped fine with an admixture of wine: the salads and herbs are lettuce, celery or the green top of horseradish and parsley: for the lemon-juice, vinegar[101] or salted water is used.

According to Brauer, Yemenite Jews call ḥaroseth duqah, "pounded stuff,"[102] and it consists of almonds, raisins, cardamom, apples, walnuts, pomegranates, dates, cloves, cinnamon, wine and vinegar. The fruit, nuts and spices are pounded in a mortar, the liquids are added at table. When the bitter herbs are eaten with ḥaroseth they are wrapped in the latter – a reversal of the Iraqi practice – then moulded into a ball and swallowed. In the Yemen, the *seder* tray is placed on a low, round table and the family sit on the ground round it. Each person has a cushion or cushions at his left to assist the traditional "leaning at ease." On the tray beans, lettuce and parsley are arranged in an outer circle "like a wreath" and this, Brauer says, is called *adama*, "earth,"

---

[99] See Drower (Stevens), *Folk-Tales of Iraq*, Oxford: Oxford University Press 1931.
[100] Namely, that one empire devours another, but that the Almighty who is above all, commands the Angel of Death and guides human history.
[101] Brauer, p. 341.
[102] Iraqi Jewesses concoct a Passover sweetmeat for children, a paste called *madquqa* (the pounded). It is made of dates, almonds, hazel-nuts and other nuts pounded in a mortar, and moistened with date-syrup (see note 96, just above).

because the blessing over "fruit of the earth" is pronounced over it.[103] At the recital of the ten plagues, a little wine is dropped for every one into a pot-sherd. When they recite "How countless are the proofs of care," every time in it the refrain in *Dayyenu* occurs, all lift the table and bring it down with a thump. According to our head servant in Baghdad, the Kurdish Jew mentioned elsewhere, this custom is practised also by Kurdish Jews.

To review the *seder*: it is obvious, when the various foods and items of the *seder* tray are compared with other seasonal ritual tables and trays in Iraq and neighbouring countries that this sacred meal is related to them, and is an adaptation of the ancient folk-magic performed in lands where life itself is dependent on the health of flocks and fields. The grafting of the narrative with its political import on to a spring festival in which already nomad and farmer rituals had met and married, must have presented difficulties. For instance, explanation becomes strained when *ḥaroseth* is said to represent mortar used by the Israelites for Egyptian taskmasters, for the so-called bitter herbs, said to represent the "bitter sufferings" of the Hebrews in Egypt, are in fact the wholesome salads in which everyone rejoices at that time of year. They are found on most ritual trays. As to the dipping into lemon-juice or vinegar, these recall *Nau Roz* picnics in Persia, on which I have gone in past years. The great feature of these is picking fresh lettuce or other salads and then sitting round a bowl of sweetened vinegar or lemon-juice into which everyone in the circle dips his or her freshly-gathered leaves.

Christians at Easter, Mandaeans at *Parwanaiia,* Yazidis at their spring feast and Parsis at their "mid-spring" *muktads* welcome the final defeat of winter as a victory of life over death, and so celebrate rites for their dead.

On the second night of the feast a *seder* meal is again eaten. In Jerusalem Passover is celebrated for seven days; in Iraq it lasts eight days, the first two and last two being holidays. The four middle days are half-holidays; they are called the days of *Ḥol Ha'mo'ed.*

On the first day, at morning service, dew is prayed for instead of rain, and that lovely poem of joy and desire, the Song of Songs, is appointed to be read. Could any Old Testament poetry be better suited to the Oriental spring?

> For lo, the winter is over and past,
> The rain is over and gone.

---

[103]Brauer, p. 341.

On the second night of Passover the "counting of the *Omer*" – that is, of the "Sheaf," begins. It is represented only by the recitation of certain prayers. The first "counting" opens with the words,

> Blessed art Thou, O Eternal our God, King of the Universe, who hath sanctified us with His commandments and ordered us to count the days of the *Omer*. May it be Thy will, O Eternal our God and God of our fathers, speedily to rebuild Thy Holy Temple in our days....

Thus the theme which recurs so often, the Messianic restoration of the Temple, has taken the place of what may have been the pious prayer of an agricultural community for a plentiful harvest. Harvest means reaping, "cutting-down," and this may possibly be why marriage is forbidden during the days of "counting the *Omer*."[104] (Taboos on marriage at harvest-time exist elsewhere, as in Southern India.) During this period, too, pious Jews refrain from cutting their hair and women abstain from house-work after dark.

The thirty-third day of the Omer, *Lag Ba-Omer*, the 18th of Ayyar, is traditionally observed as a feast. In Europe a day of joy, often spent by Jewish children picnicking in the fields, in Iraq orthodox Jews observe it only by omitting the *Taḥanun* (penitential prayer) in the synagogues. Kabbalists, however, celebrate the day with rejoicing as the anniversary of the Talmudic teacher R. Simeon Bar Yohai, to whom they attribute the authorship of the Zohar. The eve of the day is called *Hillulah*, a reference to the divine union of the saint's soul with God on the day of his death. In Iraq, crowds gathered in the Jewish quarters. Hundreds of oil-lamps and candles were lit, food and drink were provided lavishly, and passages from the Zohar read aloud with enthusiasm and emotion. Songs were sung in praise of the Master and at the close of the evening ceremonies, whilst the women shrilled their high, kite-like joy-notes, a large bonfire was kindled in an open space, into the flames of which those who desired a boon threw some precious possession such as a silk garment, a jewel or other treasured adornment, as a "ransom." Many continued to dance and sing by the glowing embers until the first grey of early dawn appeared in the sky.

We have wandered ahead of the calendar for, immediately after Passover, usually during the four middle days – the *Ḥol Ha-mo'ed* – Iraqi Jews visit the fruit-orchards in order to perform the "Blessing of

---

[104] The reason for the prohibition given by Talmudists is that the disciples of R. Akiba, a great Talmudic teacher at the time of Bar Kokhba's revolt against Rome, all died in a plague during the days of *Omer*, and that ever since then, they have been observed as days of mourning. The plague is said to have been halted on the 33rd day, and this is a day of rejoicing (Eb. 62b).

Evergreen Elijah 57

the Trees."[105] They set off in groups of not less than ten males over twelve years of age, and must perform the rite, if possible, within sight of two flowering fruit-trees, usually a date-palm and a citrus tree of some kind, a bitter or sweet orange or a lemon-tree. The ceremony consists of reading from the Talmud and Zohar and the recitation of prayers for the dead, that is, the *Ḳaddish* and the *Hashkavah*.

By invitation, the ceremony was arranged one year in our Baghdad garden. Both Tigris and spring were in full tide. Roses of every kind, European and Persian, filled the air with perfume; stocks, verbena, larkspurs, poppies and other flowers, native and imported, were blooming in profusion and straying often unbidden on to the lawns and round the trees.

We stood for the readings and prayers beside a lemon-tree in the glory of young and tender leaf; its waxy stars gleamed ivory amidst the green. Above us soared a female date-palm: her spikes of pale gold newly fertilized by the male bloom gave promise of amber harvest in the autumn. Here our guests stood in a semi-circle, books in hand, and chanted their Hebrew and Aramaic; turning to face Jerusalem when the two prayers for the dead were to be repeated. At their conclusion, each in a different key, they raised a harsh Oriental hymn. Some faces were work-lined and pale, for the Jewish quarter they came from was housebound in the heart of the thickly-built city.

They believed that in meeting here to bless the trees, they might perhaps grant release to souls imprisoned for their sins in the stately palm-tree or in the pomegranate, quince or other fruit-trees about us. For their merit in aiding these tree-bound souls they might one day receive like redemption themselves.

The fiftieth day of Counting of *Omer* brings the Jewish year to Pentecost, the "Feast of Weeks." This festival, known variously as *Shabu'oth* as "the Giving of the Law" and as "the Harvest Festival" might be fitly described by any of these names. As "Feast of Weeks" it is held seven weeks after the second day of Passover; the synagogue service relates the giving of the Mosaic code on Sinai; and, as to the last name, it concerns the wheat harvest, for the story of Ruth is read in the synagogue, about that Ruth who "stood in tears amid the alien corn" and gleaned amidst the sheaves.

---

[105]Compare the blessing pronounced on the vegetable creation recited by Zoroastrians, the *khshunam*, "for the good holy trees created by Mazda." (See iv, above.)

I have been told that in Europe and for instance in England, synagogues and houses are decorated with flowers and greenery[106] for this feast, but in Iraq there is little to mark the festival, except the readings in the synagogue. The service there and the Ḳiddush at home are performed as at Passover, the name of the feast being inserted in the proper place in the prayers. On the eve of the festival, however, Jews gather in congregations of at least ten males to read portions of the Torah, Mishnah and *Idhra Rabba* (the Great Assembly from the Zohar) as on the night of *Hosha'nah Rabba*,[107] and, as then, they burn candles for their dead, distribute three kinds of food with the appropriate benedictions, and recite the Ḳaddish and *Hashkavah*. This solemn gathering which lasts most of the night is called in Iraq the *Ḥathīmah*, the "sealing" or "conclusion."

The feast lasts for two days, and at the morning meal on the first day a special kind of pastry is eaten, called *kahi*. The women make it by beating eggs and sprinkling in flour. Soaked in melted sheep's butter, these are fried like pancakes, and are round. When eaten, they are dipped into date-syrup *(dibis)*, honey or other sweet syrup and powdered with sugar. The very poor eat *marrīs* as a substitute, that is, crumbs of bread soaked in sheep's butter and *dibis*. Pious Jews in Baghdad eat no meat on the first two days of the feast, but are allowed butter and cream.

In Iraq this feast is known also as *'Id-ul-Ziyārah*, (Feast of Pilgrimage), for at this season thousands of pilgrims, Moslems as well as Jews, visit the tombs of Ezekiel at Kifl and of Ezra near Qurna, whole families camping out near the shrines. The pilgrimage is of high antiquity and has been mentioned by travellers many times over the centuries. Moslem women, veiled and unveiled, and Jewesses, some still wearing black blinkers to cover their faces, jostle one another amicably in the small chambers of the two holy buildings, selecting at Kifl two phallic stones for special attention.

vii. Evergreen Elijah

The prophet Elijah, in Semitic folk-lore, has donned the mantle of some rain-bringing deity or genius of fertility.[108] Indian miniature

---

[106]In the Yemen the Feast of Weeks is called "the little Greenery Feast" (*'id al-Khudhaira*).

[107]See iii, p. 34, above.

[108]Even in the Old Testament Elijah is a rain-maker (I Kg. xviii, 45): he is credited with power over lightning, "fire from heaven" (I Kg. xvii); has power over water and streams (II Kg. ii, 8); revives the dead (I Kg. xvii, 21-22); and does not die a natural death but, like Enoch, is translated to the skies.

artists of the Mogul period represent him as a hoary old man wearing a green dress, for he is the Green One, *al-Khidhr, Khidhr Elias*.

His cult survives with Ashkenazi Jews in the cup set for him on the *seder* table: Iraqi Jews place a chair for him in the *sukkah* at the Feast of Tabernacles[109] and Elijah's chair, the Chair of *Khidhr Elias*, is placed prominently in both house and synagogue when a Jewish boy is circumcised. On the eve of the circumcision male guests are invited to eat a meal in honor of the coming event. Guests are invited to the house and entertainment is as lavish as the father can afford. Wine and *'araq* are drunk, and a spirit of geniality pervades the assembly. Near the table a chair is placed for *Khidhr Elias*, empty save for a copy of the Torah wrapped in a cloth.

At a circumcision I attended the chair itself was covered with a woman's silken *izār* and it was adorned with sprigs of myrtle, rue, *rihān* (basil) and flowers. The evening is called *Lailat 'Aqd el-Yās* (the night of the myrtle-contract?). Later in the evening, the chair should be placed on the mother's bed as a protection against Lilith,[110] who might, without its protection, attack the babe that night. Fearful mothers of the older generation, in their fear that this demon might attempt to strangle the child, often kept him in their laps till the break of day.

One circumcision at which I was present in Baghdad was that of our head-servant's child. He was a Kurdish Jew of Sulimaniyah and was with us for many years. He himself was to be the *sandaq* – as the man who holds the boy is called – and the Chair of *Khidhr Elias* was placed to his right, for its position always is to the right of the person who undertakes this office. The chair was on a low platform facing north, and was a small arm-chair such as might be used by a child. On the four extremities of its back and arms were silver posts with tops shaped like pomegranates *(rimmonim)* from which eleven silver bells were suspended by silver chains. The chair, called *Kursi Khidhr Elias an-Nebi* (the Chair of the Green One, Elijah the Prophet) was "dressed," that is, almost entirely covered by a loose cover of pale pink cloth – the color had no ritual significance. The copy of the Torah on the seat was wrapped in a cloth: there were also cushions and many sprigs of freshly-cut myrtle.

---

[109] See iii, p. 32, above.
[110] In Jewish folk-lore Adam had a first wife, Lilith. In her jealousy of Eve, this female demon attacks Eve's descendants and babes suffer from her malice. To protect a new-born child and its mother from her, seven white onions and a chicken's leg are fastened to the wall by a long nail above the bed where they lie. This charm protects them also from the Evil Eye. It should remain until the mother has taken her ritual bath.

When the rabbi arrived the father, who had earlier distributed nosegays of fresh green myrtle, marigolds and basil to all who stood there, took his place on the platform with his back to Jerusalem. A small thin mattress was placed on his knees. I was asked to take the baby from its mother and put it on the father's lap. He arranged the child so that it lay on the mattress with its head towards his body. Many charms and talismans had been placed round the little neck.

When the swaddling clothes had been removed, the child's legs were parted and tucked firmly beneath the coverlet on either side. The rabbi approached, and after examining the penis, placed a silver instrument over it after pushing the foreskin together. Then he made a deft swift incision round a circular aperture in the instrument with his knife, removed the instrument and foreskin together and threw the latter on the floor. Pushing back what was left of the foreskin he sucked the wound, spitting out the blood. I was told that before he took the penis into his mouth he first filled his mouth with wine. I noticed that some of the women who were watching the act kissed their fingertips and pressed them against their eyes. I was told that until recently – for now it is discouraged – if a sterile woman was present she would pounce on the severed foreskin and swallow it, hoping that it would produce pregnancy. Nowadays it is usually picked up and dropped into a hole for sewage. To any childless woman present it is usual for pitying friends to say at this moment of the rite, "*Allah yakhadh dherech!*" in the vernacular Arabic, i.e. "God make thee green!"

After the operation was over, the child's penis was wrapped by an assistant in a strip soaked in disinfectant and a bandage tied over that whilst the rabbi inhaled the perfume of three myrtle-sprigs held in his left hand, reciting a blessing over it and then a special *Ḳiddush* over the wine, which he held in his right hand. He drank of it, moistened the lips of the child with wine and then handed the cup to the bystanders that they might sip from it. The parents do not usually drink of the wine, but it is a privilege eagerly sought by childless women, for the wine is thought to cure infertility.

The circumcision which Brauer saw in the Yemen[111] resembled in most particulars those performed in Baghdad. He says, however, that a vessel of water is placed beneath *Khidhr Elias*'s chair. Barren women seek to drink of it so that their reproach may be removed. A little ritual wine is put into the child's mouth. In Aden the ceremony takes place in the father's house: rosewater is sprinkled on guests as they arrive and a sprig of myrtle is distributed to each. This sprig is

---

[111]Brauer, p. 193ff.

returned to the child's father when guests leave, and he places all the myrtle upon the prophet's chair.

Mandaeans do not refer to Elijah in their prayers, nor do they pay him any honor. He is completely ignored by them, which is curious since his cult exists in Iraq and elsewhere amongst both the Moslems and the Christians. The former, especially Shi'as, when seeking a boon, the granting of a wish or the cure of one who is sick, form a frail bark (usually cut from the base of a datepalm frond) upon which they set lighted candles, held firmly in place by daubs of clay. On any Thursday evening, provided there is little wind to roughen the waves, these glittering little barges may be seen slipping down the Tigris. If the owner who has launched one sees hers drift out of sight with lights undimmed and unextinguished, she believes that her petition will be heard. If some go out in a puff of wind, her prayer may be only partially granted: but should disaster overtake the tiny float, the omen is bad.

Christians look on the prophet as a wonder-worker and make vows to him, especially at his feast, which falls in early spring a little before the Lenten fast of fifty days. My old friend Lili, narrator of some of the stories in my *Folk-Tales of Iraq*,[112] used to delight to relate an experience which gave her proof of his visit. She was ill, and on the eve of his feast, whilst the rest of the house were asleep, she lay on her bed. Suddenly an unseen hand touched her eyelids and a voice said, "Rise! Light a candle for thyself." She left her bed, lit a candle and added it to those already burning on the tray in the living-room, and the next day found herself recovered from her illness.

The *Khidhr Elias* tray resembles in its essential points those of most seasonal ritual trays and tables. The cult of "the Green One" is wide-spread in Iraq. *Kidhr Elias* has his room, a small chamber called *Qubbat Eliyahu an-Nabi* at Ezekiel's tomb at Kifl on the Hillah branch of the Euphrates. Jews believe that this tiny room will expand to hold any number of pilgrims. Sick children are laid there for a short time in the hope that the prophet will cure them. Some stones set into the walls in this room resemble phallic emblems and these are considered to confer fertility if touched or kissed. (See end of vi, above.)

Elijah has shrines at other places of pilgrimage such as Ezra's tomb on the Tigris, and these are visited by Moslems and Christians as well as by Jews. Legends abound concerning persons whose poverty is relieved by a plate placed on their road by *Khidhr Elias,* and a woman whose husband is setting out on a journey often says to him, *"Leyqat Eliyahu en-Nebi bidarbak!"* (Mayst thou encounter the Prophet Elijah on thy

---

[112]See note 99, above.

road!); and Iraqi Jews bidding a traveller farewell may add *"Eliyahu en-Nebi biwajhak!"* (May Elijah the Prophet countenance thee!).

Postscript

I came to Iraq at the conclusion of the First World War. At that time the Jews were no worse off than the members of any other minority; indeed, in many respects their position was stronger, for most of the trade was in their hands. They were on good terms with Moslems and neighbors and proud of an ancestry which in most cases stretched back into pre-Islamic times. When, under the tolerant rule of Cyrus Jews were accorded permission to return to Judaea, the majority then resident in Babylonia preferred to remain in the land of Abraham. Here they multiplied and flourished, and Jewish academies at Pumbeditha and Sura were justly famed for dialectic and learning.

When Iraq acquired independence after the First World War and Faisal I became king, this first cabinet included a highly respected and able Jew as Minister of Finance. The Jews were useful citizens: they had their own schools, hospitals, clinics and charities and their knowledge of language and their ability enabled many to find employment in Government offices.

Even when trouble broke out in Palestine between Palestinian Arabs and Jewish settlers, there was little rancor in Iraq, a country where Jewish shrines such as the tombs of Ezra, Ezekiel, Jonah and Nahum are as sacred to Moslems and Christians as to Jews.

It was only when the Nazis came to power and when their propaganda used the situation in Palestine to heighten anti-British and anti-Jewish feeling that the Moslem Iraqi became "conscious" of his Jewish neighbor. During the time of waning British prestige with the German star in the ascendant, anti-Jewish feeling was fanned into a flame. Baghdad hooligans looted the Jewish quarter and committed the usual excesses. This anti-Jewish feeling, in abeyance after the return of the British and expulsion of Rashid 'Ali, smouldered on in the form of dislike and suspicion. Events in Palestine at the arrival of Palestinian refugees in Iraq made the situation impossible. Any Jew was now looked upon as a fifth columnist. Incident followed incident, and the terror of the Jews increased. In March 1950 Jews were told that they could register for emigration and applications flowed in a mighty stream. By March 1951 about 60.000 Jews had left the country. A law was passed "freezing" the property of emigrants and intending emigrants; in other words, these people were deprived of their property since they had no intention of returning. As transportation to Israel by aircraft of so vast a number was necessarily slow, about 40,000 whose names were registered waited penniless, to subsist on the charity of those who remained.

To those of us who had lived in the Middle East for many years, watching the ebb and flow of politics, the tragic events in both Palestine and Iraq came as no surprise; victims there had to be, and a number of innocent and inoffensive people, both Arab and Jews, were cruelly torn from homes which both held dear.

As for the Iraqi Jews – a venerable community now uprooted from the land which had harbored them for two thousand years and more, a community which had preserved intact much of its ancient heritage – many traditions and time-honored customs are bound to disappear. Modern Israel has set its face resolutely Westwards.

For this reason I am privileged to have been able to chronicle a few aspects of Babylonian Jewry as it survived into my day.

Editor's Note

I would like to thank Dr. Margaret Hackforth-Jones for making Lady Drower's *Evergreen Elijah* material available to me. Also, I thank Jesse Buckley for re-drawing the illustration of the *seder* table.

Part Two
INSTITUTIONS OF ANCIENT JUDAISM

2

Palestinian Synagogues before 70 C.E.: A Review of the Evidence

Paul Virgil McCracken Flesher
Northwestern University

The origins of the synagogue have long been a matter of debate.[1] While scholars have believed for several decades that the synagogue originated in Babylonia during the exile after 587 B.C.E. and was then brought into Palestine during the return from exile, there has been a distinct lack of evidence to support this belief.[2] Two recent articles,

---

[1] This article is a revised version of a paper given at the Midwest SBL meeting, Jan. 31, 1989. It grew out of a series of lectures I gave to the NEH Summer Seminar for College Teachers at Brown University in the summer of 1988. I am grateful to A. J. Levine of Swarthmore College for encouraging me to pursue these studies further. For reading and commenting on this paper in different drafts, I want to thank A. J. Levine, Roger Brooks, Dennis Groh, William R. Stegner and Walter Aufrecht. Their efforts have helped me improve the work. Needless to say, the responsibility for any shortcomings should be laid at my door.

[2] For the standard position, see Emil Schürer, *The History of the Jewish People in the Age of Jesus Christ*, revised and edited by G. Vermes and F. Miller, (Edinburgh: T & T Clark, 1973, 1979, etc.) esp. vol. 2, pp. 423-463; John Bright, *A History of Israel*, 3rd. ed., (Philadelphia: Westminster, 1981); Finkelstein, L., "The Origin of the Synagogue," PAAJR, 1(1930); L. I. Levine, "The Second Temple Synagogue: The Formative Years," pp. 7-32 in L. I. Levine, ed., *The Synagogue in Late Antiquity*, (Philadelphia: ASOR, 1987) and L. I. Levine, "Ancient Synagogues – A Historical Introduction," in L. I. Levine, ed., *Ancient Synagogues Revealed* (Detroit: Wayne State, 1982). For critiques and reassessment of that position, see Ellis Rivkin, "Ben-Sira and the Nonexistence of the Synagogue: A Study in Historical Method," pp. 320-354 in *In the Time of Harvest: Essays in Honor of Abba Hillel Silver*, (New York: Macmillan, 1963); M. J. Chiat, "First-Century Synagogue Architecture: Methodological Problems,"

when seen together, have set the stage for a new direction on the question of early synagogues. The first article, by J. Gwyn Griffiths, argues a convincing case for tracing the synagogue's origins to Egypt.[3] Griffiths shows that the synagogue is evidenced first in the third century by pointing to the well-known dedication of a synagogue (prayer house, *proseuche*) to Ptolemy III Euergetes, who reigned from 246-221 B.C.E., as well as to the contemporary dedication of a synagogue at Arsinoë-Crocodilopolis. He further points to several inscriptions dated from the second and first centuries revealing the existence of synagogues in both Lower Egypt and the Fayum. During the second century B.C.E. inscriptions concerning synagogues begin to appear in other places around the Mediterranean, most notably at Delos and Antioch, revealing the spread of synagogues beyond Egypt.[4] Although briefly mentioned by Griffiths, the startling contrast with the situation in Palestine is brought out most prominently in the second article mentioned, that by Lester L. Grabbe.[5] Grabbe shows that information concerning Palestine does not indicate the existence of synagogues prior to the "Post-Maccabean" period. Indeed, Grabbe indicates, "when we look at Palestine itself, evidence for the existence of synagogues is lacking before the first century B.C.E. and perhaps even until the first C.E."[6]

Taken together, these two articles suggest that the synagogue in Palestine has been imported from the larger Mediterranean world.

---

pp. 49-60 in J. Gutmann, *Ancient Synagogues: The State of Research* (Chico, CA: Scholars Press, 1981); S. B. Hoenig, "The Ancient City-Square: The Forerunner of the Synagogue," *ANRW* II 19.1, pp. 448-476. See also J. Gutmann, "Synagogue Origins: Theories and Facts," pp. 1-6 in J. Gutmann, ed., *Ancient Synagogues: The State of Research* (Chico, CA: Scholars Press, 1981) and S. Hoenig, "The Supposititious Temple-Synagogue," pp. J. Gutman, *The Synagogue: Studies in Origins, Archaelogy and Architecture* (New York: KTAV, 1975).

[3]J. Gwyn Griffiths, "Egypt and the Rise of the Synagogue," *JThS*, 38 (1987) 1, pp. 1-15. Much of the inscriptional evidence Griffiths cites is well-known and has been discussed by other scholars. See, for example, E. Schürer, revised by G. Vermes, *et al.*, *The History of the Jewish People in the Age of Jesus Christ*, (Edinburgh: T & T Clark, 1979) vol. ii, p. 425, n. 5; and *Theological Dictionary of the New Testament*, (Grand Rapids, MI: Eerdmans, 1964-76), vol. vii, pp. 811-2. The importance of Griffiths' article is that he uses this evidence to articulate a well-argued claim that the synagogue began in Egypt. See also Paul-Eugène Dion, "Synagogues et Temples dans l'Égypte Hellénistique," *Science et Esprit*, 29 (1977), pp. 45-75.

[4]See Griffiths, p. 4, notes 9-10.

[5]Lester L. Grabbe, "Synagogues in Pre-70 Palestine: A Re-Assessment," *JThS* 39 (1988) 2, pp. 401-410.

[6]Grabbe, p. 410.

Indeed, we can document its existence in Egypt nearly two centuries before any evidence of its penetration into Palestine appears. While this conclusion may finally resolve the scholarly debate on origins, it opens up a new set of questions. Not least of these is, how was the synagogue – this foreign import – received in Palestine? The question is particularly acute because the synagogue and the activities that take place in it constitute an inherently different Judaism from that of the Jerusalem Temple, the cultic center of Israelite religion. This difference must be emphasized.

The Temple cult was a system of holiness and purity mediated through sacrifices offered by a holy caste of people, the priests. The ability of the common Israelite to participate was limited in general to two types of activity, (1) watching, and (2) supporting the Temple cult with taxes, tithes and animals for sacrifice. The priests were the only class of people who were permitted to conduct the rites within the heightened holiness of the Temple and its inner Court. Indeed, they alone could safely enter that space. There were a few exceptions to this division of worship, most notably with regard to the Passover sacrifice and the Nazirite oath, but the distinction between priest and common Israelite remained; the priest carried out the activities of the Temple cult, the Israelite had few responsibilities with regard to the actual performance of worship.

The synagogue, by contrast, arose in a region without access to the Temple cult (i.e., in Egypt) and in a sense comprised a substitute for it. It served as a gathering place for all Israelites – priests and commoners – where they took part in worship. That worship seems to have consisted of prayers and Scripture reading, as far as the limited evidence indicates. There were no sacrifices and hence there existed no need to distinguish among the Israelite castes. Indeed, the only synagogue activity related to the Temple cult at Jerusalem seems to have been the collection of the annual Temple tax.[7] So the synagogue lacked the high levels of holiness that infused the Temple cult. From the perspective of the common Israelite, the non-priest, there were thus really two different Judaisms: the Temple cult from which he was generally excluded from meaningful participation, and the Judaism of the synagogue in which he was a full participant.

---

[7]Josephus, in *Antiquities* xvi 164-173, indicates that Ceasar Augustus and other Roman officials decreed that, among other things, the Jews be permitted to store money for the Temple tax in their synagogues and to transport that money to the Jerusalem Temple without hindrance. It should also be noted that at one time there was a Jewish Temple on the island of Elephantine in the Nile near Aswan. A discussion of that temple is beyond the scope of this paper.

Given the essential differences between the synagogue and the Temple cult, the question must be asked, what was the synagogue's reception when it entered Palestine? Since the synagogue originated in a region where there was no access to the Jerusalem Temple, an easy introduction of the synagogue into an area where such access was available should not be taken for granted. The Temple priests may have viewed the synagogue as an unholy competitor (after all, the Hebrew Scriptures provide no support for it). It is also possible that such a stance was unnecessary; the proximity of the Temple cult may have made the synagogue seem inappropriate and unappealing to Jews native to Jerusalem. Conversely, the synagogue and the Temple cult may have cooperated and filled distinct but compatible roles in Palestinian society. Unfortunately, we lack the evidence to answer any of these questions or even to provide an extensive analysis of this problem. But we can investigate it in a general manner by taking a demographic perspective and, in essence, doing a survey. By asking, "where and when, in pre-70 Palestine, do we find evidence concerning the establishment of the synagogue?" we can discover the distribution of synagogues in pre-70 Palestine. The pattern of distribution will reveal, to the limits of the data, the relationship between the synagogue and the Temple cult. We shall focus our analysis first on evidence from literary sources, then move to an investigation of the archaeological evidence.[8] At each stage, we shall probe the reliability of the evidence so that the strength of the conclusions we ultimately draw will be clear.

In general terms what we shall discover is this: Palestine itself can be divided into two areas with regard to the success of establishing the synagogue as an institution. In the region around Jerusalem, which for the sake of this paper is roughly coextensive with the political boundaries of Judea, we find no evidence that the synagogue

---

[8]This article will not include the rabbinic literature in its investigations; to be properly understood, rabbinic information concerning synagogues requires an extensive study of its own, which I have begun. I will point out, however, that none of the rabbinic texts published prior to about 250 C.E. refer to synagogues prior to 70. The tannaitic midrashim – the Mekhiltas, Sifra, the two Sifrés – rarely mention synagogues at all and never in a pre-70 context. The Mishnah, while it discusses synagogues in a number of places, never depicts them prior to 70 either. The prayers and activities that the Mishnah's framers portray as happening in the post-70 synagogue are depicted as part of the pre-70 Temple cult. It is not until the later texts, such as the tosefta and the Talmuds, that synagogues are mentioned that supposedly existed prior to 70. The lateness of these texts, particularly in light of the silence of the earlier texts, renders the information from the later sources extremely suspect. Also note that Grabbe, in his article, makes a few preliminary observations.

established itself as an important institution. The Temple cult apparently held sway in this area and maintained a religious environment that prevented the synagogue from gaining a foothold in the area. Conversely, the region north of Judea (Samaria, Galilee, Decapolis, Trachonitis, and so on) provided fertile ground for the establishment of the synagogue. This area, lying beyond the immediate religious influence of the Temple cult, evidences the naturalization and development of the synagogue by the early first century C.E. To work out the extent of these conclusions and their implications, we now turn to our analysis, beginning with the literary evidence.

When we investigate the numerous Jewish documents written prior to 70 C.E., we discover this striking point: they contain little information concerning synagogues. Indeed, only three sets of texts even mention synagogues in Palestine – the New Testament, Josephus and Philo. All other documents are silent. Nowhere in the Hebrew Bible can we find anything about synagogues.[9] Furthermore, the whole corpus of apocalyptic, pseudepigraphic and other pre-70 Jewish literature is silent. No mention of any Palestinian synagogues appears in First or Second Maccabees, the Qumran texts, Jubilees, any of the Enoch texts, Aristeas or any of the testaments, to mention just a few texts.[10]

By contrast, the texts that point to the existence of Palestinian synagogues during Temple times reveal an interesting phenomenon. The synagogues they mention are primarily in places beyond the control of the Jerusalem Temple – in northern Palestine. This is certainly true for the synagogues found in Josephus. Although most of the synagogues he mentions are in the diaspora, he describes three synagogues in Palestine. All lie in areas north of the Temple's immediate control – Tiberius in Galilee, Dor and Ceasaria on the coast in northwestern Samaria.[11] Unfortunately, Philo's evidence is less substantial. He mentions Palestinian synagogues only in the context of the Essenes of

---

[9] Several passages have been identified as possibly indicating synagogues, but upon further analysis it is clear that they do not. Among these are Ezek. 11:16, Neh. 8, Is. 19:19, Psalms 74:8 and Jer. 39:8.
[10] Of course, in many of these texts we would not expect to find synagogues mentioned. But the question of this study is whether there *is* evidence, not whether we should expect evidence.
[11] For Tiberius, see *Life* 277, 280, 293. For Dor, see *Antiquities* xix 300 and for Ceasaria, see *War* ii 285-9. Josephus also mentions a synagogue in diasporan Antioch, *War* vii 44.

Palestine-Syria, not with regard to Palestinian Jews in general or in Judea in particular.[12]

As for the New Testament – the gospels and the book of Acts, to be specific – it follows Josephus in providing a clear picture of synagogues in Galilee and northern Palestine, but reveals little solid evidence of them in Judea. The synoptic gospels almost unanimously place the synagogues with which Jesus interacts in Galilee. They mention, for example, specific instances in which Jesus teaches in synagogues at Nazareth and Capernaum, and frequently state that Jesus went to synagogues throughout Galilee.[13] The only possible exception appears at Luke 4:44, which states that Jesus taught in the synagogues of Judea. Joseph Fitzmyer, however, makes clear that the term "Judea" here has a general reference implying areas where Jews live (i.e., northern Palestine), rather than the territory of Judea proper.[14] This point is supported by the parallel passages (Mt. 4:23, Mk 1:39) which clearly state that Jesus taught in the synagogues in Galilee. Furthermore, in the following section, to which this remark is a transition, Luke goes on to describe Jesus' activity in Galilee (Luke 5:1-11). Thus, Luke in particular, and the synoptic gospels in general, evidence synagogues only in Northern Palestine.[15]

The gospel of John echoes this emphasis on Galilee (Jn 6:59), but also repeatedly mentions, in the context of Jerusalem, that the Pharisees have threatened people who believe in Jesus with excommunication from the synagogue (Jn 9:22, 12:42, 16:2). These passages provide no evidence of synagogues in Jerusalem either, however, for scholars have shown that these descriptions reflect the poor state of relations between Jews and Christians during the period in which John is writing, probably sometime after 80, and the location in which he writes, somewhere in the diaspora, rather than the state of affairs during Jesus' lifetime.[16] John therefore provides evidence for

---

[12]*Quod omis prober liber sit*, 81. See also the mention of synagogues in Alexandria (in Egypt) in *Flaccus* 45-8 and *Spec. Legat.* 20, 132.
[13]Mt. 4:23, 9:35,13:54; Mark 1:21-29, 1:39, 3:1, 6:2; Luke 4:15-44, 7:5, 8:41; John 6:59.
[14]J. A. Fitzmyer, *The Gospel according to Luke (I-IX)*, (Garden City, NY: Doubleday, 1981), pp. 530-4.
[15]Again, the question before us is not whether we expect to find data in the synoptic gospels concerning synagogues in Judea, but whether there is such data.
[16]For discussion of this question, see R. E. Brown, *The Gospel according to John (i-xii)*, (Garden City, NY: Doubleday, 1966), pp. LXX-LXXIII, 374, 379-82, 487-8; J. L. Martyn, *History & Theology in the Fourth Gospel*, 2nd ed. (Nashville: Abingdon, 1979), pp. 37-63; R. Kimelman, "Birkat Ha-Minim and the Lack of Evidence for an Anti-Christian Jewish Prayer in Late Antiquity," in E. P. Sanders

synagogues in Galilee and perhaps for some in the Mediterranean diaspora, but none for synagogues in Jerusalem.

Acts provides a different picture; it focuses primarily on synagogues in the diaspora: Antioch, Corinth, Athens and so on. Still it includes two sets of passages that do mention synagogues in Jerusalem. First, Paul states that he persecuted Christians in Jerusalem synagogues in the three major speeches of his final captivity (Acts 22:19, 24:12, 26:11). But, unfortunately for the "Jerusalem Synagogue," Conzelmann, Haenchen and Cadbury all agree that these speeches are literary constructions composed by Luke and thus reflect a post-70 diaspora situation.[17]

Second, Acts 6:9 mentions "the synagogue which is called that of the Libertini, both Cyrenians and and Alexandrians."[18] While there are problems both with the interpretation of Acts six as a whole and with the phrase referring to synagogues in particular, scholars do not find any basis for doubting the existence of this particular synagogue.[19] So here we finally locate literary evidence for a pre-70 synagogue in Jerusalem. On the face of it, this passage shows that the distinction between Judea and Galilee intimated by the evidence above is incorrect. But if we study the passage more closely, we discover that it does not speak of a synagogue attended by Jerusalemites in general. Instead, this is the synagogue is of the "Cyrenians and Alexandrians"; it is a synagogue for foreigners, one part of which – the Alexandrians – even come from the country that has the oldest evidence concerning the establishment of synagogues. This implies, then, that the institution is for Jews from foreign lands, not for native Jerusalemites. The passage does not indicate that the synagogue as an institution has successfully moved into Jerusalem and established itself as a religious force counter to the Temple cult.

---

et al., eds., *Jewish and Cristian Self-Definition*, vol. 2 (Philadelphia: Fortress, 1981), pp. 226-243; L. H. Schiffman, *Who Was a Jew?* (Hoboken, NJ: KTAV, 1985), pp. 53-61. I think that in general this judgement is correct, even though several of these authors do not properly use the rabbinic literature.

[17]H. Conzelmann, *Acts of the Apostles* (Philadelphia: Fortress, 1987), pp. xliii-xlv,187; E. Haenchen, *The Acts of the Apostles* (Philadelphia: Westminster, 1971), pp. 103-10; H. J. Cadbury, "The Speeches in Acts," in *The Beginnings of Christianity*, vol. 5, F. J. Foakes Jackson and K. Lake, eds. (London: Macmillan, 1933), pp. 402-26.

[18]The translation is from *The Beginnings of Christianity*, vol. 4, F. J. Foakes Jackson and K. Lake, eds. (London: Macmillan, 1933), pp. 66-8.

[19]See the discussion in the previous citation.

We can shed more light on the position of synagogues in Jerusalem if we turn briefly to the Theodotus inscription.[20] This inscription was found near the site of the Jerusalem Temple and has been dated to the pre-70 period. It states that one Theodotus, a synagogue head and the grandson of a synagogue head, built this particular synagogue. If the dating is correct, scholars have suggested, then the grandfather may have headed a synagogue in Jerusalem in the early first century C.E. or even the late first century B.C.E.[21]

The important point for our purposes is that the inscription reveals that the synagogue to which it refers has a nature similar to the one mentioned in Acts six. One of the primary purposes of Theodotus' synagogue was to provide "the strangers' lodging and the chambers and the conveniences of waters for an inn for them that need it from abroad...."[22] That is, the synagogue served as a place where Jews from outside Palestine could come and stay during their visit in Jerusalem – the inscription refers to a religious boarding house. Like the passage in Acts, the inscription does not provide evidence to indicate that the synagogue had gained acceptance in Jerusalem as a religious institution alongside the Temple cult. There is no hint that this synagogue is for natives of Jerusalem. The only evidence of synagogues in Judea is for foreigners, therefore, whether they be permanent residents or visitors. Neither the Theodotus inscription nor Acts reveal the synagogue as the Temple cult's co-institution.

The evidence from literary sources, then, points to the conclusion that the synagogue as an imported institution did not gain equal acceptance in all areas of Palestine. In Galilee – whose residents, like those in the diaspora, had no immediate access to the Temple – the synagogue seemed to have become broadly established by the early first century C.E. In Judea, by contrast, where the Temple cult was the main focus of religious activity, we find no evidence of the synagogue

---

[20]See R. Weill, *La Cité de David* (Paris: Librairie Paul Geuthner, 1920), esp., pp. 186-90; L. H. Vincent, *RB*, 1921, pp. 247-277; T. Reinach, *REJ*, Jul,Sept. 1920, pp. 46-56; and A. Deissman, *Light from the Ancient East*, trans. by L. R. M. Strachan (New York: George H. Doran, 1927), pp. 439-441.

[21]Unfortunately, the date of this inscription is uncertain. The French scholars who initially studied it could not agree on the date. Some argued for a pre-70 dating, others for a Hadrianic or even Trajianic date. Furthermore, the archaeologists who found the inscription did not use the modern methods of stratigraphic analysis. Indeed, it is not even known whether the inscription was below, in or above the destruction layer of 70. Thus, the sure dating of this stone seems to be impossible. Even with these uncertainties, it seems probable that the inscription was written prior to 70 C.E.

[22]Deissman, p. 440.

gaining acceptance as a major religious institution. The only evidence of synagogues in Jerusalem is linked to the needs of foreigners. Perhaps, if I may speculate momentarily, foreign visitors needed them to assist pilgrimages, or, perhaps the synagogue served as a familiar religious and social center – a "home away from home" – for those who were more permanent residents in the city.

The evidence from documentary sources has provided an intriguing hypothesis. We can test it further if we turn to the data derived from archaeological investigations. The question now before us is whether archaeological remains confirm or contradict the distinction we have drawn between Galilee and Judea. To begin with, archaeologists have identified six potential pre-70, Palestinian synagogues. Two of these lie in Judea: Masada and Heriodium; the other four in Galilee: Migdal, Chorazin, Capernaum, and Gamla.[23] Upon close inspection, not all of these buildings live up to their tentative identification as synagogues. This is true for Migdal. Here a later structure has obliterated most of the remains of the suggested synagogue. This precludes establishing the character of the original building, and thus prevents confirming that it is a synagogue.[24] Similarly, if there ever was a first-century synagogue at Chorazin, it was lost before archaeologists were able to study it thoroughly.[25] Finally, the Capernaum "synagogue" at this

---

[23] The best statement of this position is G. Foerster, "The Synagogues at Masada and Herodium," in *JJA* 1977, 3-4:6-11, reprinted in L. I. Levine, ed., *Ancient Synagogues Revealed* (Detroit: Wayne State, 1982), pp. 24-9. The claim concerning the remains of a possible first century synagogue at Capernaum was made in a recent article by J. F. Strange and H. Shanks appearing in *Biblical Archeology Review*.

[24] M. J. S. Chiat, "Migdal," pp. 116-118, in *Handbook of Synagogue Architecture* (Chico, CA: Scholars Press, 1982). M. J. Chiat, "First-Century Synagogue Architecture: Methodological Problems," pp. 49-60 in J. Gutmann, *Ancient Synagogues: The State of Research* (Chico, CA: Scholars Press, 1981). V. Corbo, "La Citta' Romana de Magdala," pp. 355-378 in *Studia Hierosolymitana*, (Jerusalem: 1976), esp. pp. 364-372. G. Foerster, "The Synagogues at Masada and Herodium," in *JJA* 1977, 3-4:6-11. G. Foerster, "The Synagogues at Masada and Herodium," pp. 24-29 in L. I. Levine, ed., *Ancient Synagogues Revealed* (Detroit: Wayne State, 1982). F. Hüttenmeister, *Antiken Synagogen*, vol. 1, pp. 316-318.

[25] M. J. S. Chiat, "Chorozin," pp. 97-102, in *Handbook of Synagogue Architecture* (Chico, CA: Scholars Press, 1982). M. J. Chiat, "First-Century Synagogue Architecture: Methodological Problems," pp. 49-60 in J. Gutmann, *Ancient Synagogues: The State of Research* (Chico, CA: Scholars Press, 1981). G. Foerster, "The Synagogues at Masada and Herodium," in *JJA* 1977, 3-4:6-11. G. Foerster, "The Synagogues at Masada and Herodium," pp. 24-29 in L. I. Levine, ed., *Ancient Synagogues Revealed* (Detroit: Wayne State, 1982). F.

stage remains pure speculation, based only on the discovery of a first-century structure. Thus there are only three structures for which sufficient evidence exists to discuss their possible identification as pre-70 Palestinian synagogues: two in Judea – Masada and Herodium, and one in Galilee – Gamla.

Even these buildings do not provide overwhelming amounts of information confirming their identity, however. First, none of these structures have any features that would identify them as specifically Jewish, let alone as synagogues. Their Jewish character is evident only from their location within an area identified with Jews. In fact, the architectural features that have been used to identify them as synagogues – the benches around the walls and the columns – appear also in structures not identified as synagogues, and only some of these are Jewish.[26] While it appears certain that the buildings were built and used by Jews, their lack of specifically Jewish features indicates the difficulty facing investigators who wish to ascertain their function. Second, although the discipline of archeology has prided itself on the development of scientific methods that carefully record the site and permit later study and reconstruction and although excavation reports of this information enable scholars to study and interpret the site, these methods have not been fully applied to these so-called synagogues. Only a single preliminary report has appeared for Masada, for example.[27] Thus, while excavators have suggested that these buildings are synagogues, they have not always provided the hard evidence to support those suggestions. We need to keep these caveats in mind as we review the individual buildings.

The so-called synagogue at Masada is the best known of the three structures.[28] Yigael Yadin has identified a building attached to the

---

Hüttenmeister, *Antiken Synagogen*, vol. 1, pp. 275-81. Z. Yeivin, "Ancient Chorazin Comes back to Life, " *BAR* 13 (1987) 5:22-39

[26]See the discussion of *ekklesia* and *bouleterion* by Zvi Maoz on p. 41 of "The Synagogue of Gamla and the Typology of Second-Temple Synagogues," pp. 35-41 in L. I. Levine, ed., *Ancient Synagogues Revealed* (Detroit: Wayne State, 1982). See also Foerster's discussion of the *pronaos*, pp. 26-28, in "The Synagogues at Masada and Herodium," pp. 24-29 in L. I. Levine, ed., *Ancient Synagogues Revealed* (Detroit: Wayne State, 1982). See also Yadin, *Preliminary Report*, pp. 79.

[27]Y. Yadin, *The Excavation of Masada 1963/64: Preliminary Report* (Jerusalem: IES, 1965), pp. 76-79.

[28]D. Chen, "The Design of the Ancient Synagogues in Judea: Masada and Herodium" in *BASOR*, 1980, 239:37-40. M. J. S. Chiat, "Masada," pp. 248-251, in *Handbook of Synagogue Architecture* (Chico, CA: Scholars Press, 1982). M. J. Chiat, "First-Century Synagogue Architecture: Methodological Problems," pp. 49-60 in J. Gutmann, *Ancient Synagogues: The State of Research* (Chico, CA:

casemate wall as a synagogue. This structure was originally erected under Herod and later taken over by the rebels during the first revolt against Rome (68-73 C.E.). The rebels, Yadin claims, converted it into a synagogue.[29] They accomplished this by removing a wall, adding a floor, constructing a storage room and adding four levels of stone benches around the inside walls. Why does Yadin identify this structure as a synagogue? (1) It is an assembly hall; (2) the "entrance faced east, and it was wholly oriented towards Jerusalem," as is expected of some later synagogues; (3) fragments of Deuteronomy and Ezekiel were found buried in the storage room.[30] Although the building clearly is an assembly hall, the step from that identification to one of a synagogue is problematic. First of all, the orientation of the building derives not from the rebels but from the original Herodian structure. In fact, the modifications that the rebels made indicate that the orientation was unimportant to them, for they built a room halfway across the wall facing Jerusalem. Thus the wall towards which the worship would have been directed was irregular – hardly a suitable focus of worship. Second, Yadin's claim regarding orientation is actually a combination of two, mutually exclusive, theories regarding orientation. A building's orientation – at least as it has been applied in the study of synagogue remains – usually refers to the direction faced by the facade or main entrance. If the facade faces Jerusalem, then the synagogue is oriented towards Jerusalem. The other theory, found in Tosefta Megilla 3:22, requires the synagogue to be oriented in the same direction as the Jerusalem Temple, namely, towards the east. By conflating the two theories – which use incompatible criteria to orient the synagogue – Yadin makes his case less persuasive. Third, according to Yadin's preliminary report, the original (Herodian) floor of the building was

---

Scholars Press, 1981). G. Foerster, "The Synagogues at Masada and Herodium," in *JJA* 1977, 3-4:6-11. G. Foerster, "The Synagogues at Masada and Herodium," pp. 24-29 in L. I. Levine, ed., *Ancient Synagogues Revealed* (Detroit: Wayne State, 1982). F. Hüttenmeister, *Antiken Synagogen*, vol. 1, pp. 314-315. Z. Maoz, "The Synagogue of Gamla and the Typology of Second-Temple Synagogues," pp. 35-41 in L. I. Levine, ed., *Ancient Synagogues Revealed* (Detroit: Wayne State, 1982). Norman Mirsky, *Unorthodox Judaism*, (Columbus: Ohio State, 1978), pp. 151-171. A. Ovadiah and T. Michaeli, "Observations on the Origin of the Architectual Plan of Ancient Synagogues," pp. 234-241 in *JJS* Vol. 38, #2, Autumn, 1987. Y. Yadin, *Masada: Herod's Fortress and the Zealots' Last Stand* (New York, 1966), pp. 181-192. Y. Yadin, *The Excavation of Masada 1963/64: Preliminary Report* (Jerusalem: IES, 1965), pp. 76-79. Y. Yadin, "The Synagogue at Masada," pp. 19-23 Foerster, in L. I. Levine, ed., *Ancient Synagogues Revealed* (Detroit: Wayne State, 1982).
[29]Yadin, *Preliminary Report*, pp. 76-9.
[30]Yadin, *Masada*, pp. 184 & 187-8.

covered with a deep layer of animal dung, indicating that it had been a barn. The dung was not removed before the new floor was laid down.[31] Given the sanctity and respect accorded a synagogue, it seems incongruent – if not sacrilegious – to build one over a dung heap. Fourth, the buried scrolls by themselves hardly prove that this was a synagogue. For example, the literary and archaeological evidence at Qumran show that there was no synagogue there. Since Qumran's scrolls are nowhere associated with a synagogue, Masada's fragments cannot on their own indicate such a structure. It is clear, therefore, that the identification of this structure as a synagogue is highly uncertain. Indeed, it could have been a place for the rebels to meet and plan strategy, a need common to most armies. Certainly, it is well situated for that purpose, overlooking the area where the Romans built their siege ramp.

The structure at Herodium has the same uncertainties as the Masada building.[32] First, although the building – probably remodeled by rebels in the first war against Rome – clearly is an assembly hall, we have no indication that it was used for religious purposes. Second, its orientation is a matter of the original structure and cannot be attributed to the remodelers. Third, the site was again the location of a rebel army who, like the rebels at Masada, would have needed a place of conference and assembly for military reasons. The structure at Herodium therefore provides no sure evidence of a pre-70 synagogue.

Even if these two structures were synagogues, they would not provide information that could counter the distinction between Galilee and Judea evidenced by the literary data. Neither of them appear in

---

[31]Yadin, *Preliminary Report*, p. 77. He seems to have ignored this when he suggests in *Masada*, p. 185, that Herod may have used the building as a synagogue also.

[32]D. Chen, "The Design of the Ancient Synagogues in Judea: Masada and Herodium" in *BASOR*, 1980, 239:37-40. M. J. S. Chiat, "Herodium," pp. 204-7, in *Handbook of Synagogue Architecture* (Chico, CA: Scholars Press, 1982). M. J. Chiat, "First-Century Synagogue Architecture: Methodological Problems," pp. 49-60 in J. Gutmann, *Ancient Synagogues: The State of Research* (Chico, CA: Scholars Press, 1981). V. Corbo, "L'Herodion de Giabel Fureidis," *LA* XVII, 1967, pp. 101ff. V. Corbo, "The Excavation at Herodium," *Qad.* I, 4 (1968), 132-36. G. Foerster, "The Synagogues at Masada and Herodium," in *JJA* 1977, 3-4:6-11. G. Foerster, "The Synagogues at Masada and Herodium," pp. 24-29 in L. I. Levine, ed., *Ancient Synagogues Revealed* (Detroit: Wayne State, 1982). F. Hüttenmeister, *Antiken Synagogen*, vol. 1, pp. 173-4. Z. Maoz, "The Synagogue of Gamla and the Typology of Second-Temple Synagogues," pp. 35-41 in L. I. Levine, ed., *Ancient Synagogues Revealed* (Detroit: Wayne State, 1982). A. Ovadiah, and T. Michaeli, "Observations on the Origin of the Architectual Plan of Ancient Synagogues," pp. 234-241 in *JJS* Vol. 38, #2, Autumn, 1987.

villages, towns, or cities and thus they provide no evidence about the typical day-to-day behavior of the Judean citizenry. Furthermore, they come late in the pre-70 period – it would be difficult to date the so-called "synagogue" stage of their existence to a point much before 68 C.E. But what of the structure in Galilee?

The final building that has been suggested as a pre-70 synagogue, and the only viable possibility in Galilee, stands in Gamla.[33] It is not a remodeled building, like Masada and Herodium, but one designed and constructed for a specific purpose from the beginning. It has no later buildings constructed on it, as at Migdal, because the site was abandoned after its destruction. So here we have a clear example of a building that was built for the function it served. The question is whether this function was that of a synagogue.

The building was erected between 20 B.C.E. and 40 C.E., and was used until the Romans destroyed Gamla in the war. Taken as a whole, its design differs significantly from that of the other two buildings. Like the others, it was a rectangular building with tiers of benches going around all four sides. Unlike them, however, it had four rows of columns arranged as a rectangle around the inside of the benches. It was large enough to hold a great number of people, being almost three times the size of the Masada structure. Furthermore, it seems to be an official structure in a community setting; the length of its use indicates that the people at Gamla endorsed its construction and used the building.

Two items indicate that this structure was probably a synagogue. First, on the lintel over the doorway, the builders carved a six-

---

[33]"Gamla and Gaulanitis," *ZDPV*, 92 (1976) 54-71. Anonymous, "Gamla: the Masada of the North," pp. 12-19 in *BAR*, 1979, Vol. 5, # 1. M. J. S. Chiat, "Gamla," pp. 282-4, in *Handbook of Synagogue Architecture* (Chico, CA: Scholars Press, 1982). M. J. Chiat, "First-Century Synagogue Architecture: Methodological Problems," pp. 49-60 in J. Gutmann, *Ancient Synagogues: The State of Research* (Chico, CA: Scholars Press, 1981). G. Foerster, "The Synagogues at Masada and Herodium," in *JJA* 1977, 3-4:6-11. G. Foerster, "The Synagogues at Masada and Herodium," pp. 24-29 in L. I. Levine, ed., *Ancient Synagogues Revealed* (Detroit: Wayne State, 1982). S. Gutman, "The Synagogue at Gamla," pp. 30-34 in L. I. Levine, ed., *Ancient Synagogues Revealed* (Detroit: Wayne State, 1982). S. Gutmann, "Gamla – 1983," pp. 26-7 in *Excavations and Surveys in Israel*, 1984, vol. 3, (Jerusalem, 1984) [items selected and translated from *HA*). S. Gutmann, "Gamla – 1984/1985/1986," pp. 38-41 in *Excavations and Surveys in Israel*, 1986, vol. 5, (Jerusalem, 1986) [items selected and translated from *HA*, 88-89]. F. Hüttenmeister, *Antiken Synagogen*, vol. 1, pp. 524. Z. Maoz, "The Synagogue of Gamla and the Typology of Second-Temple Synagogues," pp. 35-41 in L. I. Levine, ed., *Ancient Synagogues Revealed* (Detroit: Wayne State, 1982). A. Ovadiah and T. Michaeli, "Observations on the Origin of the Architectual Plan of Ancient Synagogues," pp. 234-241 in *JJS* Vol. 38, #2, Autumn, 1987.

petalled rosette, a Jewish ornament commonly associated with religious contexts during this period. This suggests that the structure was not simply a civic meeting house, but that it had a religious purposes, namely, those of a synagogue. Second, the center of the meeting room was unpaved. As Zvi Maoz has pointed out, this area was probably one where people did not freely walk (otherwise it would have been paved), and it presumably was covered with carpets.[34] In other words, this was an important focus of attention, but not casually accessed. In addition, a foundation stone was carefully placed within the unpaved area. Its location is well-suited for the placement of a *bema* (for which it would have served as a support), the table from which the Torah scroll is read. Although none of this data provides total certainty, it seems probable that this building was a synagogue.

The archaeological evidence thus provides conclusions similar to those we derived from the literary evidence. That is to say, the data points to the existence of synagogues in Galilee prior to 70, but provides no firm evidence concerning Judea. While we would be overstating the case to claim that the archaeological data demonstrates that there were no synagogues in Judea prior to the Temple's destruction, it is not incorrect to state that, apart from the evidence of synagogues for foreigner, there is no indication that synagogues became part of the way of worship in Judea or in Jerusalem.

When we attempt to take seriously the data currently available to modern scholarship, therefore, we discover an important phenomenon. Within the limits of the evidence, it appears that an incompatibility existed between the synagogue and the Temple cult. The synagogue, which originated in regions where there was no practical access to the Jerusalem Temple, did best in places that also lacked this access. In Galilee and other areas in northern Palestine, the synagogue established itself and became an important community institution. By contrast, in regions where the Temple cult exercised some control and where people lived close enough to attend sacrifices, bring tithes and so on without major expenditures of time, the synagogue is not evidenced as being broadly accepted by the populace. Thus Jerusalem and Judea provide no data to indicate that the synagogue was an important institution alongside the Temple.

The evidence, little as it is, also suggests that the synagogues known to have stood in Jerusalem belonged to or provided services for Jews from outside Palestine. This reinforces the hypothesis that the synagogue originated outside the Palestine – according to Griffiths, in Egypt. When Jews from abroad permanently resided in Jerusalem, they

---

[34] Maoz, p. 38-9.

brought their foreign institution – the synagogue – with them. They apparently established it in their own sub-community, but there is no evidence to indicate that it spread throughout the native Jerusalem population. Although the synagogue became naturalized in Galilee after its introduction, that does not seem to have happened in Jerusalem.

Abbreviations

ANRW	*Aufstieg und Niedergang der römischen Welt*
BAR	*Biblical Archeology Review*
BASOR	*Bulletin of the American School of Oriental Research*
HA	*Hadashot Archeologot*
JJA	*Journal of Jewish Art*
JJS	*Journal of Jewish Studies*
JThS	*Journal of Theological Studies*
LA	*Liber Annus*
Qad	*Qadmoniot*
RB	*Revue biblique*
REJ	*Revue des études juives*
ZDPV	*Zeitschrift für des deutschen Palästina-Vereins*

Part Three
THE LITERATURE OF ANCIENT JUDAISM

3

The Three Stages in the Formation of Rabbinic Writings

Jacob Neusner
The Institute for Advanced Study and Brown University

Each of the score of documents that make up the canon of Judaism in late antiquity exhibits distinctive traits in logic, rhetoric, and topic, so that we may identify the purposes and traits of form and intellect of the authorship of that document. It follows that documents possess integrity and are not merely scrapbooks, compilations made with no clear purpose or aesthetic plan. But, as is well known, some completed units of thought – propositional arguments, sayings, and stories for instance – travel from one document to another. It follows that the several documents intersect through shared materials. Furthermore, writings that peregrinate by definition do not carry out the rhetorical, logical, and topical program of a particular document. In framing a theory to accommodate the facts that documents are autonomous but also connected through such shared materials, therefore, we must account for the history of not only the documents in hand but also the completed pieces of writing that move from here to there. We have at present no theory of the formation of the various documents of the rabbinic literature that derives from an inductive sifting of the evidence. Nor do we have even a theory as to the correct method for the framing of a hypothesis for testing against the evidence.

My theory on the literary history of the rabbinic canon posits three stages in the formation of writing. Moving from the latest to the earliest, one stage is marked by the definition of a document, its topical program, its rhetorical medium, its logical message. The document as we know it in its basic structure and main lines therefore comes at the end. It follows that writings that clearly serve the program of that document and carry it the purposes of its authorship were made up in connection with the formation of *that* document. Another, and I think, prior stage is marked by the preparation of writings that do not serve the needs of a particular document now in our hands, but can have carried out the purposes of an authorship working on a document of a *type* we now have. The existing documents then form a model for defining other kinds of writings worked out to meet the program of a documentary authorship.

But there are other types of writings that in no way serve the needs or plans of any document we now have, and that, furthermore, also cannot find a place in any document of a type that we now have. These writings, as a matter of fact, very commonly prove peripatetic, traveling from one writing to another, equally at home in, or alien to, the program of the documents in which they end up. These writings therefore were carried out without regard to a documentary program of any kind exemplified by the canonical books of the Judaism of the Dual Torah. They form what I conceive to be the earliest in the three stages of the writing of the units of completed thought that in the aggregate form the canonical literature of the Judaism of the Dual Torah of late antiquity.

As a matter of fact, therefore, a given canonical document of the Judaism of the Dual Torah draws upon three classes of materials, and these were framed in temporal order. Last comes the final class, the one that the redactors themselves defined and wrote; prior is the penultimate class that can have served other redactors but did not serve these in particular; and earliest of all in the order of composition (at least, from the perspective of the ultimate redaction of the documents we now have) is the writing that circulated autonomously and served no redactional purpose we can now identify within the canonical documents.

i. The Correct Starting Point

In beginning the inquiry with the traits of documents seen whole, I reject the assumption that the building block of documents is the smallest whole unit of thought, the lemma, nor can we proceed in the premise that a lemma traverses the boundaries of various documents and is unaffected by the journey.[1] The opposite premise is that we start

---

[1] As a matter of fact, the identification of the lemma as the primary unit of inquiry rests upon the premise that the person to whom a saying is assigned really said that saying. That premise is untenable. But for the sake of

our work with the traits of documents as a whole, rather than with the traits of the lemmas of which documents are (supposedly) composed. In a variety of books[2] I have set forth the documentary hypothesis for the analysis of the rabbinic literature of late antiquity. But how shall we proceed, if we take as our point of entry the character and conditions of the document, seen whole? And what are the results of doing so?

Having demonstrated beyond any doubt that a rabbinic text is a document, that is to say, a well-crafted text and not merely a compilation of this and that, and further specified in acute detail precisely the aesthetic, formal, and logical program followed by each of those texts, accordingly, I am able to move to the logical next step. That is to show that in the background of the documents that we have is writing that is *not* shaped by documentary requirements, writing that is not shaped by the documentary requirements of the compilations we now have, and also writing that is entirely formed within the rules of the documents that now present that writing. These then are the three kinds of writing that form, also, the three stages in the formation of the classics of Judaism.

ii. Redaction and Writing: The Extreme Case of the Mishnah

My example of a document that is written down essentially in its penultimate and ultimate stages, that is, a document that takes shape within the redactional process and principally there, is, of course, the Mishnah. In that writing, the patterns of language, e.g., syntactic structures, of the apodosis and protasis of the Mishnah's smallest whole units of discourse are framed in formal, mnemonic patterns. They follow a few simple rules. These rules, once known, apply nearly everywhere and form stunning evidence for the document's cogency. They permit anyone to reconstruct, out of a few key phrases, an entire cognitive unit, and even complete intermediate units of discourse. Working downward from the surface, therefore, anyone can penetrate into the deeper layers of meaning of the Mishnah. Then and at the same time, while discovering the principle behind the cases, one can easily memorize the whole by mastering the recurrent rhetorical pattern dictating the expression of the cogent set of cases. For it is easy

---

argument, I bypass that still more fundamental flaw in the methodology at hand.

[2]Particularly *From Tradition to Imitation. The Plan and Program of Pesiqta deRab Kahana* and *Pesiqta Rabbati, Canon and Connection: Intertextuality in Judaism, Midrash as Literature: The Primacy of Documentary Discourse,* and *The Bavli and its Sources: The Question of Tradition in the Case of Tractate Sukkah,* as well as *The Talmud of the Land of Israel.* 35. *Introduction. Taxonomy,* and *Judaism. The Classic Statement. The Evidence of the Bavli.*

to note the shift from one rhetorical pattern to another and to follow the repeated cases, articulated in the new pattern downward to its logical substrate. So syllogistic propositions, in the Mishnah's authors' hands, come to full expression not only in *what* people wish to state but also in *how* they choose to say it. The limits of rhetoric define the arena of topical articulation.

Now to state my main point in heavy emphasis: *the Mishnah's formal traits of rhetoric indicate that the document has been formulated all at once, and not in an incremental, linear process extending into a remote (mythic) past, (e.g., to Sinai).* These traits, common to a series of distinct cognitive units, are redactional, because they are imposed at that point at which someone intended to join together discrete (finished) units on a given theme. The varieties of traits particular to the discrete units and the diversity of authorities cited therein, including masters of two or three or even four strata from the turn of the first century to the end of the second, make it highly improbable that the several units were formulated in a common pattern and then preserved, until, later on, still further units, on the same theme and in the same pattern, were worked out and added. The entire indifference, moreover, to historical order of authorities and concentration on the logical unfolding of a given theme or problem without reference to the sequence of authorities, confirm the supposition that the work of formulation and that of redaction go forward together.

The principal framework of formulation and formalization in the Mishnah is the intermediate division rather than the cognitive unit. The least-formalized formulary pattern, the simple declarative sentence, turns out to yield many examples of acute formalization, in which a single distinctive pattern is imposed upon two or more (very commonly, groups of three or groups of five) cognitive units. While an intermediate division of a tractate may be composed of several such conglomerates of cognitive units, it is rare indeed for cognitive units formally to stand wholly by themselves. Normally, cognitive units share formal or formulary traits with others to which they are juxtaposed and the theme of which they share. It follows that the principal unit of formulary formalization is the intermediate division and not the cognitive unit. And what that means for our inquiry, is simple: we can tell when it is that the ultimate or penultimate redactors of a document do the writing. Now let us see that vast collection of writings that exhibit precisely the opposite trait: a literature in which, while doing some writing of their own, the redactors collected and arranged available materials.

iii. When the Document Does Not Define the Literary Protocol: Stories Told But Not Compiled

Now to the other extreme. Can I point to a kind of writing that in no way defines a document now in our hands or even a type of document we can now imagine, that is, one that in its particulars we do not have but that conforms in its definitive traits to those that we do have? Indeed I can, and it is the writing of stories about sages and other exemplary figures. To show what might have been, I point to the simple fact that the final organizers of the Bavli, the Talmud of Babylonia had in hand a tripartite corpus of inherited materials awaiting composition into a final, closed document. First, the first type of material, in various states and stages of completion, addressed the Mishnah or took up the principles of laws that the Mishnah had originally brought to articulation. These the framers of the Bavli organized in accord with the order of those Mishnah-tractates that they selected for sustained attention. Second, they had in hand received materials, again in various conditions, pertinent to Scripture, both as Scripture related to the Mishnah and also as Scripture laid forth its own narratives. These they set forth as Scripture-commentary. In this way, the penultimate and ultimate redactors of the Bavli laid out a systematic presentation of the two Torahs, the oral, represented by the Mishnah, and the written, represented by Scripture.

And, third, the framers of the Bavli also had in hand materials focused on sages. These in the received form, attested in the Bavli's pages, were framed around twin biographical principles, either as strings of stories about great sages of the past or as collections of sayings and comments drawn together solely because the same name stands behind all the collected sayings. These can easily have been composed into biographies. In the context of Christianity and of Judaism, it is appropriate to call the biography of a holy man or woman, meant to convey the divine message, a gospel.[3] This is writing that is utterly

---

[3] I use the word "gospel" with a small G as equivalent to "didactic life of a holy man, portraying the faith." Obviously, the Christian usage, with a capital G, must maintain that there can be a Gospel only about Jesus Christ. Claims of uniqueness are, of course, not subject to public discourse. In the present context, I could as well have referred to lives of saints, since Judaism of the dual Torah produced neither a gospel about a central figure nor lives of saints. Given the centrality of Moses "our rabbi," for example, we should have anticipated a "Gospel of Moses" parallel to the Gospels of Jesus Christ, and, lacking that, at least a "life of Aqiba," scholar, saint, martyr, parallel to the lives

outside of the documentary framework in which it is now preserved; nearly all narratives in the rabbinic literature, not only the biographical ones, indeed prove remote from any documentary program exhibited by the canonical documents in which they now occur.

The Bavli as a whole lays itself out as a commentary to the Mishnah. So the framers wished us to think that whatever they wanted to tell us would take the form of Mishnah commentary. But a second glance indicates that the Bavli is made up of enormous composites, themselves closed prior to inclusion in the Bavli. Some of these composites – around 35% to 40% of Bavli's, if my sample is indicative[4] – were selected and arranged along lines dictated by a logic other than that deriving from the requirements of Mishnah commentary. The components of the canon of the Judaism of the Dual Torah prior to the Bavli had encompassed amplifications of the Mishnah, in the Tosefta and in the Yerushalmi, as well as the same for Scripture, in such documents as Sifra to Leviticus, Sifré to Numbers, another Sifré, to Deuteronomy, Genesis Rabbah, Leviticus Rabbah, and the like. But there was no entire document, now extant, organized around the life and teachings of a particular sage. Even The Fathers According to Rabbi Nathan, which contains a good sample of stories about sages, is not so organized as to yield a life of a sage, or even a systematic biography of any kind. Where events in the lives of sages do occur, they are thematic and not biographical in organization, e.g., stories about the origins, as to Torah-study, of diverse sages; death-scenes of various sages. The sage as such, whether Aqiba or Yohanan ben Zakkai or Eliezer b. Hyrcanus, never in that document defines the appropriate organizing principle for sequences of stories or sayings. And there is no other in which the sage forms an organizing category for any material purpose.[5]

---

of various saints. We also have no autobiographies of any kind, beyond some "I"-stories, which themselves seem to me uncommon.

[4]I compared Bavli and Yerushalmi tractates Sukkah, Sanhedrin, and Sotah, showing the proportion of what I call Scripture-units of thought to Mishnah-units of thought. See my *Judaism. The Classic Statement. The Evidence of the Bavli* (Chicago, 1986: University of Chicago Press).

[5]The occasion, in the history of Judaism, at which biography defines a generative category of literature, therefore also of thought, will therefore prove noteworthy. The model of biography surely existed from the formation of the Pentateuch, with its lines of structure, from Exodus through Deuteronomy, set forth around the biography of Moses, birth, call, career, death. And other biographies did flourish prior to the Judaism of the dual Torah. Not only so, but the wall of the Dura synagogue highlights not the holy people so much as saints, such as Aaron and Moses. Accordingly, we must regard as noteworthy and requiring explanation the omission of biography from the literary genres of

The Three Stages in the Formation of Rabbinic Writings

Accordingly, the decision that the framers of the Bavli reached was to adopt the two redactional principles inherited from the antecedent century or so and to reject the one already rejected by their predecessors, even while honoring it. [1] They organized the Bavli around the Mishnah. But [2] they adapted and included vast tracts of antecedent materials organized as scriptural commentary. These they inserted whole and complete, not at all in response to the Mishnah's program. But, finally, [3] while making provision for small-scale compositions built upon biographical principles, preserving both strings of sayings from a given master (and often a given tradent of a given master) as well as tales about authorities of the preceding half millennium, they *never* created redactional compositions, of a sizable order, that focused upon given authorities. But sufficient materials certainly lay at hand to allow doing so.

We have now seen that some writings carry out a redactional purpose. The Mishnah was our prime example. Some writings ignore all redactional considerations we can identify. The stories about sages in the Fathers According to Rabbi Nathan for instance show us kinds of writing that are wholly out of phase with the program of the document that collects and compiles them. We may therefore turn to Midrash-compilations and find the traits of writing that clearly are imposed by the requirements of compilation. We further identify writings that clearly respond to a redactional program, but not the program of any compilation we now have in hand. There is little speculation about the identification of such writings. They will conform to the redactional patterns we discern in the known-compilations, but presuppose a collection other than one now known to us. Finally, we turn to pieces of writing that respond to no redactional program known to us or susceptible to invention in accord with the principles of defining compilation known to us.

iv. Pericopes Framed for the Purposes of the Particular Document in Which They Occur

My analytical taxonomy of the writings now collected in various Midrash-compilations point to not only three stages in the formation of the classics of Judaism. It also suggests that writing went on outside of the framework of the editing of documents, and also within the limits of the formation and framing of documents. Writing of the former kind then constituted a kind of literary work to which redactional planning

---

the canon of the Judaism of the Dual Torah. One obvious shift is marked by Hasidism, with its special interest in stories about saints and in compiling those stories.

proved irrelevant. But the second and the third kinds of writing responds to redactional considerations. So in the end we shall wish to distinguish between writing intended for the making of books – compositions of the first three kinds listed just now – and writing not response to the requirements of the making of compilations.

The distinctions upon which these analytical taxonomies rest are objective and no no way subjective, since they depend upon the fixed and factual relationship between a piece of writing and a larger redactional context.

[1] We know the requirements of redactors of the several documents of the rabbinic canon, because I have already shown what they are in the case of a large variety of documents. When, therefore, we judge a piece of writing to serve the program of the document in which that writing occurs, it is not because of a personal impulse or a private and incommunicable insight, but because the traits of that writing self-evidently respond to the documentary program of the book in which the writing is located.

[2] When, further, we conclude that a piece of writing belongs in some other document than the one in which it is found, that too forms a factual judgment.

My example is a very simple one: writing that can serve only as a component of a commentary on a given scriptural book has been made up for the book in which it appears (or one very like it, if one wants to quibble). My example may derive from any of the ten Midrash-compilations of late antiquity. Here is one among innumerable possibilities.

Sifré to Numbers I:VII

1. A. "[The Lord said to Moses, 'Command the people of Israel that they put out of the camp every leper and every one having a discharge, and every one that is unclean through contact with the dead.] You shall put out both male and female, putting them outside the camp, that they may not defile their camp, in the midst of which I dwell'" (Gen. 5:1-4).

   B. I know, on the basis of the stated verse, that the law applies only to male and female [persons who are suffering from the specified forms of cultic uncleanness]. How do I know that the law pertains also to one lacking clearly defined sexual traits or to one possessed of the sexual traits of both genders?

   C. Scripture states, "...putting *them* outside the camp." [This is taken to constitute an encompassing formulation, extending beyond the male and female of the prior clause.]

   D. I know, on the basis of the stated verse, that the law applies only to those who can be sent forth. How do I know that the law pertains also to those who cannot be sent forth?

The Three Stages in the Formation of Rabbinic Writings 93

- E. Scripture states, "...putting them outside the camp." [This is taken to constitute an encompassing formulation, as before.]
- F. I know on the basis of the stated verse that the law applies only to persons. How do I know that the law pertains also to utensils?
- G. Scripture states, "...putting *them* outside the camp." [This is taken to constitute an encompassing formulation.]

I:VII
2. A. [Dealing with the same question as at 1.F,] R. Aqiba says, "'You shall put out both male and female, putting them outside the camp.' Both persons and utensils are implied."
- B. R. Ishmael says, "You may construct a logical argument, as follows:
- C. "Since man is subject to uncleanness on account of *negaim* ["plagues"], and clothing [thus: utensils] are subject to uncleanness on the same count, just as man is subject to being sent forth [ostracism], likewise utensils are subject to being sent forth."
- D. No, such an argument is not valid [and hence exegesis of the actual language of Scripture, as at A, is the sole correct route]. If you have stated the rule in the case of man, who imparts uncleanness when he exerts pressure on an object used for either sitting or lying, and, on which account, he is subject to ostracism, will you say the same rule of utensils, which do not impart uncleanness when they exert pressure on an object used for sitting and lying? [Clearly there is a difference between the uncleanness brought about by a human being from that brought about by an inanimate object, and therefore the rule that applies to the one will not necessarily apply to the other. Logic by itself will not suffice, and, it must follow, the proof of a verse of Scripture alone will suffice to prove the point.]
- E. [No, that objection is not valid, because we can show that the same rule does apply to both an inanimate object and to man, namely] lo, there is the case of the stone affected with a *nega*, which will prove the point. For it does not impart uncleanness when it exerts pressure on an object used for sitting or lying, but it does require ostracism [being sent forth from the camp, a rule that Scripture itself makes explicit].
- F. Therefore do not find it surprising that utensils, even though they in general do not impart uncleanness when they exert pressure on an object used for sitting or lying, are to be sent forth from the camp." [Ishmael's logical proof stands.]

I:VII
3. A. R. Yosé the Galilean says, "'You shall put out both male and female, putting them outside the camp, that they may not defile their camp, in the midst of which I dwell.'
- B. "What marks as singular male and female is that they can be turned into a generative source of uncleanness [when they die and are corpses], and, it follows, they are to be sent forth from the camp when they become unclean [even while alive], so anything

94   *The Literature of Ancient Judaism*

which can become a generative source of uncleanness will be subject to being sent forth from the camp.

C. "What is excluded is a piece of cloth less than three by three fingerbreadths, which in the entire Torah is never subject to becoming a generative source of uncleanness."

I:VII
4. A. R. Isaac says, "Lo, Scripture states, '[And every person that eats what dies of itself or what is to torn by beasts, whether he is a native or a sojourner, shall wash his clothes and bathe himself in water and be unclean until the evening; they he shall be clean.] But if he does not wash them or bathe his flesh, he shall bear his iniquity' (Lev. 17:15-16).
   B. "It is on account of failure to wash one's body that Scripture has imposed the penalty of extirpation.
   C. "You maintain that it is on account of failure to wash one's body that Scripture has imposed the penalty of extirpation. But perhaps Scripture has imposed a penalty of extirpation only on account of the failure to launder one's garments.
   D. "Thus you may construct the argument to the contrary [*su eipas*]: if in the case of one who has become unclean on account of corpse-uncleanness, which is a severe source of uncleanness, Scripture has not imposed a penalty merely because of failure to launder one's garments, as to one who eats meat of a beast that has died of itself, which is a minor source of uncleanness, it is a matter of reason that Scripture should not impose a penalty on the account of having failed to launder the garments."

Why do I maintain that the composition can serve only the document in which it occurs? The reason is that we read the verse in a narrow framework: what rule do we derive from the *actual* language at hand. No. 1 answers the question on the basis of an exegesis of the verse. No. 2 then provides an alternative proof. Aqiba provides yet another reading of the language at hand. Ishmael goes over the possibility of a logical demonstration. I find it difficult to see how Yosé's pericope fits in. It does not seem to me to address the problem at hand. He wants to deal with a separate issue entirely, as specified at C. No. 4 pursues yet another independent question. So Nos. 3, 4 look to be parachuted down. On what basis? No. 3 deals with our base verse. But No. 4 does not. Then what guided the compositors to introduce Nos. 1, 2, 3, and 4? Nos. 1, 2 deal with the exegesis of the limited rule at hand: how do I know to what classifications of persons and objects ostracism applies? No. 1 Answers to questions, first, the classifications, then the basis for the rule. No. 2 introduces the second question: on what basis do we make our rule? The answer, as is clear, is Scripture, not unaided reason. Now at that point the issue of utensils emerges. So Yosé the Galilean's interest in the rule governing a utensil – a piece of cloth – leads to the intrusion of his item. And the same theme – the rule governing utensils, garments – accounts for the introduction of I:VII.4 as well. In sum, the redactional principle is looks to be clear: treat the verse, then the theme generated by the verse. Then this piece of writing can have been formed only for the purpose of a commentary to the book of Numbers: Sifré to Numbers is the only one we have. Q.E.D.

v. Pericopes Framed for the Purposes of a Particular Document but Not of a Type We Now Possess

A piece of writing that serves no where we now know may nonetheless conform to the rules of writing that we can readily imagine and describe in theory. For instance, a propositional composition, that runs through a wide variety of texts to make a point autonomous of all of the texts that are invoked, clearly is intended for a propositional document, one that (like the Mishnah) makes points autonomous of a given prior writing, e.g., a biblical book, but that makes points that for one reason or another cohere quite nicely on their own. Authors of propositional compilations self-evidently can imagine that kind of redaction. We have their writings, but not the books that they intended to be made up of those writings. In all instances, the reason that we can readily imagine a compilation for that will have dictated the indicative traits of a piece of writing will prove self-evident: we have compilations of such a type, if not specific compilations called for by a given composition. A single example suffices. It derives from Sifra.

If the canon of Judaism included a major treatise or compilation on applied logic and practical reason, then a principal tractate, or set of tractates, would be devoted to proving that reason by itself cannot produce reliable results. And in that treatise would be a vast and various collection of sustained discussions, which spread themselves across Sifra and Sifré to Numbers and Sifré to Deuteronomy, the Yerushalmi and the Bavli, as well as other collections. Here is a sample of how that polemic has imposed itself on the amplification of Lev. 1:2 and transformed treatment of that verse from an exegesis to an example of an overriding proposition. It goes without saying that where we have this type of proof of the priority of Scripture over logic, or of the necessity of Scripture in the defining of generative taxa, the discussion serves a purpose that transcends the case, and on that basis I maintain the proposition proposed here. It is that there were types of collections that we can readily imagine but that were not made up. In this case, it is, as is clear, a treatise on applied logic, and the general proposition of that treatise is that reliable taxonomy derives only from Scripture.

Sifra Parashat Vayyiqra Dibura Denedabah Parashah 2=III.I

1. A. "Speak to the Israelite people [and say to them, 'When any [Hebrew: Adam] of you presents an offering of cattle to the Lord, he shall choose his offering from the herd or from the flock. If his offering is a burnt-offering from the herd, he shall offer a male without blemish; he shall offer it at the door of the tent of meeting, that he may be accepted before the Lord;] he shall lay [his hand upon the head of the burnt-offering, and it shall be accepted for him to make atonement for him]'" (Lev. 1:2):
   B. "He shall lay his hand": Israelites lay on hands, gentiles do not lay on hands.
   C. [But is it necessary to prove that proposition on the basis of the cited verse? Is it not to be proven merely by an argument of a logical order, which is now presented?] Now which measure [covering the applicability of a rite] is more abundant, the measure of wavings or the measure of laying on of hands?
   D. The measure of waving [the beast] is greater than the measure of laying on of hands.
   E. For waving [the sacrifice] is done to both something that is animate and something that is not animate, while the laying on of hands applies only to something that is animate.
   F. If gentiles are excluded from the rite of waving the sacrifice, which applies to a variety of sacrifices, should they not be excluded from the rite of laying on of hands, which pertains to fewer sacrifices? [Accordingly, I prove on the basis of reason the rule that is derived at A-B from the verse of Scripture.]
   G. [I shall now show that the premise of the foregoing argument is false:] [You have constructed your argument] from the angle that yields waving as more common and laying on of hands as less common.
   H. But take the other angle, which yields laying on of hands as the more common and waving as the less common.
   I. For the laying on of hands applies to all partners in the ownership of a beast [each one of whom is required to lay hands on the beast before it is slaughtered in behalf of the partnership in ownership of the beast as a whole],
   J. but the waving of a sacrifice is not a requirement that applies to all partners in the ownership of a beast.
   K. Now if I eliminate [gentiles' laying on of hands] in the case of the waving of a beast, which is a requirement applying to fewer cases, should I eliminate them from the requirement of laying on of hands, which applies to a larger number of cases?
   L. Lo, since a rule pertains to the waving of the sacrifice that does not apply to the laying on of hands, and a rule pertains to the laying on of hands that does not apply to the waving of the sacrifice, it is necessary for Scripture to make the statement that it does, specifically:
   M. "He shall lay his hand": Israelites lay on hands, gentiles do not lay on hands.

The basic premise is that when two comparable actions differ, then the more commonly performed one imposes its rule upon further actions, the rule governing which is unknown. If then we show that action A is more commonly performed than action B, other actions of the same classification will follow the rule governing A, not the rule governing B. Then the correct route to overturn such an argument is to show that each of the actions, the rule governing which is known, differs from the other in such a way that neither the one nor the other can be shown to be the more commonly performed. Then the rule governing the further actions is not to be derived from the one governing the two known actions. The powerful instrument of analytical and comparative reasoning proves that diverse traits pertain to the two stages of the rite of sacrifice, the waving, the laying on of hands, which means that a rule pertaining to the one does not necessarily apply to the other. On account of that difference we must evoke the specific ruling of Scripture. The polemic in favor of Scripture, uniting all of the components into a single coherent argument, then insists that there really is no such thing as a genus at all, and Scripture's rules and regulations serve a long list of items, each of them *sui generis*, for discovering rules by the logic of analogy and contrast is simply not possible.

vi. Pericopes Framed for the Purposes Not Particular to a Type of Document Now in Our Hands

Some writings stand autonomous of any redactional program we have in an existing compilation or of any we can even imagine on the foundations of said writings. Compositions of this kind, as a matter of hypothesis, are to be assigned to a stage in the formation of classics prior to the framing of all available documents. For, as a matter of fact, all of our now exant writings adhere to a single program of conglomeration and agglutination, and all are served by composites of one sort, rather than some other. Hence we may suppose that at some point prior to the decision to make writings in the model that we now have but in some other model people also made up completed units of thought to serve these other kinds of writings. These persist, now, in documents that they do not serve at all well. And we can fairly easily identify the kinds of documents that they can and should have served quite nicely indeed. These then are the three stages of literary formation in the making of the classics of Judaism.

Of the relative temporal or ordinal position of writings that stand autonomous of any redactional program we have in an existing compilation or of any we can even imagine on the foundations of said writings we can say nothing. These writings prove episodic; they are commonly singletons. They serve equally well everywhere, because they demand no traits of form and redaction in order to endow them with sense and meaning. Why not? Because they are essentially freestanding and episodic, not referential and allusive. They are stories that contain their own point and do not invoke, in the making of that point, a given verse of Scripture. They are sayings that are utterly ad hoc. A variety of materials fall into this – from a redactional perspective – unassigned, and unassignable, type of writing. They do not belong in books at all. By that I mean, whoever made up these pieces of writing did not imagine that what he was forming required a setting beyond the limits of his own piece of writing; the story is not only complete in itself but could stand entirely on its own; the saying spoke for itself and required no nurturing context; the proposition and its associated proofs in no way was meant to draw nourishment from roots penetrating nutriments outside of its own literary limits.

Where we have utterly hermetic writing, able to define its own limits and sustain its point without regard to anything outside itself, we know that here we are in the presence of authorships that had no larger redactional plan in mind, no intent on the making of books out of their little pieces of writing. We may note that, among the "unimaginable" compilations is not a collection of parables, since parables rarely[6] stand free and never are inserted for their own sake. Whenever in the rabbinic canon we find a parable, it is meant to serve the purpose of an authorship engaged in making its own point; and the point of a parable is rarely, if ever, left unarticulated. Normally it is put into words, but occasionally the point is made simply by redactional setting. It must follow that, in this canon, the parable cannot have constituted the generative or agglutinative principle of a large-scale compilation. It further follows, so it seems to me, that the parable always takes shape within the framework of a work of composition for the purpose of either a large-scale exposition or, more commonly still, of compilation of a set of expositions into what we should now call the chapter of a book; that is to say, parables link to purposes that transcend the tale that they tell (or even the point that the tale makes). Let me now give one example of what I classify as a free-standing piece of writing, one with no place for itself in accord with the purposes of compilers either of documents we now have in hand or of documents we can readily envisage or imagine. My example again derive from Sifra, although, as a matter of fact, every document of the canon yields illustrative materials for all three types of writing.

---

[6]I should prefer to say "never," but it is easier to say what is in the rabbinic literature than what is never there.

The issue of the relationship between the Mishnah and Scripture deeply engaged a variety of writers and compilers of documents. Time and again we have evidence of an interest in the scriptural sources of laws, or of greater consequence in the priority of Scripture in taxonomic inquiry. We can show large-scale compositions that will readily have served treatises on these matters. But if I had to point to a single type of writing that is quite commonplace in the compilations we do have, but *wholly* outside of the repertoire of redactional possibilities we have or can imagine, it must be a sustained piece of writing on the relationship of the Mishnah to Scripture. Such a treatise can have been enormous, not only because, in theory, every line of the Mishnah required attention. It is also because, in practice, a variety of documents, particularly Sifra, the two Sifrés, and the Talmuds, contain writing of a single kind, meant to amplify the Mishnah by appeal to Scripture (but never to amplify Scripture by appeal to the Mishnah!). It is perfectly clear that no one imagined compiling a commentary to the Mishnah that would consist principally of proofs, of a sustained and well-crafted sort, that the Mishnah in general depends upon Scripture (even though specific and sustained proofs that the principles of taxonomy derive from Scripture are, as I said, susceptible of compilation in such treatises). How do we know that fact? It is because, when people did compile writings in the form of sustained commentaries to the Mishnah, that is to say, the two Talmuds, they did not focus principally upon the scriptural exegesis of the Mishnah; that formed only one interest, and, while an important one, it did not predominate; it certainly did not define the plan and program of the whole; and it certainly did not form a center of redactional labor. It was simply one item on a list of items that would be brought into relationship, where appropriate, with sentences of the Mishnah. And even then, it always was the intersection at the level of sentences, not sustained discourses, let alone with the Mishnah viewed whole and complete.

And yet – and yet if we look into compilations we do have, we find sizable sets of materials that can have been joined together with the Mishnah, paragraph by paragraph, in such a way that Scripture might have been shaped into a commentary to the Mishnah. Let me now give a sustained example of what might have emerged, but never did emerge, in the canonical compilations of Judaism. I draw my case from Sifra, but equivalent materials in other Midrash-compilations as well as in the two Talmuds in fact are abundant. In boldface type are direct citations of Mishnah-passages. I skip Nos. 2-12, because these are not germane to this part of my argument.

Sifra Parashat Behuqotai Parashah 3
CCLXX:I
1. A. ["The Lord said to Moses, Say to the people of Israel, When a man makes a special vow of persons to the Lord at your Valuation, then your Valuation of a male from twenty years old up to sixty years old shall be fifty shekels of silver according to the shekel of the sanctuary. If the person is a female, your Valuation shall be thirty shekels. If the person is from five years old up to twenty years old, your Valuation shall be for a male twenty shekels and for a female ten shekels. If the person is from a month old up to five years old, your Valuation shall be for a male five shekels of silver and for a female your Valuation shall be three shekels of silver. And if the person is sixty years old and upward, then your Valuation for a male shall be fifteen shekels and for a female ten shekels. And if a man is too poor to pay your Valuation, then he shall bring the person before the priest, and the priest shall value him; according to the ability of him who vowed the priest shall value him" (Lev. 27:1-8).]
   B. "Israelites take vows of Valuation, but gentiles do not take vows of Valuation [M. Ar. 1:2B].
   C. "Might one suppose they are not subject to vows of Valuation?
   D. "Scripture says, 'a man,'" the words of R. Meir.
   E. Said R. Meir, "After one verse of Scripture makes an inclusionary statement, another makes an exclusionary statement.
   F. "On what account do I say that gentiles are subject to vows of Valuation but may not take vows of Valuation?
   G. "It is because greater is the applicability of the rule of subject to the pledge of Valuation by others than the applicability of making the pledge of Valuation of others [T. Ar. 1:1A].
   H. "For lo, a deaf-mute, idiot, and minor may be subjected to vows of Valuation, but they are not able to take vows of Valuation [M. Ar. 1:1F]."
   I. R. Judah says, "Israelites are subject to vows of Valuation, but gentiles are not subject to vows of Valuation [M. Ar. 1:2C].
   J. "Might one suppose that they may not take vows of Valuation of third parties?
   K. "Scripture says, 'a man.'"
   L. Said R. Judah, "After one verse of Scripture makes an inclusionary statement, another makes an exclusionary statement.
   M. "On what account do I say that gentiles are not subject to vows of Valuation but may take vows of Valuation?
   N. "It is because greater is the applicability of the rule of pledging the Valuation of others than the applicability of being subject to the pledge of Valuation by others [T. Ar. 1:1C].
   O. "For a person of doubtful sexual traits and a person who exhibits traits of both sexes pledge the Valuation of others but are not subjected to the pledge of Valuation to be paid by others" [M. Ar. 1:1D].
13. A. And how do we know that the sixtieth year is treated as part of the period prior to that year?

	B.	Scripture says, "from twenty years old up to sixty years old" –
	C.	this teaches that the sixtieth year is treated as part of the period prior to that year.
	D.	I know only that that is the rule governing the status of the sixtieth year. How do I know the rule as to assigning the fifth year, the twentieth year?
	E.	It is a matter of logic:
	F.	Liability is incurred when one is in the sixtieth year, the fifth year, and the twentieth year.
	G.	Just as the sixtieth year is treated as part of the period prior to that year,
	H.	so the fifth and the twentieth years are treated as part of the period prior to that year.
	I.	But if you treat the sixtieth year as part of the prior period, imposing a more stringent law [the Valuation requiring a higher fee before than after sixty],
	J.	shall we treat the fifth year and the twentieth year as part of the period prior to that year, so imposing a more lenient law in such cases [the Valuation being less expensive]?
	K.	Accordingly, Scripture is required to settle the question when it refers repeatedly to "year,"
	L.	thus establishing a single classification for all such cases:
	M.	just as the sixtieth year is treated as part of the prior period, so the fifth and the twentieth years are treated as part of the prior period.
	N.	And that is the rule, whether it produces a more lenient or a more stringent ruling [M. Ar. 4:4M-Q, with somewhat different wording].
14.	A.	R. Eliezer says, "How do we know that a month and a day after a month are treated as part of the sixtieth year?
	B.	"Scripture says, 'up...':
	C.	"Here we find reference to 'up...,' and elsewhere we find the same. Just as 'up' used elsewhere means that a month and a day after the month [are included in the prior span of time], so the meaning is the same when used here. [M. Ar. 4:4R: R. Eleazar says, "The foregoing applies so long as they are a month and a day more than the years which are prescribed."]
15.	A.	I know only that this rule applies after sixty. How do I know that the same rule applies after five or twenty?
	B.	It is a matter of logic:
	C.	One is liability to pay a pledge of Valuation if the person to be evalued is old than sixty, and one is liable if such a one is older than five or older than twenty.
	D.	Just as, if one is older than sixty by a month and a day, the person is as though he were sixty years of age, so if the one is after five years or twenty years by a month and a day, lo, these are deemed to be the equivalent of five or twenty years of age.
16.	A.	"And if a man is too poor to pay your Valuation":
	B.	this means, if he is too impoverished to come up with your Valuation.
17.	A.	"...then he shall bring the person before the priest":
	B.	this then excludes a dead person.

	C.	I shall then exclude a corpse but not a dying person?
	D.	Scripture says, "then he shall bring the person before the priest, and the priest shall value him" –
	E.	one who is subject to being brought is subject to being valuated, and one who is not subject to being brought before the priest [such as a dying man] also is not subject to the pledge of Valuation.
18.	A.	Might one suppose that even if someone said, "The Valuation of Mr. So-and-so is incumbent on me," and he died, the man should be exempt?
	B.	Scripture says, "and the priest shall value him."
	C.	That is so even if he is dead.
19.	A.	"...and the priest shall value him":
	B.	This means that one pays only in accord with the conditions prevailing at the time of the Valuation.
20.	A.	"...according to the ability of him who vowed the priest shall value him":
	B.	It is in accord with the means of the one who takes the vow, not the one concerning whom the vow is taken,
	C.	whether that is a man, woman or child.
	D.	In this connection sages have said:
	E.	The estimate of ability to pay is made in accord with the status of the one who vows;
	F.	and the estimate of the years of age is made in accord with the status of the one whose Valuation is vowed.
	G.	And when this is according to the Valuations spelled out in the Torah, it is in accord with the status, as to age and sex, of the one whose Valuation is pledged.
	H.	And the Valuation is paid in accordance with the rate prescribed at the time of the pledge of Valuation [M. Ar. 4:1A-D].
21.	A.	"...the priest shall value him":
	B.	This serves as the generative analogy covering all cases of Valuations, indicating that the priest should be in charge.

The program of the Mishnah and the Tosefta predominates throughout, e.g., Nos. 1, 12, 13, 14-15. The second methodical inquiry characteristic of our authorship, involving exclusion and inclusion, accounts for pretty much the rest of this well-crafted discussion. Now we see a coherent and cogent discussion of a topic in accord with a program applicable to all topics, that trait of our document which so won our admiration. Thus Nos. 2-11, 17-20, involve inclusion, exclusion, or extension by analogy. I should offer this excellent composition as an example of the best our authorship has to give us, and a very impressive intellectual gift at that. The point throughout is simple. We know how the compilers of canonical writings produced treatments of the Mishnah. The one thing that they did not do was to create a scriptural commentary to the Mishnah. That is not the only type of writing lacking all correspondence to documents we have or can imagine, but it is a striking example.

vii. The Three Stages of Literary Formation

Now to return to my starting point, namely, those sizable selections of materials that circulated from one document to another and why I tend to think they were formed earlier than the writings particular to documents. The documentary hypothesis affects our reading of the itinerant compositions, for it identifies what writings are extra-documentary and non-documentary and imposes upon the hermeneutics and history of these writings a set of distinctive considerations. The reason is that these writings serve the purposes not of compilers (or authors or authorships) of distinct compilations, but the interests of a another type of authorship entirely: one that thought making up stories (whether or not for collections) itself an important activity; or making up exercises on Mishnah-Scripture relationships; or other such writings as lie beyond the imagination of the compilers of the score of documents that comprise the canon. When writings work well for two or more documents therefore they must be assumed to have a literary history different from those that serve only one writing or one type of writing, and, also, demand a different hermeneutic.

My "three stages" in ordinal sequence correspond, as a matter of fact, to a taxic structure, that is, three types of writing. The first – and last in assumed temporal order – is writing carried out in the context of the making, or compilation, of a classic. That writing responds to the redactional program and plan of the authorship of a classic. The second, penultimate in order, is writing that can appears in a given document but better serves a document other than the one in which it (singularly) occurs. This kind of writing seems to me not to fall within the same period of redaction as the first. For while it is a type of writing under the identical conditions, it also is writing that presupposes redactional programs in no way in play in the ultimate, and definitive, period of the formation of the canon: when people did things this way, and not in some other. That is why I think it is a kind of writing that was done prior to the period in which people limited their redactional work and associated labor of composition to the program that yielded the books we now have.

The upshot is simple: whether the classification of writing be given a temporal or merely taxonomic valence, the issue is the same: have these writers done their work with documentary considerations in mind? I believe I have shown that they have not. Then where did they expect their work to makes its way? Anywhere it might, because, so they assumed, fitting in nowhere in particular, it found a suitable locus everywhere it turned up. But I think temporal, not merely taxonomic, considerations pertain.

The third kind of writing seems to me to originate in a period prior to the other two. It is carried on in a manner independent of all redactional considerations such as are known to us. Then it should derive from a time when redactional considerations played no paramount role in the making of compositions. A brief essay, rather than a sustained composition, was then the dominant mode of writing. My hypothesis is that people can have written both long and short compositions – compositions and composites, in my language – at one and the same time. But writing that does not presuppose a secondary labor of redaction, e.g., in a composite, probably originated when authors or authorships did not anticipate any fate for their writing beyond their labor of composition itself.

Along these same lines of argument, this writing may or may not travel from one document to another. What that means is that the author or authorship does not imagine a future for his writing. What fits anywhere is composed to go nowhere in particular. Accordingly, what matters is not whether a writing fits one document or another, but whether, as the author or authorship has composed a piece of writing, that writing meets the requirements of any document we now have or can even imagine. If it does not, then we deal with a literary period in which the main kind of writing was ad hoc and episodic, not sustained and documentary.

Now extra- and non-documentary kinds of writing seem to me to derive from either [1] a period prior to the work of the making of Midrash-compilations and the two Talmuds alike; or [2] a labor of composition not subject to the rules and considerations that operated in the work of the making of Midrash-compilations and the two Talmuds. As a matter of hypothesis, I should guess that non-documentary writing comes prior to making any kind of documents of consequence, and extra-documentary writing comes prior to the period in which the specificities of the documents we now have were defined. That is to say, writing that can fit anywhere or nowhere is prior to writing that can fit somewhere but does not fit anywhere now accessible to us, and both kinds of writing are prior to the kind that fits only in what documents in which it is now located.

And given the documentary propositions and theses that we can locate in all of our compilations, we can only assume that the non-documentary writings enjoyed, and were assumed to enjoy, ecumenical acceptance. That means, very simply, when we wish to know the consensus of the entire textual (or canonical) community[7] – I mean simply the people, anywhere and any time, responsible for everything we now have – we turn not to the distinctive perspective of documents, but the (apparently universally acceptable) perspective of the extra-documentary compositions. That is the point at which we should look for the propositions everywhere accepted but no where advanced in a distinctive way, the "Judaism beyond the texts" – or behind them.

Do I place a priority, in the framing of a hypothesis, over taxonomy or temporal order? Indeed I do. I am inclined to suppose that non-documentary compositions took shape not only separated from, but in time before, the documentary ones did. My reason for thinking so is worth rehearsing, even though it is not yet compelling. The kinds of non-documentary writing I have identified in general focus on matters of very general interest. These matters may be assembled into two very large rubrics: virtue, on the one side, reason, on the other. Stories about sages fall into the former category; all of them set forth in concrete form the right living that sages exemplify. Essays on right thinking, the role of reason, the taxonomic priority of Scripture, the power of analogy, the exemplary character of cases and precedents in the expression of general and encompassing rules – all of these intellectually coercive writings set forth rules of thought as universally applicable, in their way, as are the rules of conduct contained in stories about sages, in theirs. A great labor of generalization is contained in both kinds of non-documentary and extra-documentary writing. And the results of that labor are then given concrete expression in the documentary writings in hand; for these, after all, do say in the setting of specific passages or problems precisely what, in a highly general way, emerges from the writing that moves hither and yon, never with a home, always finding a suitable resting place.

Now, admittedly, that rather general characterization of the non-documentary writing is subject to considerable qualification and clarification. But it does provide a reason to assign temporal priority, not solely taxonomic distinction, to the non-documentary compositions. We can have had commentaries of a sustained and systematic sort on Chronicles, on the one side, treatises on virtue, on the second, gospels, on the third – to complete the triangle. But we do not have these kinds of books.

In conclusion, let me confess that I wish our sages had made treatises on right action and right thought, in their own idiom to be

---

[7] I prefer Brian Stock's "textual community," see his *Implications of Literacy* (Princeton, 1986: Princeton University Press).

sure, because I think these treatises will have shaped the intellect of generations to come in a more effective way than the discrete writings, submerged in collections and composites of other sorts altogether, have been able to do. Compositions on correct behavior made later on filled the gap left open by the redactional decisions made in the period under study; I do not know why no one assembled a Midrash on right action in the way in which, in Leviticus Rabbah and Genesis Rabbah, treatises on the rules of society and the rules of history were compiled. And still more do I miss those intellectually remarkable treatises on right thought that our sages can have produced out of the rich resources in hand: the art of generalization, the craft of comparison and contrast, for example. In this regard the Mishnah, with its union of (some) Aristotelian modes of thought and (some) neo-Platonic propositions forms the model, if a lonely one, for what can have been achieved, even in the odd and unphilosophical idiom of our sages.[8] The compositions needed for both kinds of treatises – and, as a matter of fact, many, many of them – are fully in hand. But no one made the compilations of them.

The books we do have not only preserve the evidences of the possibility of commentaries and biographies. More than that, they also bring to rich expression the messages that such books will have set forth. And most important, they also express in fresh and unanticipated contexts those virtues and values that commentaries and biographies ("gospels") meant to bring to realization, and they do so in accord with the modes of thought that sophisticated reflection on right thinking has exemplifed in its way as well. So when people when about the work of making documents, they did something fresh with something familiar. They made cogent compositions, documents, texts enjoying integrity and autonomy. But they did so in such a way as to form of their distinct documents a coherent body of writing, of books, a canon, of documents, a system. And this they did in such a way as to say, in distinctive and specific ways, things that, in former times, people had expressed in general and broadly applicable ways.

---

[8]This is fully explained in my *Philosophical Mishnah* (Atlanta, 1989: Scholars Press for Brown Judaic Studies) I-IV, and in my *The Philosophy of Judaism: The First Principles* (in press).

4

Documentary Hermeneutics and the Interpretation of Narrative in the Classics of Judaism

Jacob Neusner
The Institute for Advanced Study and Brown University

A common attitude of mind among scholars of the literature of formative Judaism is to examine a story or a fable entirely in its own terms. That viewpoint treats as null the interests of the compilers of a document, who may not only have selected a story or fable for preservation but also revised its indicative traits – whether of narrative or of proposition – to conform to the larger program for which they make their compilation. Indifference to the imperatives of the documentary setting may or may not represent a valid hermeneutic in the analysis of literary and even folkloristic materials. When should we seek the marks of a documentary framing of a piece of writing, and when are we justified in ignoring the documentary interests in an otherwise autonomous tale? In point of fact, a systematic account of the matter, in theory with one sustained and I think compelling example, will answer these complementary questions.[1]

i. The Starting Point

We do not now know how the various classics of the Judaism of the Dual Torah that reached closure in late antiquity, by the seventh century, took shape. The reason is that the books all are anonymous.

---

[1] I present here some of the principal propositions of my *Making the Classics in Judaism: The Three Stages in Documentary Formation* (Atlanta, 1989: Scholars Press for Brown Judaic Studies).

We not only do not know who wrote or compiled them, we also do not know when any one of them reached closure. The sole evidence in hand is inductive: the characteristic traits, as to rhetoric, logic of cogent discourse, and topic, of the writings themselves. The manner in which that evidence is to be interpreted has to be carefully considered. But, short of believing that all sayings assigned to named authorities were really said by those to whom said sayings are attributed – and such an act of utter gullibility is inconceivable – we have no clear notion of the history of the canonical writings of Judaism from the Mishnah, ca. 200, through the Bavli, ca. 600. Nor do we even know where to begin the work of framing a hypothesis for rigorous testing.

But two starting points present themselves: the whole or the smallest part. That is to say, do we start from the document as a whole and examine its indicative traits? Then the reading of the parts will be in the light of the program of the whole. We shall define the norm on the base-line of the whole and ask where, how, and why the parts diverge from the norm. That is the mode of comparison and contrast that will generate our hypotheses of literary history and purpose – and also, therefore our hermeneutics. The manner of analysis dictated by the entry from the outermost layer is simple.

We commence our analytical inquiry from a completed document and unpeel its layers, from the ultimate one of closure and redaction, to the penultimate, and onward into the innermost formation of the smallest whole units of thought of which a document is comprised. In so doing, we treat the writing as a document that has come to closure at some fixed point and through the intellection of purposeful framers or redactor. We start the analytical process by asking what those framers – that authorship – have wanted their document to accomplish and by pointing to the means by which that authorship achieved its purposes. Issues of prevailing rhetoric and logic, as well as the topical program of the whole, guide us in our definition of the document as a whole. The parts then come under study under the aspect of the whole. Knowing the intent of the framers, we ask whether, and how, materials they have used have been shaped in response to the program of the document's authorship.

The alternative point of entry is to begin with the smallest building block of any and all documents, which is the lemma or irreducible minimum of completed thought, and working upward and outward from the innermost layer of the writing. That point of entry ignores the boundaries of discrete documents and asks what we find common within and among all documents. There is the starting point, and the norm is defined by the traits of the saying or lemma as it moves from here to there. Within this theory of the history of the literature, the boundary-lines of documents do not demarcate important classifications of data; all data are uniform, wherever they occur. The stress then lies not on the differentiating traits of documents, but the points shared in common among them; these points are sayings that occur in two or more places. Literary history consists in the inquiry into the fate of sayings as they move from one place to another. The hermeneutics of course will focus upon the saying and its history, rather than on the program and plan of documents that encompass, also, the discrete saying. The advantage of this approach, of course, is that it takes account of what is shared among documents, on the one side, and also of what exhibits none of the characteristic traits definitive of given documents, on the other.

ii. The Hypothesis: The Three Stages of Literary Formation

As to method, I maintain that we begin with the whole and work inward, as we peel an onion. As to the parts, we classify them by their indicative traits of relationship with the plan and program of the whole. That is to say, are writings responsive to the program of the compilation in which they occur? Are they responsive to the program of some other compilation, not the one where they now are? Or are they utterly autonomous of the requirements of any redactional setting we have or can envisage?

It is the simple fact that rabbinic documents – particularly Midrash-compilations – in some measure draw upon a fund of completed compositions of thought that have taken shape without attention to the needs of the compilers of those documents. The second is that some of these same documents draw upon materials that have been composed with the requirements of the respective documents in mind. Within the distinction between writing that serves a redactional purpose and writing that does not, we shall see four types of completed compositions of thought. Each type may be distinguished from the others by appeal to a single criterion of differentiation, that is to say, to traits of precisely the same sort. The indicative traits concern relationship to the redactional purpose of a piece of writing, viewed overall.

[1] Some writings in a given Midrash-compilation clearly serve the redactional program of the framers of the document in which those writings occur.

[2] Some writings in a given Midrash-compilation serve not the redactional program of the document in which they occur, but some other document, now in our hands. There is no material difference, as to the taxonomy of the writing of the classics in Judaism, between the first

and second types; it is a problem of transmission of documents, not their formation.

[3] Some writings in a given Midrash-compilation serve not the purposes of the document in which they occur but rather a redactional program of a document, or of a type of document, that we do not now have, but can readily envision. In this category we find the possibility of imagining compilations that we do not have, but that can have existed but did not survive; or that can have existed and were then recast into the kinds of writings that people clearly preferred (later on) to produce. Numerous examples of writings that clearly have been redacted in accord with a program and plan other than those of any document now in our hands will show precisely what I mean here. Not only so, but the entire appendix is devoted to showing that stories about sages were told and recorded, but not compiled into complete books, e.g., hagiographies about given authorities. In *Why No Gospels in Talmudic Judaism?* I was able to point out one kind of book that we can have received but were not given. The criterion here is not subjective. We can demonstrate that materials of a given type, capable of sustaining a large-scale compilation, were available; but no such compilation was made, so far as extant sources suggest or attest.

[4] Some writings now found in a given Midrash-compilation stand autonomous of any redactional program we have in an existing compilation or of any we can even imagine on the foundations of said writings.

The first of those four kinds of completed units of thought (pericopes) as matter of hypothesis fall into the final stage of literary formation. That is to say, at the stage at which an authorship has reached the conclusion that it wishes to compile a document of a given character, that authorship will have made up pieces of writing that serve the purposes of the document it wishes to compile. The second through fourth kinds of completed units of thought come earlier than this writing in the process of the formation of the classics of Judaism represented by the compilation in which this writing now finds its place.

The second of the four kinds of completed units of thought served a purpose other than that of the authorship of the compilation in which said kind of writing now occurs. It is therefore, as a matter of hypothesis, to be assigned to a stage in the formation of classics prior to the framing of the document in which the writing now occurs; in the context of a given compilation that now contains that writing, it is in a relative sense earlier than a piece of writing that the framers have worked out to serve their own distinctive and particular purposes. It is then earlier than a writing that has been made up to serve the document in which it now occurs. But it is also later in its formation than what we find in the third kind of writing.

The third of the four kinds of completed units of thought clearly presupposes a location in a document of a kind we do not have. But the characteristics of a set of such writings permits us to identify and define the kind of writing that can readily have contained, and been well served by, pericopes of this kind. Compositions of this kind, as a matter of hypothesis, are to be assigned to a stage in the formation of classics prior to the framing of all available documents. For, as a matter of fact, all of our now extant writings adhere to a single program of conglomeration and agglutination, and all are served by composites of one sort, rather than some other. Hence we may suppose that at some point prior to the decision to make writings in the model that we now have but in some other model people also made up completed units of thought to serve these other kinds of writings. These persist, now, in documents that they do not serve at all well. And we can fairly easily identify the kinds of documents that they can and should have served quite nicely indeed. These then are the three stages of literary formation in the making of the classics of Judaism.

Type four in the list above stands outside of the three stages of literary formation, because these are kinds of writings that fall outside of any relationship with a redactional program we either have in hand or can even imagine. These free-standing units can have been written any time; the tastes as to redaction of a given set of compilers of documents make no impact upon the writing of such materials. When we find them in existing documents – and they are everywhere – they are parachuted down and bear no clear role in the accomplishment, through the writing, of the redactors' goals for their compilation. They are given, by way of rich example, in my presentation here of the treatment in the compilation, Ruth Rabbah, of Ruth 3:13.

Of the relative temporal or ordinal position of writings that stand autonomous of any redactional program we have in an existing compilation or of any we can even imagine on the foundations of said writings we can say nothing.[2] These writings prove episodic; they are commonly singletons. They serve equally well everywhere, because they demand no traits of form and redaction in order to endow them with sense and meaning. Why not? Because they are essentially free-standing and episodic, not referential and allusive. They are stories that contain their own point and do not invoke, in the making of that point, a given verse of Scripture. They are sayings that are utterly ad hoc. A variety of materials fall into this – from a redactional

---

[2] But I shall qualify this judgment later on.

perspective – unassigned, and unassignable, type of writing. They do not belong in books at all. By that I mean, whoever made up these pieces of writing did not imagine that what he was forming required a setting beyond the limits of his own piece of writing; the story is not only complete in itself but could stand entirely on its own; the saying spoke for itself and required no nurturing context; the proposition and its associated proofs in no way was meant to draw nourishment from roots penetrating nutriments outside of its own literary limits.

My analytical taxonomy of the writings now collected in various Midrash-compilations points to not only three stages in the formation of the classics of Judaism. It also suggests that writing went on outside of the framework of the editing of documents, and also within the limits of the formation and framing of documents. Writing of the former kind then constituted a kind of literary work on which redactional planning made no impact. But the second and the third kinds of writing responds to redactional considerations. So in the end we shall wish to distinguish between writing intended for the making of books – compositions of the first three kinds listed just now – and writing not response to the requirements of the making of compilations – compositions of the fourth kind.

The distinctions upon which these analytical taxonomies rest are objective and no no way subjective, since they depend upon the fixed and factual relationship between a piece of writing and a larger redactional context.

[1] We know the requirements of redactors of the several documents of the rabbinic canon, because I have already shown what they are in the case of a large variety of documents. When, therefore, we judge a piece of writing to serve the program of the document in which that writing occurs, it is not because of a personal impulse or a private and incommunicable insight, but because the traits of that writing self-evidently respond to the documentary program of the book in which the writing is located.

[2] When, further, we conclude that a piece of writing belongs in some other document than the one in which it is found, that too forms a factual judgment.

[3] A piece of writing that serves no where we now know may nonetheless conform to the rules of writing that we can readily imagine and describe in theory. For instance, a propositional composition, that runs through a wide variety of texts to make a point autonomous of all of the texts that are invoked, clearly is intended for a propositional document, one that (like the Mishnah) makes points autonomous of a given prior writing, e.g., a biblical book, but that makes points that for one reason or another cohere quite nicely on their own. Authors of

propositional compilations self-evidently can imagine that kind of redaction. We have their writings, but not the books that they intended to be made up of those writings. Another example, as I have already pointed out, is a collection of stories about a given authority, or about a given kind of virtue exemplified by a variety of authorities. These and other types of compilations we can imagine but do not have are dealt with in the present rubric.

[4] And, finally, where we have utterly hermetic writing, sealed off from any broader literary context and able to define its own limits and sustain its point without regard to anything outside itself, we know that here we are in the presence of authorships that had no larger redactional plan in mind, no intent on the making of books out of their little pieces of writing. Here the judgment of what belongs and what does not is not at all subjective, as I shall show in through my concrete examples.

These distinctions form the first step in the analysis of the formation of the rabbinic documents viewed not in isolation from one another but in relationship both to one another and also to shared antecedent writings to which we have access only in the re-presentation of the now completed documents. I have now completed the bulk of my re-presentation and analysis of the documents of the Judaism of the Dual Torah one by one. Here I begin the analysis of those documents seen not in isolation from one another, but rather in relationship to what may be a common fund of materials framed without. The work of analysis begins with the data *in situ*: as we have them. That is why I give a sizable sample of two of the types I regard as indicative: writing for redactional purposes, writing not at all for redactional purposes, and writing for redactional purposes, but not of the redactors of the document in which that writing appears.

Specifically, in my sample of Ruth Rabbah, the first entry, marked LXII:i, is composed in response to the requirements of a sustained commentary on the verses, read in succession, of the book of Ruth. The second entry, LXII:ii, is made up entirely on its own and organized and set forth in response to an inner-facing interest in narrative. However we divide the bits and pieces that are assembled here, there can be no doubt that the whole hangs together without attention to any broader compilation in which the vast entry may be included. The third entry, LXII:iii, serves to demonstrate a proposition. That proposition is not particular to the book of Ruth, of course. But a treatise of pertinent propositions, e.g., theological-moral virtues, can well have been served by precisely the composition before us. So while we do not have a document the needs of which can have generated the item we shall examine, we can readily imagine such a document and identify the traits of the writing before us as documentary and not free-standing and internally generated.

iii. Our Case: Ruth Rabbah to Ruth 3:13

    3:13   "*Remain this night and in the morning, if he will do the part of the next of kin for you, well; let him do it; but if he is not willing to do the part of the next of kin for you, then, as the Lord lives, I will do the part of the next of kin for you. Lie down until the morning.*"

LXII:i
1. A   "Remain this night:"
   B.   "This night you will spend without a husband, but you will not spend another night without a husband."

The opening gloss is trivial. But it clearly serves only the passage at hand, no broader proposition (by contrast to the utilization of our base-verse in LXII:iii). This writing conforms to the most limited definition of the redactional requirements of the compilers of a commentary to the book of Ruth. The contrast with what follows is stunning. For what we see is an item parachuted down into this compilation but wholly indifferent to the documentary program of the compilers. It has been made up on its own, not for service in this document.

Let me explain what I mean. Elsewhere[3] I point out some simple facts. The final organizers of the Bavli, the Talmud of Babylonia had in hand a tripartite corpus of inherited materials awaiting composition into a final, closed document. First, the first type of material, in various states and stages of completion, addressed the Mishnah or took up the principles of laws that the Mishnah had originally brought to articulation. These the framers of the Bavli organized in accord with the order of those Mishnah-tractates that they selected for sustained attention. Second, they had in hand received materials, again in various conditions, pertinent to Scripture, both as Scripture related to the Mishnah and also as Scripture laid forth its own narratives. These they set forth as Scripture-commentary. In this way, the penultimate and ultimate redactors of the Bavli laid out a systematic presentation of the two Torahs, the oral, represented by the Mishnah, and the written, represented by Scripture. And, third, the framers of the Bavli

---

[3]In my *Why No Gospels in Talmudic Judaism?* (Atlanta, 1988: Scholars Press for Brown Judaic Studies) I explain why no other document in the rabbinic canon of late antiquity can have been compiled out of such materials either. In fact there was every possibility of compiling biographies, but it is something that the framers of canonical documents never undertook.

Documentary Hermeneutics

also had in hand materials focused on sages. These in the received form, attested in the Bavli's pages, were framed around twin biographical principles, either as strings of stories about great sages of the past or as collections of sayings and comments drawn together solely because the same name stands behind all the collected sayings.

These stories, exemplified in what follows, can easily have been composed into biographies. In the context of Christianity and of Judaism, it is appropriate to call the biography of a holy man or woman, meant to convey the divine message, a gospel. Hence the question I raised there: why no gospels in Judaism? The question is an appropriate one, because, as I shall show, there could have been. The final step – assembling available stories into a coherent narrative, with a beginning, middle, and end, for example – was not taken. This suffices for the present to underline that what follows here is simply beyond the framework of compilation – ultimate organization, closure, and redaction – of documents. Hence this writing belongs into the fourth class among those differentiated just now.

LXII:ii

1. A. "...and in the morning, if he will do the part of the next of kin for you, well; let him do it; but if he is not willing to do the part of the next of kin for you, then, as the Lord lives, I will do the part of the next of kin for you. [Lie down until the morning]:"
    B. On the Sabbath R. Meir was in session and expounding in the school of Tiberias, and Elisha, his master, was passing in the market riding a horse.
    C. They said to R. Meir, "Lo, Elisha your master is passing by in the market."
    D. He went out to him.
    E. He [Elisha] said to him [Meir], "With what were you engaged?"
    F. He said to him, "'So the Lord blessed the latter end of Job more than his beginning' (Job 42:12)."
    G. He said to him, "And what do you have to say about it?"
    H. He said to him, "'Blessed' means that he gave him twice as much money as he had before."
    I. He said to him, "Aqiba, your master, did not explain it in that way. This is how he explained it: "'So the Lord blessed the latter end of Job more than his beginning:" it was on account of the repentance and the good deeds that were in his hand to begin with.'"
    J. He said to him, "And what else did you say?"
    K. He said to him, "'Better is the end of a thing than the beginning thereof' (Qoh. 7:8)."
    L. He said to him, "And what do you have to say about it?"
    M. He said to him, "You have the case of someone who buys merchandise in his youth and loses on it, while in his old age he profits through it.

N. "Another matter: 'Better is the end of a thing than the beginning thereof' (Qoh. 7:8): you have the case of someone who does wicked deeds in his youth, but in his old age he does good deeds.

O. "Another matter: 'Better is the end of a thing than the beginning thereof' (Qoh. 7:8): you have the case of someone who studies Torah in his youth but forgets it, and in his old age it comes back to him. [Since Elisha was an apostate who had earlier been a great master of the Torah, these interpretations bear a personal message to him from his disciple, Meir.]

P. "Thus 'Better is the end of a thing than the beginning thereof' (Qoh. 7:8)."

Q. He said to him, "Aqiba, your master, did not explain matters in this way.

R. "Rather, 'Better is the end of a thing than the beginning thereof' (Qoh. 7:8): the end of a matter is good when it is good from the very beginning.'

S. "And there is this case [which illustrates Aqiba's view]: Abbuyah, my father, was one of the leading figures of the generation, and when the time came to circumcise me, he invited all the leading men of Jerusalem, and he invited R. Eliezer and R. Joshua with them.

T. "And when they had eaten and drunk, these began to say psalms, and those began to say [Rabinowitz, p. 77:] alphabetical acrostics.

U. "Said R. Eliezer to R. Joshua, 'These are engaged with what matters to them, so should we not devote ourselves to what matters to us?'

V. "They began with [verses of] the Torah, and from the Torah, they went on to the prophets, and from the prophets to the writings. And the matters gave as much joy as when they were given from Sinai, so fire leapt round about them.

W. "For was not the very act of giving them through fire? 'And the mountain burned with fire to the heart of heaven' (Dt. 4:11).

X. "[My father] said, 'Since such is the great power of Torah, this son, if he survives for me, lo, I shall give him over to the Torah.'

Y. "But since his true intentionality was not for the sake of Heaven [but for the ulterior motive of mastering the supernatural power of the Torah], my Torah did not endure in me.

Z. [Elisha continues in his talk with Meir:] "And what [else] did you say?"

AA. [Meir said to Elisha,] "'Gold and glass cannot equal it' (Job 28:17)."

BB. He said to him, "And what did you have to say about it?"

CC. He said to him, "This refers to teachings of the Torah, which are as hard to acquire as golden utensils and as easy to break as glass."

DD. He said to him, "Aqiba, your master, did not explain matters in this way.

EE. "Rather: 'just as golden and glass utensils, should they break, can be repaired, so a disciple of the sages who loses his master of the Mishnah can regain it.'"

FF. [Meir said to Elisha,] "Turn back."

GG. He said to him, "Why?"

Documentary Hermeneutics

	HH.	[Elisha] said to [Meir], "Up to here is the Sabbath limit [and within this space alone are you permitted to walk about]."
	II.	[Meir] said to him, "How do you know?"
	JJ.	[Elisha] said to him, "It is from the hooves of my horse, for the horse has already travelled two thousand cubits."
	KK.	[Meir] said to [Elisha], "And all this wisdom is in your possession, and yet you do not return?"
	LL.	He said to him, "I don't have the power to do so."
	MM.	He said to him, "Why not?"
	NN.	He said to him, "I was riding on my horse and sauntering past the synagogue on the Day of Atonement that coincided with the Sabbath. I heard an echo floating in the air: '"Return, O backsliding children" (Jer. 3:14), "Return to me and I will return to you" (Mal. 3:7) – except for Elisha b. Abbuyah.
	OO.	"'For he knew all my power, but he rebelled against me.'"
2.	A.	And how did he come to do such a deed? They tell the following:
	B.	One time he was sitting and repeating [Torah-sayings] in the valley of Gennesaret.
	C.	He saw a man climb up a palm tree on the Sabbath, take the dam with the offspring, and climb down whole and in one piece. Then at the end of the Sabbath he saw another man climb up a palm tree and take the offspring but send away the dam, and he came down, and a snake bit him and he died.
	D.	He said, "It is written, 'You shall in any manner let the dam go, but the young you may take for yourself, that it may be well with you and that you may live a long time' (Dt. 22:7).
	E.	"Now where is the goodness and the long life of this man?"
	F.	But he did not know that R. Aqiba had expounded in a public address: "'...that it may be well with you:' in the world that is entirely good.
	G.	"'...and that you may live a long time:' in the world that lasts for ever."
3.	A.	And some say that it was because he saw the tongue of R. Judah the baker being carried out in the mouth of a dog.
	B.	He said, "If this tongue, which has labored in the Torah throughout the man's life, is treated in this way, a tongue of one who does not know and does not labor in the Torah – all the more so!"
	C.	He said, "If so, then there is no granting of a reward for the righteous and no resurrection of the dead."
4.	A.	And some say that it was because when his mother was pregnant with him, she passed by temples of idolatry and smelled the odor,
	B.	and they gave her some of [the offering to the idol] to eat, and she ate it, and it diffused in her like the poison of an insect.
5.	A.	After some time Elisha b. Abbuyah fell ill.
	B.	They came and told R. Meir, "Elisha, your master, is sick."
	C.	He came to him.
	D.	He said to him, "Repent."
	E.	He said to him, "Even to this point do they accept [repentance]?"
	F.	He said to him, "Is it not written, 'You turn man to contrition' (Ps. 90:3) – until the very crushing of the spirit."

	G.	At that moment Elisha b. Abbuyah wept, and died.
	H.	And R. Meir rejoiced, saying, "It appears that it was from the midst of repentance that my master has gone away."
6.	A.	And when they buried him, a fire came to burn up his grave.
	B.	They came and told R. Meir, "The grave of your master is burning."
	C.	He came and spread his cloak over it."
	D.	He said to him, "'Remain this night:' in this world, the whole of which is night.
	E.	"'...and in the morning, if he will redeem you [lit.: do the part of the next of kin for you], well; let him do it:'
	F.	"'and in the morning:' in the world that is wholly good.
	G.	"'...if he will redeem you, well and good, he will redeem you:' this refers to the Holy One, blessed be He: 'The Lord is good to all' (Ps. 145:9).
	H.	"'...but if he is not willing to redeem you, you, then, as the Lord lives, I will redeem you. Lie down until the morning.'"
	I.	[Rabinowitz:] And the fire subsided.
7.	A.	They said to him, "My lord, in the world to come, if they say to you, whom do you want, your father or your master, what will you say?"
	B.	He said to them, "Father, then my master."
	C.	They said to him, "Will they listen [when you ask for Elisha, who was an apostate]?"
	D.	He said to them, "Is it not an explicit teaching of the Mishnah? **The case of a scroll may on the Sabbath may be saved from a fire together with the scroll, and the case of tefillin together with the tefillin [M. Shab. 16:1].**
	E.	"They will save Elisha because of the merit of his Torah-learning."
8.	A.	After some time, his daughters came and begged for charity from our lord [Judah the Patriarch].
	B.	He said, "'Let there be none to extend kindness to him, neither let there be any to be gracious to his orphaned children' (Ps. 109:12)."
	C.	They said, "My lord, do not focus upon his deeds, focus upon his Torah."
	D.	At that moment our lord wept and made the decree concerning them that they were to receive their requirements.
	E.	He said, "If one whose mastery of Torah was not for the sake of Heaven has produced such as these, one whose Torah is for the sake of Heaven how much the more so!"

This entire composition is parachuted down because of the appeal to our base-verse as a prooftext at one point in the narrative. The whole has been assembled – much of it a sustained, unitary and flowing story – to make the points at the end about the power of repentance and of Torah-study. But the exposition of the relationship between the sinning master and the disciple transcends the requirement of an exemplary account of virtue. Our interest is of course limited; but the selection of a powerful and enormous piece of writing, obviously composed for its own purposes, shows us how the compilers of the document broadened the conception of what a compilation should, and

Documentary Hermeneutics 119

need not, encompass. The impact upon their recasting of the book of Ruth is at once nearly nil and also profound and encompassing.

Now to a passage composed with a document in mind, but not the document in which the passage now appears. The base-verse is here subordinated; there are three cases to prove a point. Hence a document that wished to present syllogistic arguments in behalf of propositions can have been served by what follows, but a document meant to form a commentary to the book of Ruth is not well served. The following falls into the second of the four classes of materials set forth earlier.

LXXII:iii
1. A. Said R. Yosé, "There were three who were tempted by their inclination to do evil, but who strengthened themselves against it in each case by taking an oath: Joseph, David, and Boaz.
   B. "Joseph: 'How then can I do this great wickedness and sin against God' (Gen. 39:9).
   C. [Yosé continues, citing] R. Hunia in the name of R. Idi: 'Does Scripture exhibit defects? What Scripture here says is not, "and sin against the Lord," but "and sin against God."
   D. "'For he had sworn [in the language of an oath] to his evil inclination, saying, "By God, I will not sin or do this evil."'
   E. "David: 'And David said, 'As the Lord lives, no, but the Lord shall smite him' (1 Sam. 26:10).
   F. "To whom did he take the oath?
   G. "R. Eleazar and R. Samuel b. Nahman:
   H. "R. Eleazar said, 'It was to his impulse to do evil.'
   I. "R. Samuel b. Nahman said, 'It was to Abishai b. Zeruiah. He said to him, "As the Lord lives, if you touch him, I swear that I will mix your blood with his."'
   J. "Boaz: 'as the Lord lives, I will do the part of the next of kin for you. Lie down until the morning.'
   K. "R. Judah and R. Hunia:
   L. "R. Judah said, 'All that night his impulse to do evil was besieging him and saying to him, "You are a free agent and on the make, and she is a free agent and on the make. Go, have sexual relations with her, and let her be your wife!"'
   M. "'And so he took an oath against his inclination to do evil, saying, "as the Lord lives."'
   N. "'And to the woman he said, "Remain this night and in the morning, if he will do the part of the next of kin for you, well; let him do it; but if he is not willing to do the part of the next of kin for you, then...I will do the part of the next of kin for you. Lie down until the morning."'
   O. "And R. Hunia said, 'It is written, "A wise man is strong [beoz]. Yes, a man of knowledge increases strength" (Prov. 24:5).
   P. "'Read the word for strong [beoz] as Boaz:
   Q. "'A wise man is Boaz.
   R. "'"...and a man of knowledge increases strength," because he strengthened himself with an oath."'

Now we see what a passage serving our base-verse can accomplish. But even here, of course, our base-verse is made to address the interest of a proposition not particular to the passage at hand. The proposition of Yosé is that one should strengthen himself against temptation by taking an oath, and he gives three examples of that fact, of which ours is third only by reason of the redactional requirement of our compilers. Otherwise any order will serve as well. I have represented matters as though the whole were Yosé's statement, but of course, that is hardly required. In fact each item is autonomous of the others, with its independent exposition of its case. Thus B-D form an independent statement on Joseph, then D-E on David, with the appended expansion of F-I. J then stands on its own, with the appended and essential materials of Kff. An alternative theory is that to Yosé are to be attributed only the barebones of the proposition, consisting of B, E, and J, with the rest inserted to expand on his point; that seems to me entirely plausible. In this treatment of the base-verse, therefore, we find three quite distinct compositions. LXII:i is particular to the base-verse, but only a minor gloss; LXII:ii is an astonishing composition on its own, formed around the figure of Elisha b. Abbuyah. LXII:iii assembles three cases to establish a proposition.

iv. What Is at Stake: The Three Stages of Literary Formation and the Formation of a New Hermeneutics

Once we recognize, as I have shown we must, that the rabbinic documents constitute texts, not merely scrapbooks or random compilations of *ad hoc* and episodic materials. both the hermeneutics and the (theoretical) history of the texts are recast. For our criteria for interpreting a passage is now the program of the document. Our interest in philology – meanings of words scattered over a variety of documents – correspondingly diminishes. The context now predominates; meanings of words and phrases, while interesting, move away from center stage. And the texts now are seen to have histories – the texts, that is, the completed documents, and not merely the materials that the texts (happen, adventitiously, to) contain. And yet, we recognize, within these same thirteen well-crafted documents, sizable selections of materials did circulate from one document to another. The documentary hypothesis affects the itinerant compositions, for it identifies what writings are extra-documentary and non-documentary and imposes upon the hermeneutics and history of these writings a set of distinctive considerations too. For these writings serve the purposes not of compilers (or authors or authorships) of distinct compilations, but those of a variety of compilers; that means some writings are particular to a

Documentary Hermeneutics 121

document and immediately express the purposes of a distinct authorship or group of compilers, while other writings work well for two or more documents.

Let me expand on this point, since the movement of materials from compilation to compilation has always enjoyed prominence in such literary history and theory as have been shaped for the canon before us. By definition, according to the results of the present experiment, these other writings have been made up not with a given document's requirements in mind, but within a different theory altogether of the purpose and meaning of writing. Not only so, but, as we saw, there is a class of writings, associated with the kind in Ruth Rabbah LXII:iii in its independence of existing documentary compilations, that clearly means to serve the purposes of compilers of a document – but not the document(s) in which these writings now find their place. Writings of this class permit us to speculate on the existence of compilations now no longer in our hands, or, more to the point, *types* of compilations we (no longer) possess.

v. The Priority of Documentary Hermeneutics

Before proceeding, let me restate the premise of the whole. The analysis of the types of compositions of which rabbinic compilations are made up rests upon one fundamental premise. It is that rabbinic documents are texts and not scrapbooks,[4] that we moreover may identify the traits that characterize one piece of compilation and distinguish those traits from the ones that mark another compilation within the canon of the Judaism of the Dual Torah. My argument in favor of the documentary integrity of rabbinic compilations can stand reiteration.

In my study of Leviticus Rabbah I proposed to demonstrate in the case of that compilation of exegeses of Scripture that a rabbinic document constitutes a text, not merely a scrapbook or a random compilation of episodic materials. A text is a document with a purpose, one that exhibits the traits of the integrity of the parts to the whole

---

[4]But it must be said that some of the compilations, e.g., Leviticus Rabbah and Genesis Rabbah and Sifra, exhibit much more cogency than do others, e.g., Lamentations Rabbah and Esther Rabbah. However, I am not inclined to dismiss even Lamentations Rabbah, Esther Rabbah, and Ruth Rabbah as no more than scrapbooks. There is considerable attention among their compilers devoted to formal patterns, for one thing, and a well-crafted propositional program emerges in each of these compilations, for another. I find them admirable in their documentary cogency, but it is a different kind of coherence from that exhibited in the great Sifra or the two Sifrés. And, I hasten to add, formally we do not deal with the decadence of the form defined by Genesis Rabbah and Leviticus Rabbah, but in a revision of that form.

and the fundamental autonomy of the whole from other texts. I showed that the document at hand therefore falls into the classification of a cogent composition, put together with purpose and intended as a whole and in the aggregate to bear a meaning and state a message.

I therefore disproved the claim, for the case before us, that a rabbinic document serves merely as an anthology or miscellany or is to be compared only to a scrapbook, made up of this and that. In that exemplary instance I pointed to the improbability that a document has been brought together merely to join discrete and ready-made bits and pieces of episodic discourse. A document in the canon of Judaism thus does not merely define a context for the aggregation of such already completed and mutually distinct materials. Rather, I proved, that document constitutes a text. So at issue in my study of Leviticus Rabbah is what makes a text a text, that is, the textuality of a document. At stake is how we may know when a document constitutes a text and when it is merely an anthology or a scrapbook.

The importance of that issue for the correct method of comparison is clear. If we can show that a document is a miscellany, then traits of the document have no bearing on the contents of the document – things that just happen to be preserved there, rather than somewhere else. If, by contrast, the text possesses its own, integrity, then everything in the text must first of all be interpreted in the context of the text, then in the context of the canon of which the text forms a constituent. Hence my stress on the comparison of whole documents, prior to the comparison of the results of exegesis contained within those documents, rests upon the result of the study of Leviticus Rabbah. Two principal issues frame the case. The first is what makes a text a text. The textuality of a text concerns whether a given piece of writing hangs together and is to be read on its own The second is what makes a group of texts into a canon, a cogent statement all together. At issue is the relationship of two or more texts of a single, interrelated literature to the worldview and way of life of a religious tradition viewed whole.

Now it may be claimed by proponents of the view that redactional, hence documentary, considerations are of negligible importance that powerful evidence contradicts my emphasis on the documentary origin of much writing now located in Midrash-compilations.[5] They point to

---

[5] These proponents are not fictive. David Weiss Halivni concentrates on sayings and their solitary journeys through various pericopes, scarcely attending to the traits of documents at all. I have dealt with his contrary approach to literary history in *Making the Classics in Judaism: The Three Stages of Literary Formation* (Atlanta, 1990: Scholars Press for Brown Judaic Studies).

the fact that stories and exegeses move from document to document. The travels of a given saying or story or exegesis of Scripture from one document to another validate comparing what travels quite apart from what stays home. And that is precisely what comparing exegeses of the same verse of Scripture occurring in different settings does. Traveling materials enjoy their own integrity, apart from the texts – the documents – that quite adventitiously give them a temporary home. The problem of *integrity* therefore is whether or not a rabbinic document stands by itself or right at the outset forms a scarcely differentiated segment of a larger and uniform canon, one made up of materials that travel everywhere and take up residence indifferent to the traits of their temporary abode.

The reason one might suppose that, in the case of the formative age of Judaism, a document does not exhibit integrity and is not autonomous is simple. The several writings of the rabbinic canon of late antiquity, formed from the Mishnah, ca. A.D. 200, through the Talmud of Babylonia, ca. A.D. 600, with numerous items in between, do share materials – sayings, tales, protracted discussions. Some of these shared materials derive from explicitly-cited documents. For instance, passages of Scripture or of the Mishnah or of the Tosefta, cited verbatim, will find their way into the two Talmuds. But sayings, stories, and sizable compositions not identified with a given, earlier text and exhibiting that text's distinctive traits will float from one document to the next.

That fact has so impressed students of the rabbinic canon as to produce a firm consensus of fifteen hundred years' standing. It is that one cannot legitimately study one document in isolation from others, describing its rhetorical, logical, literary, and conceptual traits and system all by themselves. To the contrary, all documents contribute to a common literature, or, more accurately, religion – Judaism. In the investigation of matters of rhetoric, logic literature, and conception, whether of law or of theology, all writings join equally to given testimony to the whole. For the study of the formative history of Judaism, the issue transcends what appears to be the simple, merely literary question at hand: when is a text a text? In the context of this book: when do the interests of the framers of a text participate in the writing of their text? and when do they merely compile from ready-made materials whatever suits their purpose? In the larger context of that question we return to the issue of the peripatetic sayings, stories, and exegeses.

vi. The Three Stages of Literary Formation Revisited

When I frame matters of literary theory, including literary history ("the three stages of literary formation") in terms of the problem of the rabbinic document, I ask what defines a document as such, the text-ness, the textuality, of a text. How do we know that a given book in the canon of Judaism is something other than a scrapbook? The choices are clear. One theory is that a document serves solely as a convenient repository of prior sayings and stories, available materials that will have served equally well (or poorly) wherever they took up their final location. In accord with that theory it is quite proper in ignorance of all questions of circumstance and documentary or canonical context to (to take the example of Comparative Midrash as presently performed) compare the exegesis of a verse of Scripture in one document with the exegesis of that verse of Scripture found in some other document.

The other theory is that a composition exhibits a viewpoint, a purpose of authorship distinctive to its framers or collectors and arrangers. Such a characteristic literary purpose – by this other theory – is so powerfully particular to one authorship that nearly everything at hand can be shown to have been (re)shaped for the ultimate purpose of the authorship at hand, that is, collectors and arrangers who demand the title of authors. In accord with this other theory context and circumstance form the prior condition of inquiry, the result, in exegetical terms, the contingent one. To resort again to a less than felicitous neologism, I thus ask what signifies or defines the "document-ness" of a document and what makes a book a book. I therefore wonder whether there are specific texts in the canonical context of Judaism or whether all texts are merely contextual. In framing the question as I have, I of course lay forth the mode of answering it. We have to confront a single rabbinic composition, and ask about its definitive traits and viewpoint.

vii. Itinerancy and Documentary Integrity: The Problem of the Peripatetic Composition

But we have also to confront the issue of the traveling sayings, the sources upon which the redactors of a given document have drawn. For there are sayings that do travel from one document to another without exhibiting much wear from the journey, and, as I shall show in Part Three, there also are sources that are equally at home everywhere because they belong no where. And such sources call into question the documentary theory of the making of the classics in Judaism that I present in this book. So let us turn to the matter of what is called "the sources."⁶

By "sources" I mean (for the purposes of argument here) simply passages in a given book that occur, also, in some other rabbinic book. Such sources – by definition prior to the books in which they appear – fall into the classification of materials general to two or more compositions and by definition not distinctive and particular to any one of them. The word "source" therefore serves as an analogy to convey the notion that two or more sets of authors have made use of a single, available item. About whether or not the shared item is prior to them both or borrowed by one from the other at this stage we cannot speculate.⁷

Let me now summarize this phase of the argument. We ask about the textuality of a document – is it a composition or a scrap book? – so as to determine the appropriate foundations for comparison, the correct classifications for comparative study. We seek to determine the correct context of comparison, hence the appropriate classification. My claim is simple: once we know what is unique to a document, we can investigate the traits that characterize all the document's unique and so definitive materials. We ask about whether the materials unique to a document also cohere, or whether they prove merely miscellaneous. If they do cohere, we may conclude that the framers of the document have followed a single plan and a program. That would in my view justify the claim that the framers carried out a labor not only of conglomeration, arrangement and selection, but also of genuine authorship or composition in the narrow and strict sense of the word. If

---

⁶This is defined at great length in my treatment of Halivni's theory of sources and traditions cited above. I redefine "sources" and "traditions" at the end of that paper, in terms that I think far more suitable.

⁷To state the consequences for Comparative Midrash, which has received attention in its own terms: These shared items, transcending two or more documents and even two or more complete systems or groups, if paramount and preponderant, would surely justify the claim that we may compare [3] exegeses of verses of Scripture without attention to [2] context. Why? Because there is no context defined by the limits of a given document and its characteristic plan and program. All the documents do is collect and arrange available materials. The document does not define the context of its contents. If that can be shown, then *comparative midrash* may quite properly ignore the contextual dimension imparted to sayings, including exegeses of Scripture, by their occurrence in one document rather than some other. In this connection, see my *Comparative Midrash: The Plan and Program of Genesis Rabbah and Leviticus Rabbah* (Atlanta, 1986: Scholars Press for Brown Judaic Studies.) *Comparative Midrash II. The Plan and Program of Lamentations Rabbah, Esther Rabbah, Ruth Rabbah, and Song of Songs Rabbah* is planned.

so, the document emerges from authors, not merely arrangers and compositors. For the same purpose, therefore, we also take up and analyze the items shared between that document and some other or among several documents. We ask about the traits of those items, one by one and all in the aggregate. In these stages we may solve for the case at hand the problem of the rabbinic document: do we deal with a scrapbook or a cogent composition? A text or merely a literary expression, random and essentially promiscuous, of a larger theological context? That is the choice at hand.

Since we have reached a matter of fact, let me state the facts as they are. To begin with, I describe the relationships among the principal components of the literature with which we deal. The several documents that make up the canon of Judaism in late antiquity relate to one another in three important ways.

First, all of them refer to the same basic writing, the Hebrew Scriptures. Many of them draw upon the Mishnah and quote it. So the components of the canon join at their foundations.

Second, as the documents reached closure in sequence, the later authorship can be shown to have drawn upon earlier, completed documents. So the writings of the rabbis of the talmudic corpus accumulate and build from layer to layer.

Third, as I have already hinted, among two or more documents some completed units of discourse, and many brief, discrete sayings, circulated, for instance, sentences or episodic homilies or fixed apophthegms of various kinds. So in some (indeterminate) measure the several documents draw not only upon one another, as we can show, but also upon a common corpus of materials that might serve diverse editorial and redactional purposes.

The extent of this common corpus can never be fully known. In my exemplary materials, Ruth Rabbah LXII:ii and iii present what can have formed a common corpus. But we know only what we have, not what we do not have. So we cannot say what has been omitted, or whether sayings that occur in only one document derive from materials available to the editors or compilers of some or all other documents. That is something we never can know. We can describe only what is in our hands and interpret only the data before us. Of indeterminates and endless speculative possibilities we need take no account. In taking up documents one by one, do we not obscure their larger context and their points in common?

In fact, shared materials proved for Leviticus Rabbah not many and not definitive. They form an infinitesimal proportion of Genesis Rabbah, under 3-5% of the volume of the *parashiyyot* for which I conducted probes.⁸ Materials that occur in both Leviticus Rabbah and some other document prove formally miscellany and share no single viewpoint or program; they are random and brief. What is unique to Leviticus Rabbah and exhibits that document's characteristic formal traits also predominates and bears the message of the whole. So much for the issue of the peripatetic exegesis. To date I have taken up the issue of homogeneity of "sources," in a limited and mainly formal setting, for the matter of how sayings and stories travel episodically from one document to the next.⁹ The real issue is not the traveling, but the unique, materials: the documents, and not what is shared among them. The variable – what moves – is subject to analysis only against the constant: the document itself.

viii. Theology and Hermeneutics: The Unacknowledged Participant in the Debate

To describe and analyze documents one by one violates the lines of order and system that have characterized all earlier studies of these same documents. Until now, just as people compared exegeses among different groups of a given verse of Scripture without contrasting one circumstance to another, so they tended to treat all of the canonical texts as uniform in context, that is, as testimonies to a single system and structure, that is, to Judaism. What sort of testimonies texts provide varies according to the interest of those who study them. That is why, without regard to the source of the two expositions of the same verse, people would compare one *midrash*, meaning the interpretation of a given verse of Scripture, with another *midrash* on the same verse of Scripture. True enough, philologians look for meanings of words and phrases, better versions of a text. For them all canonical documents equally serve as a treasury of philological facts and variant readings. Theologians study all texts equally, looking for God's will and finding testimonies to God in each component of the Torah of Moses our Rabbi. Why so? Because all texts ordinarily are taken to form a common

---

⁸There were two kinds of exceptions. First, entire *parashiyyot* occur in both Leviticus Rabbah and, verbatim, in Pesiqta deR. Kahana. Second, Genesis Rabbah and Leviticus Rabbah share sizable compositions. The former sort always conform to the formal program of Leviticus Rabbah. They in no way stand separate from the larger definitive and distinctive traits of the document. The latter sort fit quite comfortably, both formally and programmatically, into both Genesis Rabbah and Leviticus Rabbah, because those two documents themselves constitute species of a single genus.

⁹*The Peripatetic Saying. The Problem of the Thrice-Told Tale in Talmudic Literature* (Chico, 1985).

statement, "Torah" in the mythic setting, "Judaism" in the theological one.

But comparison cannot be properly carried out on such a basis. The hermeneutical issue dictated by the system overall defines the result of description, analysis, and interpretation. Let me give a single probative example. From the classical perspective of the theology of Judaism the entire canon of Judaism ("the one whole Torah of Moses, our rabbi") equally and at every point testifies to the entirety of Judaism. Why so? Because all documents in the end form components of a single system. Each makes its contribution to the whole. If, therefore, we wish to know what "Judaism" or, more accurately, "the Torah," teaches on any subject, we are able to draw freely on sayings relevant to that subject wherever they occur in the entire canon of Judaism. Guided only by the taste and judgment of the great sages of the Torah, as they have addressed the question at hand, we thereby describe "Judaism." And that same theological conviction explains why we may rip a passage out of its redactional context and compare it with another passage, also seized from its redactional setting. It goes without saying that the theological *apologia* for doing so has yet to reach expression; and there can be no other than a theological *apologia*. In logic I see none; epistemologically there never was one. The presence of a theological premise has yet to be acknowledged, or even recognized, by exponents of the anti-documentary hermeneutic and theory of literary history alike.

ix. Autonomy, Connection, Continuity

In fact documents stand in three relationships to one another and to the system of which they form part, that is, to Judaism, as a whole. The specification of these relationships constitutes the principal premise of this inquiry and validates the approach to the formation of compositions and composites that I offer here.

[1] Each document is to be seen all by itself, that is, as autonomous of all others.

[2] Each document is to be examined for its relationships with other documents universally regarded as falling into the same classification, as Torah.

[3] And, finally, in the theology of Judaism (or, in another context, of Christianity) each document is to be allowed to take its place as part of the undifferentiated aggregation of documents that, all together, constitute the canon of, in the case of Judaism, the "one whole Torah revealed by God to Moses at Mount Sinai."

Simple logic makes self-evident the proposition that, if a document comes down to us within its own framework, as a complete book with a beginning, middle, and end, in preserving that book, the canon presents us with a document on its own and not solely as part of a larger composition or construct. So we too see the document as it reaches us, that is, as autonomous.

If, second, a document contains materials shared verbatim or in substantial content with other documents of its classification, or if one document refers to the contents of other documents, then the several documents that clearly wish to engage in conversation with one another have to address one another. That is to say, we have to seek for the marks of connectedness, asking for the meaning of those connections. It is at this level of connectedness that we labor. For the purpose of comparison is to tell us what is like something else, what is unlike something else. To begin with, we can declare something unlike something else only if we know that it is like that other thing. Otherwise the original judgment bears no sense whatsoever. So, once more, canon defines context, or, in descriptive language, the first classification for comparative study is the document, brought into juxtaposition with, and contrast to, another document.

Finally, since the community of the faithful of Judaism, in all of the contemporary expressions of Judaism, concur that documents held to be authoritative constitute one whole, seamless "Torah," that is, a complete and exhaustive statement of God's will for Israel and humanity, we take as a further appropriate task, if one not to be done here, the description of the whole out of the undifferentiated testimony of all of its parts. These components in the theological context are viewed, as is clear, as equally authoritative for the composition of the whole: one, continuous system. In taking up such a question, we address a problem not of theology alone, though it is a correct theological conviction, but one of description, analysis, and interpretation of an entirely historical order.

In my view the various documents of the canon of Judaism produced in late antiquity demand a hermeneutic altogether different from the one of homogenization and harmonization, the ahistorical and anticontextual one definitive for the prevailing hermeneutic and theory of literary history. It is one that does not harmonize but that differentiates. It is a hermeneutic shaped to teach us how to read the compilations of exegeses first of all one by one and in a particular context, and second, in comparison with one another.

Let me review in this context out the method I applied to both Rabbah-compilations[10] and plan to apply to the four final Rabbah-compilations later on: Lamentations Rabbah, Esther Rabbah, Ruth Rabbah, and Song of Songs Rabbah.[11] It is not complicated and rests upon what seem to me self-evident premises. I have to prove that the document at hand rests upon clearcut choices of formal and rhetorical preference, so it is, from the viewpoint of form and mode of expression, cogent. I have to demonstrate that these formal choices prove uniform and paramount. So for the several compilations I have analyzed large *parashiyyot* (systematic and sustained compositions of exegeses) to show their recurrent structures. These I categorize. Then, I proceed to survey all *parashiyyot* of each of the complete compilations and find out whether or not every *parashah* of the entire document finds within a single cogent taxonomic structure suitable classifications for its diverse units of discourse. If one taxonomy serves all and encompasses the bulk of the units of discourse at hand, I may fairly claim that Leviticus Rabbah or Genesis Rabbah, or Lamentations Rabbah, Esther Rabbah, and Ruth Rabbah, respectively, do constitute a cogent formal structure, based upon patterns of rhetoric uniform and characteristic throughout.

My next step, for the several probes and documents, is to ask whether the framers of the document preserved a fixed order in arranging types of units of discourse, differentiated in accord with the forms I identified. In both documents I am able to show that, in ordering materials, the framers or redactors paid much attention to the formal traits of their units of discourse. They chose materials of one formal type for beginning their sustained exercises of argument or syllogism, then chose another formal type for the end of their sustained exercises of syllogistic exposition. This seems to me to show that the framers or redactors followed a set of rules which we are able to discern. Finally, in the case of the several documents, I outline the program and show the main points of emphasis and interest presented in each. In this way I characterize the program as systematically as I described the plan. In this way I answer the question, for the documents under study, of whether or not we deal with a text, exhibiting traits of composition, deliberation, proportion, and so delivering a message on its own. Since we do, then Leviticus Rabbah or Genesis Rabbah, on the one side, and Lamentation Rabbah, Esther Rabbah, Ruth Rabbah, and Song of Songs

---

[10]Reference is made to *The Integrity of Leviticus Rabbah* (Chico, 1985),and *Comparative Midrash: The Program and Plan of Genesis Rabbah and Leviticus Rabbah* (Atlanta, 1985).
[11]This will be *Comparative Midrash II*.

Rabbah, on the other, do demand description, analysis, and interpretation first of all each compilation on its own, as an autonomous statement. It then requires comparison and contrast with other compositions of its species of the rabbinic genus, that is to say, it demands to be brought into connection with, relationship to, other rabbinic compositions.[12]

x. The Next Stage

My "three stages" in ordinal sequence correspond, as a matter of fact, to three types of writing. The first – and last in assumed temporal order – is writing carried out in the context of the making, or compilation, of a classic. That writing responds to the redactional program and plan of the authorship of a classic. The second, penultimate in order, is writing that can appears in a given document but better serves a document other than the one in which it (singularly) occurs. This kind of writing seems to me not to fall within the same period of redaction as the first. For while it is a type of writing under the identical conditions, it also is writing that presupposes redactional programs in no way in play in the ultimate, and definitive, period of the formation of the canon: when people did things this way, and not in some other. That is why I think it is a kind of writing that was done prior to the period in which people limited their redactional work and associated labor of composition to the program that yielded the books we now have.

The upshot is simple: whether the classification of writing be given a temporal or merely taxonomic valence, the issue is the same: have these writers done their work with documentary considerations in mind? I believe I have shown that they have not. Then where did they expect their work to makes its way? Anywhere it might, because, so they assumed, fitting in no where in particular, it found a suitable locus everywhere it turned up. But I think temporal, not merely taxonomic, considerations pertain. Let me say why.

The third kind of writing seems to me to originate in a period prior to the other two. It is carried on in a manner independent of all redactional considerations such as are known to us. Then it should derive from a time when redactional considerations played no

---

[12]The quite separate question of the use and meaning of Scripture in Judaism is addressed in my *Judaism and Scripture: The Evidence of Leviticus Rabbah* (Chicago, 1986: University of Chicago Press). The beginning of my theological path is marked by *Writing with Scripture: The Authority and Uses of the Hebrew Bible in the Torah of Formative Judaism* (Minneapolis, 1989: Fortress Press) [with William Scott Green].

paramount role in the making of compositions. A brief essay, rather than a sustained composition, was then the dominant mode of writing. My hypothesis is that people can have written both long and short compositions – compositions and composites, in my language – at one and the same time. But writing that does not presuppose a secondary labor of redaction, e.g., in a composite, probably originated when authors or authorships did not anticipate any fate for their writing beyond their labor of composition itself.

Along these same lines of argument, this writing may or may not travel from one document to another. What that means is that the author or authorship does not imagine a future for his writing. What fits anywhere is composed to go nowhere in particular. Accordingly, what matters is not whether a writing fits one document or another, but whether, as the author or authorship has composed a piece of writing, that writing meets the requirements of any document we now have or can even imagine. If it does not, then we deal with a literary period in which the main kind of writing was ad hoc and episodic, not sustained and documentary.

Now this second and third kind of writing – the kind richly exemplified in Ruth Rabbah LXII:ii and iii – seems to me to derive from either [1] a period prior to the work of the making of Midrash-compilations and the two Talmuds alike; or [2] a labor of composition not subject to the rules and considerations that operated in the work of the making of Midrash-compilations and the two Talmuds. As a matter of hypothesis, I should guess that what is in LXII:ii comes prior to making any kind of documents of consequence, and what is in LXII:iii comes prior to the period in which the specific of documents we now have were subject to formation. That is to say, writing that can fit anywhere or nowhere is prior to writing that can fit somewhere but does not fit anywhere now accessible to us, and both kinds of writing are prior to the kind that fits only in what documents in which it is now located.

And given the documentary propositions and theses that we can locate in all of our compilations, we can only assume that the non-documentary writings enjoyed, and were assumed to enjoy, ecumenical acceptance. That means, very simply, when we wish to know the consensus of the entire canonical community – I mean simply the people, anywhere and any time, responsible for everything we now have – we turn not to the distinctive perspective of documents, but the (apparently universally acceptable) perspective of the extra-documentary compositions. That is the point at which we should look for the propositions everywhere accepted but no where advanced in a distinctive way, the "Judaism beyond the texts" – or behind them.

Do I place a priority, in the framing of a hypothesis, over taxonomy or temporal order? Indeed I do. I could have spoken to three types of writing, rather than speaking of the sequence of in which these types of writing took shape. Accordingly, I am inclined to suppose that non-documentary compositions took shape not only separated from, but in time before, the documentary ones did. My reason for thinking so is worth rehearsing, even though it is not yet compelling. The kinds of non-documentary writing I have assembled in Ruth Rabbah LXII:ii (and, I hasten to add, a good case can be made for the inclusion of the non-extant-documentary writing in LXII:iii) focus on matters of very general interest.

These matters may be assembled into two very large rubrics: virtue, on the one side, reason, on the other. Stories about sages fall into the former category; all of them set forth in concrete form the right living that sages exemplify. Essays on right thinking, the role of reason, the taxonomic priority of Scripture, the power of analogy, the exemplary character of cases and precedents in the expression of general and encompassing rules – all of these intellectually coercive writings set forth rules of thought as universally applicable, in their way, as are the rules of conduct contained in stories about sages, in theirs. A great labor of generalization is contained in both kinds of non-documentary and extra-documentary writing. And the results of that labor are then given concrete expression in the documentary writings in hand; for these, after all, do say in the setting of specific passages or problems precisely what, in a highly general way, emerges from the writing that moves hither and yon, never with a home, always finding a suitable resting place.

Now, admittedly, that rather general characterization of the non-documentary writing is subject to considerable qualification and clarification. But it does provide a reason to assign temporal priority, not solely taxonomic distinction, to the non-documentary compositions I have assembled for exemplary purposes in Ruth Rabbah LXII:ii and iii. We can have had commentaries of a sustained and systematic sort on (to take one example not portrayed here) the book of Chronicles, on the one side, treatises on virtue, on the second, gospels, on the third – to complete the triangle. But we do not have these kinds of books.

I wish our sages had made treatises on right action and right thought, in their own idiom to be sure, because I think these treatises will have shaped the intellect of generations to come in a more effective way than the discrete writings, submerged in collections and composites of other sorts altogether, have been able to do. Compositions on correct behavior made later on filled the gap left open by the redactional decisions made in the period under study; I do not know why no one assembled a Midrash on right action in the way in which, in Leviticus Rabbah and Genesis Rabbah, treatises on the rules of society and the rules of history were compiled. And still more do I miss those intellectually remarkable treatises on right thought that our sages can have produced out of the rich resources in hand: the art of generalization, the craft of comparison and contrast, for example. In this regard the Mishnah, with its union of (some) Aristotelian modes of thought and (some) neo-Platonic propositions forms the model, if a lonely one, for what can have been achieved, even in the odd and unphilosophical idiom of our sages.[13] The compositions needed for both kinds of treatises – and, as a matter of fact, many, many of them – are fully in hand. But no one made the compilations of them.

The books we do have not only preserve the evidences of the possibility of commentaries and biographies. More than that, they also bring to rich expression the messages that such books will have set forth. And most important, they also express in fresh and unanticipated contexts those virtues and values that commentaries and biographies ("gospels") meant to bring to realization, and they do so in accord with the modes of thought that sophisticated reflection on right thinking has exemplified in its way as well. So when people when about the work of making documents, they did something fresh with something familiar. They made cogent compositions, documents, texts enjoying integrity and autonomy. But they did so in such a way as to form of their distinct documents a coherent body of writing, of books a canon, of documents a system. And this they did in such a way as to say, in distinctive and specific ways, things that, in former times, people had expressed in general and broadly-applicable ways. We have moved beyond the wild storms of inchoate speculation, but have yet to reach the safe harbor of established fact. But the course is true, the destination in sight, the journey's end not at all in doubt.

---

[13]This is fully explain in my *Philosophical Mishnah* (Atlanta, 1989: Scholars Press for Brown Judaic Studies) I-IV, and in my *The Philosophy of Judaism: The First Principles* (in press).

Part Four
SOME SCHOLARLY CLASSICS ON ANCIENT JUDAISM REVISITED

5

Louis Jacobs, *Studies in Talmudic Logic and Methodology*

London, 1961: Valentine, Mitchell and Co. 164 pp.

Oren Tversky
Brown University

In its day, Louis Jacobs' book *Studies in Talmudic Logic and Methodology* was rightly considered pioneering work in the field of Talmudic logic and methodology. Its ideas were fresh, and exciting, and what it proposed to do was unprecedented. Without a doubt, some of its insights still dominate the modern-day study of the field. Other aspects of the book, however, do not fare as well when measured against the backdrop of time. But despite its flaws, Jacobs belief that there existed a gap in the study of Talmudic logic and methodology, resulted in a book which opened up the field to a more systematic, and scientific means of study.

Jacobs states that while Talmudic sugyas are analyzed in terms of their logic and methodology, no systematic general approach as yet exists for the study of these topics. In his own words, Jacobs claims that while "Talmudic learning has achieved wonders in delineating the background of the Talmud...there has been hardly any attempt at a systematic presentation of such matters as the structure of the Talmudic discussions, the formulation of the Talmudic arguments, the division of the sugya into its component parts, the methods of Talmudic reasoning and the literary style and character of the Amoraic debates" (p. viii). It is an investigation of this type that Jacobs proposes to undertake in his *Studies in Talmudic Logic and Methodology*. This investigation, the author tells the reader, is "not...a complete guide to the field" (p.

vii) but rather a "very small attempt to fill the gap" (p. vii). His book aims to note some of the problems in regard to logic and methodology and to "suggest some tentative solutions" (p. vii).

Jacobs addresses the logic of the Talmud in Part One of the book, attempting a systematic study of four subjects pertaining to Talmudic logic. Chapter one deals with the connection between the Aristotelian Syllogism and the Talmudic *Qal Wa-Homer*, while the second chapter compares *binyan 'abh* to John Stuart Mill's 'Method of Agreement.' In the third chapter, the author describes the relationship of the Talmudic *sebhara* to Scripture. Chapter Four investigates the role of *reductio ad absurdum* in the Talmud. Lastly, Jacobs devotes the entire second portion of the book to the study of the literary character of the Talmud. He maintains that the Talmud is a masterful, crafted document full of artifice and drama. I shall systematically review the entire program of the book.

First Jacobs argues "that the conventional identification of the *Qal Wa-Homer* with the Aristotelian Syllogism is erroneous" (p. vii). That is, Adolf Schwarz errs in his belief that the "*Qal Wa-Homer* is identical with the Aristotelian Syllogism" (p. 3). Jacobs symbolically denotes the two types of *Qal Wa-Homer* he has found as:

Simple: If A has x then B certainly has x.

Complex: If a, which lacks y, has x then B, which has y, certainly has x.

P. 4

To prove his point, Jacobs juxtaposes an Aristotelian Syllogism with a *Qal Wa-Homer*:

Syllogism:
All men are mortal;
Socrates is a man;
Therefore Socrates
is a mortal

Qal Wa-Homer:
If then in regard to such a light precept (i.e. the law of sending away the dam – Deut. xxii. 6-7) which concerns a matter that is worth but an *'issar* the Law has said that it may go well with thee and that thou mayest prolong thy days, how much more so in regard to the weightier precepts of the Law!

P. 5

The two differ because of "the obvious point that the element of 'how much more so' is lacking in the Syllogism" (p. 5). Moreover Jacobs claims the Syllogism deals with relationships of shared characteristics between classes and species; that because Socrates is a member of the class of man, he possesses the characteristics associated with that class, namely mortality. In Jacobs' view, this is not true of the *Qal Wa-Homer*: "I do not say that a weighty precept belongs to the class light precepts" (p. 6). For this and the historical reason that *Qal Wa-Homer* are found in documents which predate Aristotle, Jacobs arrives at his conclusion that *Qal Wa-Homer* and Syllogism are not one and the same.

On this point Jacobs was wrong, for in Chapter One, he argues that "there is no connection between the two forms of reasoning [the Aristotelian Syllogism and the Talmudic *Qal Wa-Homer* construction]." Citing the Talmud, Jacobs presents the following example of a *Qal Wa-Homer*:

> If priests who are not disqualified for service in the Temple by age are yet disqualified by bodily blemishes then Levites who are disqualified by age should certainly be disqualified by bodily blemishes.
> P. 4

In testing the validity of the author's hypothesis, I compare a Syllogism to his example:

Anything north of B is north of C

A is north of B

A is north of C[1]

A superficial comparison of the two substantiates Jacobs' claim, for the structure of the two constructions certainly differs. A more extensive examination, however yields contradictory results. Analyzing the structure of the Syllogism, I find it to consist of two premises and a conclusion drawn deductively from the two premises. The first premise states a general rule: "Anything north of B is north of C;"[2] and the second is a special case of the first. Hence, I apply the second premise to the first in concluding that A is indeed north of C. The same thing happens in our Talmudic example, though here the structures obscuring the hidden Syllogism.

The *Qal Wa-Homer*, like the Syllogism arrives at a conclusion based on premises; in this case the conclusion is that priests should be disqualified for service in the Temple on account of bodily blemishes. The premises are less obvious, but the basic construction of the passage still rests on the application of a specific case to a general rule. The underlying logic of the problem is as follows:

---

[1] Delton Thomas Howard, *Analytical Syllogistics* (Evanston: Northwestern University, 1946), p. 40.
[2] *Ibid.*, p. 40.

> **Premise 1)** Priests, who are not disqualified by age, are disqualified by blemishes
>
> **Premise 2)** Levites are disqualified by age.
>
> **Conclusion:** Levites are disqualified by blemishes.

In this case, the structure is syllogistic and matches the initial *Qal Wa-Homer*, but it is not entirely apparent how the conclusion can be drawn from the premises. The conclusion, however, is valid, for premise one is a general law, and two is a special case of one. The *Qal Wa-Homer* construction hinges on being able to say that if priests are, then Levites certainly are, the implication being that Levites are a special case of priests. The problem of identification of the Aristotelian Syllogism lies in the different structure of the *Qal Wa-Homer* and in the fact that the first premise is not stated as a general rule, something the Talmud does not do, but rather as a concrete example. It is up to the reader to infer premise one from the general principle behind the *Qal Wa-Homer*. In this case, the principle remains if priests, then Levites. This I derive from knowing that priests are not disqualified on account of bodily blemishes, where Levites are.

If I untangle the mystery of the *Qal Wa-Homer*, I find:

> **Premise 1)** People, who are or are not disqualified by age, are disqualified because of blemishes.
>
> **Premise 2)** Levites are disqualified because of age.
>
> **Conclusion:** Levites are disqualified because of bodily blemishes.

The Syllogism reveals that Priests are in some way higher than Levites on account of not being disqualified by age. Hence, in a case where the higher-ups are disqualified (the case of blemishes) then the lower ones certainly are. The case of the priests and the Levites is analogous to the following:

> **Premise 1)** X, who is 6'0" tall, is considered tall.
>
> **Premise 2)** Y is taller than X.
>
> **Conclusion:** Y is considered tall.

Just as Levites is a special case of priests, Y is a special case of X. Here, however, it is more explicit, for the hierarchy of Y is taller than X is clear, while determining the case and subcase of priests and Levites is less obvious. Discovering the relationship is based on understanding the relationship between Levites being disqualified on account of age, and priests not being disqualified on account of age. Applied to the height example, I could change premise two to say Y is 6'5," thus obscuring the relationship between Y and X. Regardless of how it is worded or structured, the *Qal Wa-Homer* remains an Aristotelian Syllogism.

Secondly, Jacobs proposes to show the equality of the Talmudic construction *binyan 'abh* with John Stuart Mill's method of agreement (Chapter Two). The author maintains that: "The Rabbis, in their attempt to discover general principles behind the laws of the Torah, used, apparently, a method similar in form to that classified by Mill as a means of discovering the laws of nature" (p. vii). Mill believed the laws of nature could be investigated using common factors to deduce causes and effects:

> If two or more instances of the phenomenon under investigation have only one circumstance in common, the circumstance in which alone all the instances agree is the cause (or the effect) of the phenomenon.[3]

Mill is careful to write "have only one circumstance in common" for if there are more than one there is no means of knowing which of the is the antecedent of the consequence.

Jacobs seeks to establish the validity of his argument by demonstrating that a construction of the *binyan 'abh* type agrees with Mill's definition of the Method of Comparison. One such example originates in Mishnah tractate Qiddushin which rules that "a woman can be acquired in marriage three ways: by the payment of money, *keseph*, by the delivery into her hands of a bond, *shetar*, and by cohabitation, *bi'ah*" (p. 10). The Talmud attempts to demonstrate that a *Huppah* too is a valid means of acquiring a woman for marriage. It accomplishes this by examining the common traits of the three known means of acquiring a woman. If the intersection of the traits of *keseph*, *shetar* and *bi'ah* does not yield an empty set, but rather a single trait, and *Huppah* also possesses this trait, then Huppah too is a valid means. To restate:

Premise 1)   *Keseph* has traits ABD and is a means of acquiring a wife.

Premise 2)   *Bi'ah* has traits ACD and is a means of acquiring a wife.

Premise 3)   *Shetar* has traits A E and is a means of acquiring a wife.

---

[3]John Stuart Mill, *A System of Logic: Book III*, Chaps. VIII and IX.

Premise 4)   *Huppah* has trait A

Conclusion: *Huppah* which posseses only A is a means of acquiring a wife.

P. 10-12

Jacobs argues that the Talmud's logic accords with Mill's method, for in both approaches I notice the search for the common trait, whose unique presence in all cases establishes it as the cause (or effect) of the phenomenon. In this case, the phenomenon is marriage, with the common cause being A.

Jacobs claims that the "notion that the ancients knew nothing of Induction will have to be revised" (p. vii), the revision being warranted because *binyan abh* is an inductive form. It is certainly true that this proves the existence of inductive forms in the Talmud, but it is by no means the only inductive form in the document. There are a variety of other inductive constructions in the Talmud that Jacobs' could have used in making the same point. Indeed, I should be inclined to show that not only does induction occur in many different forms in the Talmud, but that it is a necessary and fundamental part of the Talmud's reasoning process. The upshot is that while I think Jacobs is right, not much seems to me at stake in his observation on this point.

Let me expand on this matter. In "induction," Webster's Unabridged Dictionary tells us, I "observe a sufficient number of individual facts and, on the ground of analogy, extend what is true of them to others of the same class, thus arriving at general principles or laws." This means that any comparison between two laws or principles in the Talmud, a common occurrence, employs inductive logic as a means of drawing conclusions. For example, in Jacobs' own book I find a law explained by means of analogy to another law:

> Why does a rider (of a lost animal) fail to acquire it if he rides in the town? R. Kahana said: Because it is unusual for men to ride in the town....R. Ashi said to R. Kahana: If so if one lifts up a money-bag (that is abandoned and belongs to the one who acquires it) on the Sabbath (when it is forbidden to handle money)....

P. 49

The Talmud generalizes a principle, working from observed facts (in this case the law of the money-bag) to establish a law and then apply it to the case of the rider.

Third, Jacobs tackles the Talmudic *sebhara*, meaning common sense or reasonable argument. He holds that any accepted *sebhara* "requires no Scriptural warrant but enjoys of itself full Scriptural authority"

(p. 37). Identifying two types of *sebhara*, he purports that while the common sense type must be accepted since it is self-evident, the reasoned argument variety may be rejected. For example:

> R. Samuel b. Nahmani said: "How do I know that the onus of proof falls on the plaintiff (rather that the defendant, i.e. what is the Scriptural warrant for the established legal principle that possession cannot be disturbed without conclusive proof)? It is said 'If any man have any matters to do, let him come unto them' (Ex. xxiv, 14) – let him bring proof before them." R. Ashi raised an objection: "Why is a Scriptural text required? Is it not common sense (Sebhara)? One who is in pain visits the doctor."
>
> P. 16

The argument states that because a *sebhara* is a self-evident truth, it must be accepted, eliminating the need for a Scriptural proof.

Thus in this case, the *sebhara* enjoys full Scriptural status, if accepted. The hypothesis appears to possess some truth in several cases. But assessing precisely what truth that is, and what is at stake in it, is not so clear. For the author's questionable use of terminology complicates the task of either disproving or reaffirming his proposition. His ambiguous definition of *sebhara* prevents a reader from testing the validity of the stated thesis. The term, used in Jacobs' sense, means "'common sense' or 'reasonable argument'" (p. 16). But is not most of the Talmud based on reasonable arguments or common sense? What distinguishes Jacobs' *sebhara* from any other reasoned argument in the Talmud? Secondly, the word sebhara occurs frequently in the Talmud, often in a context not involving Scriptural support for a law. What Jacobs means by his usage of *sebhara* is not clear.

If however, Jacobs uses sebhara in the sense of a reasoned argument, employing the language "sabhri" in the Aramaic, then here too lies a flaw. For example:

> And the House of Hillel reckon [sebhara] that it is permitted to make use of a table unclean in the second remove, for those who eat Heave-offering [the priests] are careful.
>
> Another matter: There is no Scriptural requirement to wash the hands before eating unconsecrated food.
>
> What is the purpose of another matter?
>
> This is what the House of Hillel said to the House of Shammai: if you ask what is the difference in respect to food, concerning which I take care, and in respect to the hands, concerning which I do not care – **even in this regard [our opinion] is preferable,** for there is no Scriptural requirement concerning the washing of the hands before eating unconsecrated food.
>
> It is better that the hands should be made unclean, for there is no Scriptural basis for [washing] them, and **let not the food be made**

unclean, concerning which there is a Scriptural basis [for concern about it uncleanliness].[4]

The use of the language "even in this regard our opinion is preferable"[5] suggests the acceptance of both the Scriptural and the reasoned (*sebhara*) argument . The discovery of this passage does not however entirely refute Jacobs' claim, but rather necessitates further modification. The claim ought to read: often when both Scriptural and accepted *sebhara* proofs are offered, the Scriptural proof is unnecessary.

Next, I examine the use of *reductio ad absurdum* type arguments in the Talmud. This term refers to "a method of proving the falsity of a principle by demonstrating that the conclusion is absurd."(P. 38) For example, the argument runs:

> one need not fear that a weasel may have dragged (hametz leaven, i.e. after the house has been searched for leaven on the night before Passover) from house to house, or from place to place; for is so from courtyard to courtyard or from town to town:there is no end to the matter ('en la-dabhar soph).
>
> P. 38

The Talmud demonstrates the absurdity of searching for leaven carried by weasels from place to place, for if one must search each house, one must search each courtyard, and each town as well. The process will never end and the original premise must therefore be wrong.

This and other examples fit the definition of *reductio ad absurdum* as Jacobs uses it. Even so, considering that the author's interests seem to lie in associating classes of Talmudic arguments with argument forms from logic (as he did in Chapters One and Two), the *reductio ad absurdum* description warrants analysis in its own terms. It is not sufficient to class this argument with all the others; I do better by comparing this argument with its logical counterparts. Upon investigation, I learn that the *reductio ad absurdum* is a null hypothesis (a proof by contradiction). This method of proof demonstrates that the consequences of a certain hypothesis lead to a contradiction of some sort. Hence, the original hypothesis must be false, and its converse true. For example, the proof of the non-existence of a largest prime number in mathematics starts with the assumption that there exists a largest prime. By demonstrating that such a hypothesis proves false, the opposite is proven true, namely that there exists no

---

[4]Jacob Neusner, *Introduction to the Talmud*, (San Fransisco: Harper and Row, 1984), pp. 203-204.
[5]*Ibid.*, p. 204.

largest prime. In the case of *reductio ad absurdum*, the same argument is at play:

> If I question the decisions of the Court of Rabban Gamliel, I should have to question the decisions of every Court that has risen from the days of Moses until now.
>
> P. 41

The passage proves that I need not question the decisions of the Court of Gamliel by showing that the consequences of the opposite action are absurd. Once I refute the original assumption that I must question the decisions of the Court of Gamliel, I are forced to conclude the opposite.

Finally, after exhausting the topic of the Talmud's logic, Jacobs turns to a study of its methodology. Here he aims to show that the Talmud is a crafted, artificial document, as opposed to a verbatim record of dialogues among sages. In the time, thirty years ago, in which he did this work, the proposals of this part of the book prove daring and radical; time has validated every point that Jacobs proposes, and he must be regarded as the pioneer of the modern literary critical reading of the Talmud of Babylonia.

His thesis may be briefly stated. The style, structure and language of the Talmud are such that, far from being "a verbatim report of discussions which took place in the Babylonian schools" (p. viii). the Talmud is a "'contrived' literary product of great skill, in which the older material used has been reshaped by methods bearing close resemblance to those of literary artists throughout the ages" (p. viii). The redactors of the Talmud, argues Jacobs, crafted their arguments, "skilfully 'build[ing] up' the argument...so as to heighten the effect." For example:

> (a) First version of R. Papi quoted: All agree, even the Sages, that a Sage cannot cancel a vow before it has taken effect.
>
> (b) Attempt to prove this from Baraitha.
>
> (c) Refutation of proof – the Baraitha might follow the authority of R. Nathan.
>
> (d) Second version of R. Papi: All agree, even R. Nathan, that a sage can cancel a vow before it has taken effect.
>
> (e) Refutation of this version from Baraitha
>
> P. 58

The conclusion in the above quoted passage, might easily have been reached by omitting (a), (b) and (c), but these passages remained, Jacobs suggests, "so as to heighten the effect of the final refutation" (p. 58). The presence of such dramatic forms eliminates the possibility of a text aimed at accurately reproducing conversations. The drama involved suggests a literary creation intended to capture the reader's attention.

Jacobs makes his point clear by showing that the structure of passages in the Talmud differs from that of conversational dialogue, and that this difference exists for the purpose of dramatic effect. However, he, largely ignores linguistic analysis of the text. For example:

> The things which are between the House of Shammai and the House of Hillel in [regard to] the meal:
>
> The House of Shammai say, "One blesses over the day and afterward blesses over the wine...."
>
> And the House of Hillel say, "One blesses over the wine and afterward blesses over the day...."[6]

A simple qualitative evaluation of this text suggests that it is in no way an attempt at reproducing an exact account of past conversations. The use of the same wording by both parties, the perfectly parallel structure, and the formal traits of the language all point to artifice.

Nevertheless, Jacobs' well founded claim, supported by many passages, proves interesting, for the evidence of artifice in the Talmud implies underlying motives on the part of the authorship of the Talmud. The next logical step calls for the uncovering of the hermeneutics of the document. What is it that the authorship of the Talmud wished to accomplish by means of their dramatic devices? Why these devices and not others? Jacobs' conclusion precipitates many questions.

While his conclusion seems obvious to the modern reader. that this notion appears so simple today shows that it has taken hold. This phenomenon mirrors the progress of the field as well, for the fact that what was once radical and new, has now become axiomatic and obvious suggests the field accepted Jacobs' proposal and then surpassed it. However, the task is not only evaluate the work as it stands against time.

We have also to ask whether it stands firm when evaluated against its own stated goals. Jacobs aims at "a systematic presentation" (p. vii) of topics involving the logic and methodology of the Talmud. With this in mind, I can certainly affirm Jacobs' claim of having presented his reader with "a very small attempt to fill the gap [of knowledge]" (p. vii). Likewise, there is no doubt that Jacobs has "shed

---

[6]*Ibid.*, p. 182.

some fresh light on a difficult subject" (p. vii). But has the author presented his reader with an intelligible, cohesive book which solves problems using insightful new techniques? This is not a yes or no question, for while Jacobs' aim is intellectually ambitious and important, measured against his own goals, his results prove flawed.

First, the book in the end is simply not a sustained argument and therefore does not prove a proposition of weight. For the topics covered in the book are disparate and unrelated. They do not comprise the alleged *Studies in Talmudic Logic and Methodology* that the title suggests. How does a discussion of *reductio ad absurdum* logically follow an investigation into the relationship between the Talmudic *sebhara* and Scripture? Indeed, the first portion of the book might function more effectively as a collection of essays rather than as one half of a supposedly cohesive book.

Another problem lies in the author's presentation of evidence. For the most part the passages used by the author in support of his points are presented as paraphrases, rather than verbatim quotes (with some sort of explanation). This occurs throughout the book, and since so much depends on the actual language, exact quotes of the Talmud would aid in determining the validity of arguments. In one passage, for instance, the paraphrase appears to contradict the thesis of the chapter on *sebhara*: both a *sebhara* and a Scriptural proof are accepted. The use of the language "On which point do they [rabbis] differ? If you want I can say on the interpretation of a Scriptural verse, if you want I can say in a sebhara" (p. 23) seems to accept both Scripture and *sebhara* a valid means of proof. In all fairness to his reader, Jacobs ought to include in the book the raw data from which he drew his conclusions. In this manner, reader and author stand as equals – the reader can justifiably agree or disagree with the generalizations of the author.

Moreover, Jacobs fails to draw the required consequences and conclusions from his work; his is a total failure of generalization. What is at stake if *binyan abh* and Mill's method of agreement share many common features? What is the purpose of comparing logical forms in the Talmud with logical forms found in other literatures? Jacobs must address the consequences of his conclusions. He must tell his reader what comes next and set forth what he conceives that all of these results and conclusions mean.

While, therefore, *Studies in Talmudic Logic and Methodology* no longer carries with it the freshness that it once had, it remains a monument to its author's acumen and wit, and for all time it has left an indelible mark in its field.

6

Adin Steinsaltz, *The Essential Talmud*

Translated from the Hebrew by Chaya Galai. Bantam Books, 1977. 275 pp. Appendix, Index. $2.95

Eli Ungar
Brown University

With *The Essential Talmud* (by which he means only the Talmud of Babylonia, the Talmud of the Land of Israel being ignored), Adin Steinsaltz introduces the Talmud to the lay person. He clearly has in mind only Jewish readers; he cannot contemplate that the classics of Judaism can, or should, be studied outside the framework of the believers. "The Talmud is," he says, "the most important book in the Jewish culture....the summary of oral law that evolved after centuries of scholarly effort," and "the voice of sanity in a discordant and disunified world." Because of the Talmud's importance to Judaism, Steinsaltz, a practicing Jew, cannot limit himself to merely describing the Talmud to his reader, but must also prescribe it, as a book to study daily, and as a way of life. Unfortunately, in his zeal to convert the reader Steinsaltz converts the text from a highly formalized literary document to a compendium of anecdotes emphasizing tradition and community, devoid of literary significance. However, before criticizing *The Essential Talmud*, let us extend to Steinsaltz the courtesy he denies the Talmud – the opportunity to speak for oneself.

Steinsaltz believes that the "Talmud is not merely important on an intellectual and literary plane; it also has far-reaching socio-historical implications. It is reasonably certain that no Jewish community could survive for long without the ability to study

Talmud....In the course of Jewish history, various ethnic communities have tried to maintain their Judaism, sometimes even on a strictly traditional basis, without talmudic scholarship. The same process occurred in all of them; the components of their Judaism weakened and began to disintegrate...such communities lost their vitality and died out."[1] For Steinsaltz, then, the importance of Talmud study musn't be underestimated, as the act of convincing others to open a Talmud for the first time differs little from pulling someone out from in front of a bus. Both involve saving lives. And, this salvific goal constitutes Steinsaltz's purpose in writing *The Essential Talmud*.

Throughout the book, the author's purpose is twofold. While conveying information aimed at informing the reader of the historical context, content and basic structure of the Talmud, Steinsaltz also establishes a place for the reader within the tradition responsible for creating the Talmud. By linking the reader to the document, Steinsaltz hopes to convince the reader of the importance of incorporating the Talmud into his daily routine. The structure of Steinsaltz's book reveals this double agenda. Steinsaltz divides the book into three parts, and completes each of the segments, **History, Structure and Content,** and **Method**, with chapters that emphasize the relevance of the Talmud to the modern Jew.

Steinsaltz's first segment begins with a chapter entitled "What is the Talmud," and he discusses, in successive chapters, the Oral Law, the Tannaim, the Compilation of the Mishna, the Amoraim of both Babylonia and Palestine, the Redaction of the Bavli, Talmudic Exegesis, and then, surprisingly, the Printing of the Talmud and the Persecution and Banning of the Talmud.

The first chapters, which introduce the reader to the personalities, literature and historical context of which the Talmud is a product, contain stories useful in making the reader more aware of, and at home in, Jewish culture. Such stories, in addition to shedding light on the development of the Talmud, make the Talmud a more personal and less imposing document. For example, the following anecdote introduces a primary figure in the age of the Tannaim while also stressing characteristics the Talmud considers important. "The hereditary *nasi* of the Sanhedrin was Rabban Simeon Ben Gamaliel the Second, of the House of Hillel, who regarded himself as inferior to his colleagues, 'a fox among lions,' but nevertheless endeavored to rebuild a way of life and discipline for the people. Posterity was more appreciative of his value as a legislator and accepted his rulings in almost every case."[2]

---

[1] Adin Steinsaltz, *The Essential Talmud*, p. 269.
[2] *Ibid.*, p. 31.

By endearing the talmudic sages to the reader, Steinsaltz hopes to intensify the reader's desire to study the Talmud. The reader takes interest in the accomplishments and obstacles of the sages. The difficulty of compiling the Talmud, intimated in yet another set of anecdotes, increases the reader's desire to learn more about this book. And, having brought the reader into the world of the Talmud, Steinsaltz drives home his point with the final two chapters. Leaping from the seventh century in Chapter 9 ahead almost a millenium, to the age of the printing press in Chapter 10, Steinsaltz re-emphasizes the importance of the Talmud to the Jews. Though poor and fearful of persecution, Jews insisted on utilizing the printing press to make copies of the Talmud, regardless of expense. Though "the technical difficulties were many, and the project entailed an enormous amount of work," Jews "took a great interest in the printing press from the outset."[3] They went to great lengths in preserving the Talmud.

How, Steinsaltz silently implores the reader, can you not study the Talmud when today it is so simple to pick up a copy? If people were persecuted and killed in the thirteenth and sixteenth centuries for studying the Talmud, must not it be a document worth reading? Having brought the reader into the world of rabbinic Jewry, of Rav the "international trader" and Samuel "the outstanding physician," and having invited the reader to share in the accomplishments of Jews generations earlier, Steinsaltz hints that the reader, if he desires to share in the culture, must also take responsibility for its perpetuation.[4]

The second segment of the book, entitled Structure and Content, continues this process of bringing the reader into Jewish culture by demonstrating the importance of the Talmud. Steinsaltz examines the topics discussed in the Talmud (the Sabbath, Festivals and Dietary Laws, to name but a few) to reinforce the author's assertion that the Talmud constitutes a traditional document, restating what evolved from centuries of Oral Law, and that the reader qualifies as a member of that tradition. While discussing Judaism and the Talmud in glowing terms, the author transcends the act of description and enters into the act of prescription of the Talmud, to every person, for every day. Throughout this lengthy segment, Steinsaltz relates anecdotes in the hopes of further drawing the reader into this world of Talmud study. While reading about Sacrifice or Ritual Purity, the reader cannot help but remember (because Steinsaltz so designs the order of his chapters) that to prevent Jews from learning these very subjects, enemies of the Jews burned and banished the Talmud, persecuted the Jews and

---

[3]*Ibid.*, p. 75.
[4]*Ibid.*, p. 43.

destroyed their synagogues. If the Talmud was selected by its enemies as the surest way to destroy the Jews, must not its study be the surest way of insuring Jewish survival? The reader, Steinsaltz hopes, can no longer distinguishing himself from the tradition of sages who wrote, protected, cherished, studied and transmitted the Talmud. And, Steinsaltz hopes, the reader will begin studying the Talmud on a daily basis.

The third segment of the book brings to a close this process of prescription in the guise of description. Beginning with a chapter entitled "Midrash," and following with brief discussions of the "Talmudic Way of Thinking" and "Strange and Bizarre Problems," all designed to further impress upon the reader the distinctiveness of the Talmud, Steinsaltz prepares for the reader a place in the history of the Talmud. Chapter 33, "What Is A Scholar," informs the reader that he too can become a scholar, if he chooses to engage himself in the study of the Talmud. Before concluding, Steinsaltz reiterates "The Talmud's Importance for the People," to remind the reader of the undiminished significance of the Talmud today. The final chapter, "The Talmud Has Never Been Completed," constitutes Steinsaltz' invitation to the reader: join in the study of the Talmud, add to it, and thereby protect it, yourself, and the Jewish people. By so structuring his book, Steinsaltz adds to his description of the Talmud a prescription to engage in its study.

The Essential Talmud attempts to convey the essence of the Talmud by describing its world, those who created it, those who redacted, nurtured, transmitted and studied it. It further tries to convince the reader to study Talmud by establishing for him a place within the continuous traditional culture that the Talmud represents. Though Steinsaltz might succeed in convincing some of his readers of the importance of the Talmud, one must ask, however, if Steinsaltz's personal goal of bringing Jews to the Talmud affects his claim to objectively describe the Talmud. Is his description a textually accurate response to the question "What is the Talmud?" Or, is his book merely a compilation of select anecdotes and other Talmudic tidbits taken out of context and then strung together to support his definition of the Talmud as a traditional "summary of oral law" constituting the most important document in the Jewish canon?

In my judgment Steinsaltz has described a proselytizing Talmud, not the Talmud as a monument of culture and religion. He really is not interested in what the Talmud is, so much as whether his readers obey its rules and study its discussions. Not only so, but he presents his opinions ("The Talmud reflects mainly the methods of instruction of the academy") as facts, yet fails to produce evidence supporting them.[5] For a book dedicated to heaping such lavish praise on the Talmud, the failure of *The Essential Talmud* to quote even occasionally from the very document it claims to describe, is, to say the least, inconsistent with his alleged goals. If the Talmud resembles Steinsaltz's description of it, why not substantiate that description by citing the document itself? More troubling, Steinsaltz's refusal to cite the text contradicts the very premise of his plea to Jews to study the Talmud – that it is accessible. If it is accessible, why not cite passages from the Talmud? And if it is not, and the average person cannot readily enter into its discussions, why write a book urging Jews to engage in Talmud study?

Furthermore, judging from the authoritative tone Steinsaltz utilizes in conveying information in *The Essential Talmud*, the reader must assume that all of Steinsaltz's claims concerning the nature of the Talmud have a sound basis in the Talmud itself. However, much of what Steinsaltz presents as fact requires substantiation, and yet, none is forthcoming. One such example of Steinsaltz's presentation of a nonfact as fact concerns the alleged traditionality of the Babylonian Talmud. While a close literary analysis reveals that far from being traditional, the Bavli charts an original and unique literary path, Steinsaltz apparently considers literary matters insignificant (as evidenced by lack of a substantive discussion of them in this book) and ignores them. Because most readers of *The Essential Talmud* cannot know that what he routinely offers as fact constitutes mere speculation, Steinsaltz misleads his readership.

In addition to the problem of (a lack of) citation and substantiation, Steinsaltz omits a number of topics needed in any description of the Talmud. As a highly formalized document, how the Talmud speaks conveys meaning. Yet Steinsaltz virtually ignores the connection between structure and content in the Talmud, devoting but one chapter to structure and fourteen to content. This imbalance produces a description of a Talmud more concerned with rabbis than redaction, and with stories than structure, conclusions not necessarily validated by the text.

There is one further problem. Steinsaltz cannot be called a very good writer. The style is insipid and flaccid. Whether the result of poor translation or merely poor writing in the original Hebrew, *The Essential Talmud* is not a joy to read.

---

[5] *Ibid.*, p. 57.

7

Ephraim E. Urbach's *The Sages: Their Concepts and Beliefs*

Translated from the Hebrew by Israel Abrahams. Jerusalem: The Magnes Press, The Hebrew University, 1975. Two volumes – I. Text: pp. xxii and 692. II. Notes: pp. 383.[1] *Reprinted: Cambridge, 1987: Harvard University Press. In one volume.*

Jacob Neusner
Brown University

The reprinting of this book, nearly two decades after its initial appearance in Hebrew and fifteen years after it came out in English, justifies reconsidering the work. It has enjoyed publishing success, since it came out in both Hebrew and English in Jerusalem, and now in Cambridge, Massachusetts, as well. But that is a measure of politics, on the one side, and the nature of the market, on the other. What marks success in the academy? Influence on the on-going life of scholarship: has the author defined the method by which the subject will be investigated? Has he defined the questions that will be discussed in the future? Has he stimulated further work, critical review of his ideas, significant advances beyond the positions he worked out? In other words, is this an important book in any intellectual sense, and can we regard the work as a success in critical esteem as expressed by scholarship?

---

[1] My review was originally published in *Journal of Jewish Studies* 1976, 27:23-35. With revisions and important alterations, I made use of it in a number of essays as well. I know of no other full-scale essay review of this book, certainly not in English.

If this book of Urbach's has enjoyed a scholarly success through the media of response and expression in academic esteem, then the evidence is not easy to locate. For from its appearance, Urbach's *The Sages* influenced the course of further scholarship in no perceivable way. No monographs replicated by its method, no scholars addressed particular, important theses and tried either to validate or revise or refute them, no dissertations modeled after Urbach's approaches, either in contents or in propositions, have been published, and, in all, the work remains wholly without impact upon scholarship. Why has Urbach remained an isolated and somewhat curious figure, so that, in the European and North American universities, his work has proved barren and uninteresting? That question was answered in what follows, which I published nearly fifteen years ago, and which remains – alas – as valid now as it was then. But in the intervening fifteen years, other approaches to the history of Judaism have made their way, generating dissertations, monographs, significant criticism, serious give-and-take.

In German and Israeli (and U. S. rabbinical-academic) circles, death inflicted through ostracism, called *Todschweigen*, forms a commonplace mode of responding to work one does not like, cannot refute, or simply finds inconvenient, and to the authors of that kind of work. Is it possible that Urbach has been subjected to a campaign of *Todschweigen* by those who find his methods primitive, his results merely and narrowly theological, his book boring and barren of insight? Is that how we may account for the disaster of a book that has been bought and reprinted, translated into another language and reprinted in that language, and yet, at the same time, has been utterly without impact upon scholarship after its initial appearance? For that is the paradox of this work, a classic on the day on which it appeared, but a classic immediately consigned to the museum for scholarly curiosities, oddities of another age.

If the German-Israeli campaign of *Todschweigen* has found imitators among Urbach's many critics, these do not include this writer and his school. I have framed approaches to the same questions, defined methods for finding answers to the same issues, as are treated by Urbach, and from the beginning, when his book originally came out in English, to the present, my school has paid the closest attention to Urbach's results; whenever any one of us has touched upon a question with which he deals here (or in other work), we have always read him with care and used his work with respect. So we cannot be accused of doing to Urbach and his school what they have done to us.

But the world has moved on, with fresh approaches to the framing of the scholarly agenda, new modes of reading and analyzing the received literature, an original range of questions; Urbach's book was never "disproved," it simply ceased to define any problems anyone found worth solving. These new approaches, defined in my work and in the on-going response to it, have involved the replication of method, the discussion of particular, important theses, significant efforts at validation or refutation, the publication of dissertations modeled upon my approaches, and other concrete indications of influence. In permitting the reprinting of his book without a word of address to the many, and I think weighty, criticisms leveled against his ideas and methods, Urbach has confirmed, by his silence, his incapacity to answer his critics. What he said in 1969 he repeated without a line of revision in 1989. So he has simply repeated himself – and therefore those profound errors of conception and execution that to begin with denied him all serious hearing in the academic world are set forth for another generation. The fact that Harvard University Press has now reprinted the work must find explanation therefore in politics and preferment, rather than in the importance of the book to the progress of learning. These are not matters that bear upon learning, so let us turn instead to the book and see what to begin with went wrong.[2]

Ephraim E. Urbach, professor of Talmud at the Hebrew University and author of numerous articles and books on the Talmud and later rabbinic literature, here presents a compendious work intended "to describe the concepts and beliefs of the Tannaim and Amoraim and to elucidate them against the background of their actual life and environment." When published in Hebrew, in 1969, the work enjoyed immediate success, going into a second edition within two years. Urbach is an imposing figure in Israeli scholarly and religious-political circles, serving as president of the Israel Academy of Sciences and Humanities and running for the presidency of the State of Israel as candidate of the right-wing and "religious" political parties. Within Orthodox Judaism Urbach derives from the German stream, which proposes to combine piety with academic learning. That position would account for the

---

[2]Urbach's initial work on the history of ideas in formative Judaism began in the 1950s and produced important monographs on idolatry and art, on slavery, on the interplay of law and theology in formative Judaism, and various other topics. In their day, these papers were significant advances over all prior work, and they did generate not only much discussion but also continuation through further efforts on the same topics or using the same methods. I have reprinted, in Brown Classics in Judaica, the original publication of one of his papers, in the volume, *Papers of the Institute of Jewish Studies, London* (Lanham, 1989: University Press of America). For an important discussion of Urbach's work on slavery, showing all due respect for the originality and quality of his paper, see Paul V. McC. Flesher, *Oxen, Women or Citizens? Slaves in the System of the Mishnah* (Atlanta, 1988: Scholars Press for Brown Judaic Studies), pp. iiiff.

political success of his book, and the publishing record is written by his own university press, on the one side, and his U. S. Modern Orthodox Judaic collaborators at Harvard, on the other.³

Let us look at the book itself. The work before us has been accurately described by M.D. Heer (*Encyclopaedia Judaica* [Jerusalem, 1969] 16:4): "He [Urbach] outlines the views of the rabbis on the important theological issues such as creation, providence, and the nature of man. In this work Urbach synthesizes the voluminous literature on these subjects and presents the views of the talmudic authorities." The topics are as follows: belief in one God; the presence of God in the world; "nearness and distance – Omnipresent and heaven"; the power of God; magic and miracle; the power of the divine name; the celestial retinue; creation; man; providence; written law and oral law; the commandments; acceptance of the yoke of the kingdom of heaven; sin, reward, punishment, suffering, etc.; the people of Israel and its sages, a chapter which encompasses the election of Israel, the status of the sages in the days of the Hasmoneans, Hillel, the regime of the sages after the destruction of the Temple, and so on; and redemption. The second volume contains footnotes, a fairly brief and highly selective bibliography, and alas, a merely perfunctory index. The several chapters, like the work as a whole, are organized systematically, consisting of sayings and stories relevant to the theme under discussion, together with Urbach's episodic observations and comments on them.

Now it must be registered: Urbach really did improve upon earlier accounts of his subject, and that was in important ways. That fact makes all the more surprising the paltry impact upon further studies

---

³That is not to suggest the English edition had no reviews. But to my knowledge the only extended academic review was mine, cited above. I have located no more than perfunctory reviews, if that, in any of the other academic journals, e.g., *Journal of the American Academy of Religion, Journal of Religion, Journal of Biblical Literature, History of Religion, Religion, Religious Studies/Sciences Religieuses*, or even in *Jewish Quarterly Review*, for that matter. In the English-language theological or rabbinical journals, such as *Conservative Judaism, Journal of Reform Judaism, Tradition*, and so forth, the reception was at best routine. Nor is the record more impressive in the German, French, Spanish, and Portuguese critical literature, so far as I can tell. For a man as prominent as Urbach in Israeli scholarship, holding the presidency of the Israel Academy for instance, the record as to reviews proved rather flimsy. But, to be sure, the Israeli reception of the book, in Hebrew-language journals and newspapers, was more formidable. I remain puzzled as to why the English translation of Urbach's book enjoyed so modest a critical reception overseas. Nor have I seen a single review of the Harvard reprint (though reprints are not often reviewed), outside of one or two English-Jewish weekly newspapers.

that his book was able to make. In the context of earlier work on talmudic theology and religion. Urbach's contribution was a distinct improvement in every way. Compared to a similar, earlier compendium of talmudic sayings on theological subjects, A. Hyman's *Osar divré hakhamin ufitgamehem* (1934), a collection of sayings laid out alphabetically, according to catchword, Urbach's volumes have the advantage of supplying not merely sayings but cogent discussions of the various sayings and a more fluent, coherent presentation of them in essay form. Solomon Schechter's *Some Aspects of Rabbinic Theology* (1909, based on essays in the *Jewish Quarterly Review* printed in 1894-1896) covers exactly what it says, some aspects, by contrast to the much more ambitious dimension of the present work. The comparison to George Foot Moore's *Judaism in the First Centuries of the Christian Era: The Age of the Tannaim* (1927-1930) is somewhat more complex. Moore certainly has the advantage of elegant presentation. Urbach's prose, in I. Abraham's English translation, comes through as turgid and stodgy, while Moore's is the opposite. Morton Smith comments on Moore's work, "Although it too much neglects the mystical, magical and apocalyptic sides of Judaism, its apology for tannaitic teaching as a reasonable, humane, and pious working out of biblical tradition is conclusive..." (*Encyclopaedia Judaica* 12:293-4; compare *Harvard Library Bulletin* 15, 1967, pp. 169-179). By contrast to Moore, Urbach introduces sayings of Amoraim into the discussion of each category, and since both Urbach and Moore aim to present a large selection of sayings on the several topics, Urbach's work is on the face of it a more comprehensive collection.

Urbach's own comments on his predecessors (I, pp. 5-18) underline the theological bias present in most, though not all, former studies. Wilhelm Bousset and Hugo Gressmann, *Die Religion des Judentums im späthellenistischen Zeitalter* (1926) is wanting because rabbinic sources are used sparingly and not wholly accurately and because it relies on "external sources," meaning apocryphal literature and Hellenistic Jewish writings. Urbach's own criticism of Moore, that "he did not always go deeply enough into the essence of the problems that he discussed," certainly cannot be leveled against Urbach himself. His further reservation is that Moore "failed to give an account of the origin of the beliefs and concepts, of their struggles and evolution, of their entire chequered course till their crystallization, of the immense dynamism and vitality of the spiritual life of the Second Temple period, of the tension in the relations between the parties and sects and between the various sections of the Sages themselves." This view underlines the historical ambition of Urbach's approach and emphasizes his view of his own contribution, cited at the outset: to elucidate the concepts and beliefs of the Tannaim and Amoraim against the background of their actual life and environment. Since that is Urbach's fundamental claim, the work must be considered not only in the context of what has gone before, in which, as I said, it emerges as a substantial step forward, but also in the setting of its own definition and understanding of the historical task, its own theory of how talmudic materials are to be used for historical knowledge. In this regard it is not satisfactory.

There are some fairly obvious problems, on which we need not dwell at length. Urbach's selection of sources for analysis is both narrowly canonical and somewhat confusing. We often hear from Philo, but seldom from the Essene Library of Qumran, still more rarely from the diverse works assembled by R.H. Charles as the apocrypha and pseudepigrapha of the Old Testament, and the like. If we seek to describe the talmudic rabbis, surely we cannot ask Philo to testify to their opinions. If we listen to Philo, surely we ought to hear – at least for the purpose of comparison and contrast – from books written by Palestinian Jews of various kinds. The Targumim are allowed no place at all because they are deemed "late." (The work of historians of traditions, e.g. Joseph Heinemann, and of comparative midrash, e.g. Renée Bloch and Geza Vermes, plays no role at all in this history!) But documents which came to redaction much later than the several Targumim (by any estimate of the date of the latter) make rich and constant contributions to the discussion. Within a given chapter, the portrayal of the sources will move rapidly from biblical to Tannaitic to Amoraic sources, as though the line of development were single, unitary, and harmonious, and as though there were no intervening developments which shaped later conceptions.

The work is fundamentally ahistorical, not merely because it is gullible and uncritical, but because, even within the author's own premises, he has ignored all historical considerations, even of chronology. What I mean is very simple. Differentiation among the stages of Tannaitic and Amoraic sayings tends to be episodic. Commonly, slight sustained effort is made to treat them in their several sequences, let alone to differentiate among schools and circles within a given period. Urbach takes with utmost seriousness his title, the sages, their concepts and beliefs, and his "history," topic by topic, reveals remarkably little variation, development, or even movement. It would not be fair to Urbach to suggest that all he has done is publish his card files. But I think his skill at organization and arrangement of materials tends to outrun his interest in differentiation and comparison within and among them, let alone in the larger, sequential history of major ideas and their growth and coherent development over the centuries. One looks in vain for Urbach's effort to justify treating "the sages" as essentially a coherent and timeless group.

Let us turn, rather, to the more fundamental difficulties presented by the work, because, as I said, it is to be received as the definitive product of a long established approach to the study of talmudic religion and history. Urbach has certainly brought to their ultimate realization the methods and concepts of his predecessors.

First, let us ask, does the worldview of the talmudic sages emerge in a way which the ancient sages themselves would have recognized? From the viewpoint of their organization and description of reality, their worldview, it is certain that the sages would have organized their card files quite differently. We know that is the case because we do not have, among the chapters before us, a single one which focuses upon the theme of one of the orders, let alone tractates, within which the rabbis divided and presented their various statements on reality, e.g., Seeds, the material basis of life; Seasons, the organization and differentiation of time; Women, the status of the individual; Damages, the conduct of civil life including government; Holy Things, the material service of God; and Purities, the immaterial base of divine reality in this world. The matter concerns not merely the superficial problem of organizing vast quantities of data. The talmudic rabbis left a large and exceedingly complex, well-integrated legacy of law. Clearly, it is through that legacy that they intended to make their fundamental statements upon the organization and meaning of reality. An account of their concepts and beliefs which ignores nearly the whole of the halakhah surely is slightly awry.

In fairness to Urbach, I must stress that he shows himself well aware of the centrality of halakhah in the expression of the worldview of the talmudic rabbis. He correctly criticizes his predecessors for neglecting the subject and observes, "The Halakha does not openly concern itself with beliefs and concepts; it determines, in practice, the way in which one should walk....Nevertheless beliefs and concepts lie at the core of many Halakhot; only their detection requires exhaustive study of the history of the Halakha combined with care to avoid fanciful conjectures and unfounded explanations." Urbach occasionally does introduce halakhic materials. But, as is clear, the fundamental structure of his account of talmudic theology is formed in accord not with the equivalent structure of the Talmud – the halakhah – but with the topics and organizing rubrics treated by all nineteenth- and twentieth-century Protestant historical studies of theology: God, ethics, revelation, and the like. That those studies are never far from mind is illustrated by Urbach's extensive discussion of whether talmudic ethics was theonomous or autonomous (I, pp. 320ff.), an issue important only from the viewpoint of nineteenth-century Jewish ethical thought and its response to Kant. But Urbach's discussion on that matter is completely persuasive, stating what is certainly the last word on the subject. He can hardly be blamed for criticizing widely held and wrong opinions.

Second, has Urbach taken account of methodological issues important in the study of the literary and historical character of the sources? In particular, does he deal with the fundamental questions of how these particular sources are to be used for historical purposes? The answer is a qualified negative. On many specific points, he contributes sporadic philological observations, interesting opinions and judgments as to the lateness of one saying as against the antiquity of another, subjective opinions on what is more representative or reliable than something else. If these opinions are not systematic and if they reveal no uniform criterion, sustainedly applied to all sources, they nonetheless derive from a mind of immense learning. Not all judgment must be critical, and not all expression of personal taste systematic. The dogmatic opinions of a man of such self-evident mastery of the tradition, one who, in addition, clearly is an exemplar of the tradition for his own setting, are important evidence for the study and interpretation of the tradition itself, particularly in its modern phase.

Yet we must ask, if a saying is assigned to an ancient authority, how do we know that he really said it? If a story is told, how do we know that the events the story purports to describe actually took place? And if not, just what are we to make of said story and saying for historical purposes? Further, if we have a saying attributed to a first-century authority in a document generally believed to have been redacted five hundred or a thousand years later, how do we know that the attribution of the saying is valid, and that the saying informs us of the state of opinion in the first century, not only in the sixth or eleventh in which it was written down and obviously believed true and authoritative? Do we still hold, as an axiom of historical scholarship, *ein muqdam umeuhar* ["temporal considerations do not apply"] – in the Talmud?! And again, do not the sayings assigned to a first-century authority, redacted in documents deriving from the early third century, possess greater credibility than those first appearing in documents redacted in the fifth, tenth, or even fifteenth centuries? Should we not, on the face of it, distinguish between more and less reliable materials? The well-known tendency of medieval writers to put their opinions into the mouths of the ancients, as in the case of the Zohar, surely warns us to be cautious about using documents redacted, even formulated, five hundred or a thousand or more years after the events of which they speak. Urbach ignores all of these questions and the work of those who ask them.

There is yet a further, equally simple problem. The corpus of evidence is simply huge. Selectivity characterizes even the most thorough and compendious accounts, and I cannot imagine one more comprehensive than Urbach's. But should we not devise means for the filtering downward of some fundamental, widely- and well-attested opinions, out of the mass of evidence, rather than capriciously selecting what we like and find interesting? We have few really comprehensive accounts of the history of a single idea or concept. Urbach himself has produced some of the better studies which we do have. It seems somewhat premature to describe so vast a world in the absence of a far more substantial corpus of Vorstudien of specific ideas and the men who held them than is available. Inevitably, one must characterize Urbach's treatment of one topic after another as unhistorical and superficial, and this is despite the author's impressive efforts to do history and to do it thoroughly and in depth. He is not merely selective. He is downright capricious.

After all, Urbach has done this great work without the advantage of studies of the history of the traditions assigned over the centuries to one authority or another. He has at hand scarcely any critical work comparing various versions of a story appearing in successive compilations. He has no possibility of recourse to comprehensive inquiries into the Talmud's forms and literary traits, redactional tendencies, even definitive accounts of the date of the redaction of most of the literature used for historical purposes. He cannot consult work on the thought of any of the individual Amoraim or on the traits of schools and circles among them, for there is none of critical substance. Most collections which pass as biographies even of Tannaim effect no differentiation among layers and strata of the stories and sayings, let alone attempting to describe the history of the traditions on the basis of which historical biography is be recovered. The laws assigned, even in Mishnah-Tosefta, to a given Tanna have not been investigated as to their underlying presuppositions and unifying convictions, even their gross thematic agendum. If Urbach speaks of "the rabbis" and differentiates only episodically among the layers and divisions of sayings, in accord either with differing opinions on a given question or with the historical development of evidently uniformly held opinions, he is no better than anyone else. The episodic contributions he himself makes in large measure constitute such history of ideas as presently is in hand. And, as I said, even that history is remarkable for the pre-critical methods and uncritical presuppositions upon which it is based.

Nor have I alluded to the intractable problems of internal, philosophico-theological analysis of ideas and their inner structures, once their evident historical, or sequential, development, among various circles and schools of a given generation and over a period of hundreds of years, has been elucidated. That quite separate investigation and analysis of the logic and meaning of the concepts and beliefs of the sages requires definition in its own terms, not in accord with the limited and simple criteria of working historians. If Urbach does not attempt it, no one else has entirely succeeded either. In this regard, Urbach's cavalier dismissal of the work of Marmorstein, Heschel, and Kadushin, among others, is pure quackery. While they may not have "persuaded" Urbach of the correctness of their theses, while they may have been wrong in some of their conclusions, and while their methods may have been unrefined, they at least have attempted the task which Urbach refuses even to undertake. One of the less fortunate aspects of Urbach's book, which makes for unpleasant reading, is the way in which he treats the work of other scholars. In the case of the above-named, this is not only disgraceful, it also is disastrous for Urbach's own undertaking. And since the whole opinion on works of considerable scholarship is the single word "worthless" or "unpersuasive," it may be observed that there is certain subjectivity which seems to preclude Urbach's reasoned discussion of what he likes and does not like in the work of many others and to prevent any sort of rational exchange of ideas. That is what I mean by quackery.

Urbach's work, as I said, in the balance brings to their full realization the methods and suppositions of the past hundred years. I cannot imagine that anyone again will want, from these perspectives, to approach the task of describing all of "the concepts and beliefs of the Tannaim and Amoraim," of elucidating all of them "against the background of their actual life and environment." So far as the work can be done in accord with established methods, here it has been done very competently indeed. Accordingly, we may well forgive the learned author for the sustained homiletical character of his inquiry and its blatantly apologetic purposes:

> The aim of our work is to give an epitome of the beliefs and concepts of the Sages as the history of a struggle to instill religious and ethical ideals into the everyday life of the community and the individual, while preserving at the same time the integrity and unity of the nation and directing its way in this world as a preparation for another world that is wholly perfect....Their eyes and their hearts were turned Heavenward, yet one type was not to be found among them...namely the mystic who seeks to liberate himself from his ego and in doing so is preoccupied with himself alone. They saw their mission in work here in the world below. There were Sages who inclined to extremism in

their thoughts and deeds, and there were those who preached the way of compromise, which they did not, however, determine on the basis of convenience. Some were severe and exacting, while others demonstrated an extreme love of humanity and altruism. The vast majority of them recognized the complexities of life with its travail and joy, its happiness and tragedy, and this life served them also as a touchstone for their beliefs and concepts.

All of this may well be so, but it remains to be demonstrated as historical fact in the way in which contemporary critical historians generally demonstrate matters of fact. It requires analysis and argument in the undogmatic and unapologetic spirit characteristic of contemporary studies in the history of ideas and of religions. But in the context in which these words of Urbach are written, among the people who will read them, this statement of purpose puts forth a noble ideal, one which might well be emulated by the "sages" – exemplars and politicians of Orthodox Judaism – to whom, I believe, Urbach speaks most directly and persuasively, and by whom (alone) his results certainly will be taken as historical fact. The publishing success of the book and the recognition accorded its learned author are hopeful signs that the ideal of the sage of old indeed has not been lost upon their most recent avatars. It is by no means a reduction of learning to its sociological and political relevance to say that, if it were only for his advocacy of the humane and constructive position just now quoted, Urbach has made a truly formidable contribution to the contemporary theological life of Orthodox Judaism.

To respond to a work of such importance as Urbach's, it will not suffice to outline what is wrong with his book. Having stressed, for example, the importance of beginning the inquiry into the worldview of the talmudic rabbis with the study of the law, in particular of the earliest stratum, faithfully represented by Mishnah-Tosefta, I have now to propose the sorts of work to be done. Since I have raised the question of how we know what is assigned to a person was really said by him, and since by implication I have suggested that we cannot affirmatively answer that question, what sort of inquiry do I conceive to be possible, and upon what historical-epistemological basis? Let me here present very briefly an alternative conception of how to define and approach the formidable task accomplished by Urbach in accord with the prevailing methods and within established suppositions about the detailed and concrete historicity of talmudic evidences: the description of the worldview of "our sages." What happens when Fundamentalism dies, as it will even in Orthodox Jerusalem?

The problems that lie ahead and the line of research leading to their solution are now to be specified. Let us begin with the matter generally regarded as settled: the meaning of the texts. While philological research by Semitists and archaeological discoveries self-evidently will clarify the meanings of words and the identification of objects mentioned in the rabbinical literature, there is yet another task, the fresh exegesis of the whole of rabbinical literature within the discipline of contemporary hermeneutical conceptions. The established exegesis takes for granted an axiom which is simply false: that all texts are to be interpreted in the light of all other texts. Talmudic discussion of Mishnah and its meanings invariably shapes the received interpretation of Mishnah, for example. If Tosefta – itself a commentary – supplies a conception of Mishnah's principle or rule, then Tosefta places the imprint of its interpretation upon the meaning of Mishnah.

Now no one would imagine that the original meaning of Tanakh is regularly to be uncovered in the pages of Midrash or in the medieval commentaries to the Scriptures. On the contrary, everyone understands that Tanakh has been subjected to a long history of interpretation, and that history, while interesting, is germane to the original meaning of Tanakh only when, on objective and critical grounds, we are able to affirm it by historical criteria. By contrast, discussion of Mishnaic pericopae in Talmud and medieval commentaries and codes invariably exhausts the analysis of the meaning of Mishnaic pericopae. It is to the credit of H. Albeck (a better scholar than Urbach) that his excellent commentary to Mishnah makes the effort at many points deliberately to exclude considerations introduced only later on. This is done not merely to facilitate a simple and popular interpretation, though Albeck admirably succeeds in doing just that, but also to present what Albeck considers to be the primary and original meaning of the law. It is no criticism of Albeck, limited as he was by his form, a commentary of the most abbreviated sort, to say that the discussion of the primary meaning of Mishnah has to begin.

What is meant is simply, what did these words convey to the people who made them up, in the late first and second century? What issues can have been in their minds? True, much is to be learned from the answers to these questions supplied by the exegetes from the third to the twentieth century. But since, in the main, the supposition of the established exegetical tradition is non-historical and therefore uninterested in what pericopae meant at the outset, the established tradition, without re-evaluation, will not serve any longer. That is not to suggest it cannot be drawn upon. The contrary is the case. I know no other road into the heart of a pericope. At the same time, the established agendum – the set of issues, problems, and questions deemed worth consideration – is to be drastically reshaped, even while much that we have received will be reaffirmed, if on grounds quite different from those which motivated the great exegetes.

The classical exegetes faced the task of showing the profound interrelationships, in logic and meaning, of one law to the next, developing and expanding the subtleties and complexities of law, in the supposition that in hand is a timeless and harmonious, wholly integrated and unitary structure of law and logic. In other words, the established exegetical tradition properly and correctly ignores questions of beginnings and development, regarding these questions as irrelevant to the true meaning of the law under the aspect of eternity. And that is indeed the case – except when we claim to speak about specific, historical personalities, at some one time, who spoke the language of their own day and addressed the issues of their own epoch. Urbach claims to tell us not about "talmudic Judaism" in general – organized, as is clear, around various specific topics – but to describe the history and development of talmudic Judaism. Yet, if that is the case, then the sources adduced in evidence have to be examined with the question in mind, what did the person who made up or formulated this saying mean to tell us? And the answer to that question is not to be located either by repeating the essentially eisegetical results already in hand, or by pretending that everything is obvious.

We have to distinguish between the primary issue, present to begin with in a pericope, and secondary problems or considerations only later on attached to the pericope. How do we confidently distinguish between the primary message of a pericope and the secondary eisegesis found in the great commentaries? We have to ask, what does the narrator, legislator, or redactor propose to tell us in a particular, distinct pericope? That is to say, through the routine form-analytical and literary-critical techniques already available, we have to isolate the smallest units of tradition, and, removing them from their redactional as well as their exegetical-eisegetical framework, ask about their meaning and original intent. Modes of emphasis and stress, for example, are readily discerned. Important materials will commonly be placed at the beginning of a pericope, or underlined through balanced, contrary allegations. But stylistic considerations and formal traits are helpful primarily in isolating pericopae and establishing their primary units for analysis. What is decisive is the discernment of what the narrator includes or omits, what seem to be his obvious concerns and what he ignores.

Once the importance of a fresh exegesis of rabbinical texts is established, the next problem is to select the documents on which the work should begin. Here Urbach's work illustrates the fateful error of assuming that rabbinical literature is essentially timeless, so that there is "neither early nor late in Torah." Applied to the present work, it results in the notion that whatever is attributed to anyone was really said by the person to whom the saying is attributed, therefore tells us about the period in which he lived – and this without regard to the date at which the document in which the said saying occurs was redacted, as I have stressed. Thus side by side in Urbach's compilation are sayings in Mishnah and in late Amoraic and even medieval compilations of materials. In a fresh approach to the problem of the history of talmudic Judaism, we should, I believe, establish guidelines by which we evaluate materials first occurring in late compilations. Mishnah-Tosefta assuredly comes to redaction by ca. A.D. 200. On the face of it, Mishnah-Tosefta therefore constitutes a more reliable testimony to the mind of second-century rabbis than does Yalqut Shimeoni or Yalqut Reuveni. If that is obvious, then it follows that we have to begin our work with the analysis of the main ideas attributed to authorities in Mishnah-Tosefta. These have clearly to be worked out, and the materials occurring in later compilations, of Amoraic and medieval origin, are to be tested for conceptual and even thematic congruence against the materials occurring in earlier documents.

The question remains, If it is assumed that Mishnah-Tosefta testifies to the time in which the document was finally redacted, then how shall we know what layers of thought come before the time of the redaction of the document itself? How shall we know, furthermore, whether a person to whom a saying is attributed really said it? To deal with the latter question, I do not believe we have any way of verifying whether a person to whom a saying is attributed actually said it. Our history of talmudic Judaism will unfold by periods, may even produce significant differentiation among named authorities within the several periods, but it will, so far as I can see, not supply a definitive answer to the question of whether Aqiba really said what he is claimed to have said. While that question – whether we have *ipsissima verba* of a particular historical figure – is deemed terribly pressing in the study of the founder of Christianity, the importance of the question is for theological, not historical reasons. We do not know everything we might like to know; that does not mean what we do know is not worth knowing. Yet the other matter – how we can find out whether anything in Mishnah-Tosefta antedates the redaction of Mishnah-Tosefta – requires more considerable attention. Here we must begin with a working hypothesis and test that hypothesis against the results attained in its application.

The simplest possible hypothesis is that the attributions of sayings to named authorities may be relied upon in assigning those sayings to the period, broadly defined, in which said authorities flourished. We do not and cannot know, for example, whether Aqiba actually said what is attributed to him. Are we able to establish criteria by which we may conclude that what is assigned to Aqiba likely belongs in the period in which he lived, e.g., to his school or associates or even to the man himself? This proposition can indeed be tested. We have laws which interrelate in theme and conception and which also bear attributions to successive authorities, e.g., to a Yavnean, to an Ushan, and to an authority of the time of Rabbi. If we are able to demonstrate that what is assigned to a Yavnean is conceptually earlier than, and not dependent upon, what is assigned to an Ushan, then, on the face of it, the former indeed is an earlier tradition, the latter a later one. The unfolding of the rabbis' ideas on legal and other questions may be shown to take place through sequences of logic, with what is assigned to later masters often depending upon and generated by what is assigned to the earlier ones. When we find a correlation between such logical (not merely thematic) sequences and temporal ones, that is, if what is assigned to a later master does depend in theme, conception, principle, and inner logic upon what is attributed to an earlier master, then we have history: we know what comes earlier, what comes later. We are able therefore to describe ideas probably characteristic of authorities between the disaster of 70 and the Bar Kokhba debacle, and from that time to the period of Rabbi, and in the time of Rabbi. Doubtless work on Amoraic materials will yield the same series of disciplined sequences of correlated attributions and logical developments, showing the general reliability of the attributions by periods and making possible a description of ideas held in a given period by various authorities. On that basis, indeed, we can describe the ideas really characteristic of one period in the historical unfolding of talmudic Judaism and relate them to ideas characteristic of earlier and later periods. That sort of historical inquiry is virtually not attempted by Urbach, simply because he takes for granted, as I said, that what is assigned to a given authority really was stated by that authority. Having no problems, he obviously is unable to propose solutions and then to test them.

A further descriptive historical task is to be undertaken. When we concentrate attention on the most reliable witnesses to the mind of the earlier rabbis, those of the first and second century, we find ourselves engaged primarily in the analysis of legal texts. Mishnah-Tosefta and related literature focus attention on halakhic problems. Are there underlying unities of conception or definitions of fundamental principles to be discerned within the halakhah? No one familiar with the literature and its classical exegesis is in doubt that there are. These are to be spelled out with some care, also correlated and compared to conceptions revealed in writings of other Jews, not solely rabbinic Jews, as well as Christians and "pagans." When, for example, we describe primary concerns and perennial issues inherent in laws attributed to Ushans, we find that, in much acute detail, rather fundamental issues of physics are worked out, e.g., the nature of mixtures, which will not have surprised Stoic, natural philosophers. Again, an enduring interest of Yavnean pericopae is in the relationship between intention and action, an issue both of interest to Paul and those who told stories about Jesus, on the one side, and of concern to philosophers of disaster and rebuilding in the earlier destruction, for instance, Jeremiah. The thought of Yavneh in any event has to be brought into relationship with the context in which the rabbis did their work, the aftermath of the loss of the Temple, just as the work of the Ushans, following the much greater this-worldly catastrophe brought on by Bar Kokhba, must always be seen against the background of crisis. Indeed, the formation of earlier rabbinic Judaism, from its primitive beginnings after 70 to its full and complete expression by the end of Ushan times in 170, is the product of an age of many painful events, events deemed at the time to bear the most profound theological weight. Much of the halakhah both can and should be interpreted in this particular context, and many of its issues, not to be reduced to economic or social concerns, express profound thought on the issues and inner meanings of the age itself. It follows that once the exegetical work is complete (if provisionally) and the historical sequences of individual units of law fairly well established, the larger issues emergent in underlying unities of conception and definitions of fundamental principles are to be uncovered, so that the legal materials may produce a history of major ideas and themes, not merely sets of two or three logical-temporal sequences of minor details.

That is how we must answer the question, If Mishnah was redacted in ca. A.D. 200, then how do we know that anything in Mishnah derives from before A.D. 200? Traditionalists in Jewish scholarly circles have different answers. They posit transmission in exact words said by a given authority through oral means. They further hold what is not assigned to a given authority goes "way way back." But materials not given in the name of a particular master share not only the literary, but also the conceptual, traits of materials assigned to a great many named masters, in particular in the period from 130 to 170. The traditional view in this matter is simply wrong.

In time, when the work sketched here is done, we shall see the outlines of the much larger history of legal, therefore religious, ideas, the unfolding of the worldview of the rabbis who created rabbinic Judaism. These outlines will emerge not merely from discrete sayings, chosen more or less at random, about topics of interest chiefly to us, e.g.,

Ephraim E. Urbach's The Sages: Their Concepts and Beliefs   171

was rabbinical ethics theonomous or autonomous? what did "the rabbis" believe about life after death, the Messiah, eschaton? and so on. Rather, the morphology of the rabbinic worldview will emerge inductively, differentiated as to its historical stages and as to the distinctive viewpoints and conceptions held by individual authorities or circles within which that larger worldview originated.

Second, a new approach to the description and interpretation of the worldview of the earlier rabbis should emerge. This proceeds along critical-historical lines, taking account of the problems of dating sayings, of the diversity of the documents which purport to preserve opinions of the earlier masters, and the like. That is important, to be sure. But there are more important aspects of this work.

People do not seem to realize the immense dimensions of the evidence in our hands. We have much more than just a few sayings on this and that. We have a vast law-code, a huge exegetical corpus in respect to the Hebrew Scriptures and their translation, collections of stories about authorities, various kinds of sayings assigned to them – an extraordinarily large mass of materials. Our approach, for the first time, must encompass the totality of the evidence, cope with, take account of, sources of exceptional density and richness. The law, as I said, is the definitive source of the worldview of the earlier rabbis. What is earliest and best attested is Mishnah-Tosefta. Therefore, if we want to know what people were thinking in the first and second centuries, we have to turn, to begin with, to that document, which must serve as criterion in the assessment of whatever first appears in the later compilations of rabbinical sayings and stories. Books on rabbinic Judaism which focus upon non-legal sayings (without regard, even, to the time at which the documents containing those sayings were redacted) simply miss the point of rabbinic Judaism.

But the legal sayings deal with picayune and inconsequential matters. The major problem is to derive, from arcane and trivial details of laws of various sorts, the worldview which forms the foundations of, and is expressed by, these detailed rules. That work must be done in a systematic and comprehensive way. And, in consequence, the definition of the agendum of scholarship is to be revised, not merely in terms of the adaptation and systematic application of methods of literary-, form-, and redactional-criticism, hitherto unknown in this field, nor in terms of the introduction of historical-critical considerations, hitherto neglected or introduced in an episodic way and with a lack of historical sophistication, but in terms of its very shape and structure. The total failure of all prior approaches finds definitive illustration in Urbach's disastrous work. Critics of the old approaches could not have provided a better satire of the intellectual bankruptcy of the age that has gone before than does Urbach himself.

Let me return at the end to the question I raised at the outset: why was Urbach ignored by the academic world, even while enjoying a positive hearing in the world of Modern Orthodox Judaism? The answer is simple. The questions outlined here were not addressed by Urbach or by any of those who claimed to appreciate and follow him. His followers did no new work along the lines he laid out. And his critics, led by me, did. The result was that scholarship as it proceeded beyond Urbach's book simply ignored all but the sources he assembled, and, after all, there are now better concordances than the discursive one that he printed in 1969. Urbach did no new work on this book; in subsequent publications he simply repeated the methods and results. He ignored the sustained criticism his book received, not answering it, not learning from it, not deigning to take it seriously. But the world then moved past him, ignoring him and his book, denying him that very hearing that, after all, he denied others prior to his own day ("worthless," "unpersuasive" indeed!) and in his own time as well. The one enduring lesson we learn from Ephraim Urbach, who in retrospect has become a rather tragic figure of scholarship, is to try to learn from our critics, and, at the very least, to respond to their criticism. The person who practiced *Todschweigen* may well end up his own victim.

8

Why Schechter, Moore and Urbach are Irrelevant to Scholarship Today

Jacob Neusner
Brown University

When we investigate the history of the formative stage of the Judaism of the Dual Torah, what can we now learn from the generations of scholarship that began with Solomon Schechter and concluded with Ephraim E. Urbach? For, during that long period, the premises of learning in the rabbinic literature of late antiquity joined new historical interest with a received theological conviction. The former wished to describe in context ideas that had formerly been assigned no context at all: they were "Torah," and now were to be the history of ideas. The latter maintained that the documents of the rabbinic corpus were essentially seamless and formed one vast Dual Torah, oral and written; and that all attributions were valid, so that if a given authority was supposed to have made a statement, he really made it. On the basis of that received conviction, imputing inerrancy to the attributions (as well as to the story-tellers) just as had many generations of the faithful, but asking questions of context and development that were supposed to add up to history, Schechter, Moore, Kadushin, Urbach, and all the other great figures of the first three quarters of the twentieth century set forth their accounts.

But what if we recognize that documentary formulations play a role in the representation of compositions, so that the compositors' formulation of matters takes a critical place in the making of the documentary evidence? And what if, further, we no longer assume the inerrancy of the Oral Torah's writings, so that attributions are no longer taken at face value, stories no longer believed unless there are grounds for disbelief (as the Jerusalem canard has it)? Then the fundamental presuppositions of the writing of Schechter, Moore, Kadushin, Urbach, and lesser figures prove null. And that fact bears in its wake the further problem: since we cannot take their answers at face value, can we pursue their questions any more? In my judgment, the answer is negative. The only reason nowadays to read Schechter, Moore, Kadushin, Urbach and others is to see what they have to say about specific passages upon which, episodically and unsystematically, they have comments to make. All work in the history of the formative age of the Judaism of the Dual Torah that treats documentary lines as null and attributions as invariably valid must be dismissed as a mere curiosity; a collection and arrangement of this and that, bearing no compelling argument or proposition to be dealt with by the new generation.[1]

---

[1] William Horbury, reviewing my *Vanquished Nation, Broken Spirit* (*Epworth Review*, May, 1989), correctly observes: "Emotional attitudes form a traditional moral topic, and the recommendations on them in rabbinic ethics have often been considered, for example, in the *Rabbinic Anthology* of C. G. Montefiore and H. Loewe....This historical inquiry is closely related to the author's other work, and it is written on his own terms; he does not mention other writers on rabbinic ethics, and he gives no explicit criticism or development of modern study by others of the rabbinic passages and ideas with which he deals. He cannot be said to have fulfilled his obligation to his readers." Horbury does not seem to know my extensive writings on others who have worked on the formative history of Judaism, even though these have been collected and set forth in a systematic way, both as book reviews and as methodological essays, time and again. My *Ancient Judaism: Disputes and Debates* (Chico, 1986: Scholars Press for Brown Judaic Studies) is only one place in which I have indeed done just what Horbury asks, addressing Urbach and Moore and some of their most recent continuators in a systematic and thorough way. I am amazed that he can imagine I have not read the literature of my field; I not only have read and repeatedly criticized it, but I have done so in every accessible medium. His reviews of my work are simply uninformed and captious. His treatment of my *Incarnation of God* in *Expository Times*, which makes the same point in a more savage manner, shows the real problem; he does not find it possible to state more than the topic (the title!) of the book and cannot tell his readers what thesis or proposition is set forth in the book. Given those limitations of intellect, one can hardly find surprising his inability to grasp why Urbach, Schechter, Moore, Kadushin, and others by contemporary standards simply have nothing to teach us about the formative history of Judaism. Horbury wants us to do chemistry by appeal to not the oxygen but the phlogiston theory, and he wants geography to be carried out in accord with the convictions of the flat-earthers. But the latter have a better sense of humor about themselves.

Let me now reframe the question in a manner which will make clear the right way in which to work. For when we grasp how we must now investigate the formative history of Judaism, we shall also see why Schechter, Moore, and Urbach no longer compel attention for any serious and important purpose.

The question that demands a response before any historical issues can be formulate is this: How are we to determine the particular time and circumstance in which a writing took shape, and how shall we identify the generative problems, the urgent and critical questions, that informed the intellect of an authorship and framed the social world that nurtured that same authorship? Lacking answers to these questions, we find our work partial, and, if truth be told, stained by sterile academicism. Accordingly, the documentary method requires us to situate the contents of writings into particular circumstances, so that we may read the contents in the context of a real time and place. How to do so? I maintain that it is by reference to the time and circumstance of the closure of a document, that is to say, the conventional assignment of a piece of writing to a particular time and place, that we proceed outward from context to matrix.

Everyone down to Urbach, including Montefiore and Loewe, Schechter, Moore, and the rest, simply take at face value attributions of sayings to particular authorities and interpret what is said as evidence of the time and place in which the cited authorities flourished. When studying topics in the Judaism of the sages of the rabbinic writings from the first through the seventh centuries, people routinely cite sayings categorized by attribution rather than by document. That is to say, they treat as one group of sayings whatever is assigned to Rabbi X. This is without regard to the time of redaction of the documents in which those sayings occur or to similar considerations of literary context and documentary circumstance. The category defined by attributions to a given authority furthermore rests on the premise that the things given in the name of Rabbi X really were said by him. No other premise would justify resort to the category deriving from use of a name, that alone. Commonly, the next step is to treat those sayings as evidence of ideas held, if not by that particular person, then by people in the age in which the cited authority lived. Once more the premise that the sayings go back to the age of the authority to whom they are attributed underpins inquiry. Accordingly, scholars cite sayings in the name of given authorities and take for granted that those sayings were said by the authority to whom they were attributed and, of course, in the time in which that authority flourished. By contrast, in my method of the documentary study of Judaism, I treat the historical sequence of sayings only in accord with the order of the documents in which they first occur. Let me expand on why I have taken the approach that I have, explain the way the method works, and then, as before, set forth an example of the method in action.[2]

Since many sayings are attributed to specific authorities, why not lay out the sayings in the order of the authorities to whom they are attributed, rather than in the order of the books in which these sayings occur, which forms the documentary method for the description of the matrix of texts in context? It is because the attributions cannot be validated, but the books can. The first of the two principles by which I describe the matrix that defines the context in which texts are framed is that we compose histories of ideas of the Judaism of the Dual Torah in accord with the sequence of documents that, in the aggregate, constitute the corpus and canon of the Judaism of the Dual Torah. And

---

[2]My example is drawn from a whole series of books in which I worked on the histories of specific conceptions or problems, formulated as I think correct, out of the sequence of documents. These are in the following works of mine: *The Idea of Purity in Ancient Judaism. The Haskell Lectures, 1972-1973.* Leiden, 1973: E. J. Brill. [This was a most preliminary work, which made me aware of the problems to be addressed later on. The documentary theory of the history of ideas was worked out only in the earlier 1980s.] *Judaism and Story: The Evidence of The Fathers According to Rabbi Nathan.* Chicago, 1990: University of Chicago Press. *The Foundations of Judaism. Method, Teleology, Doctrine.* Philadelphia, 1983-5: Fortress Press. I-III. I. *Midrash in Context. Exegesis in Formative Judaism.* Second printing: Atlanta, 1988: Scholars Press for Brown Judaic Studies. *The Foundations of Judaism. Method, Teleology, Doctrine.* Philadelphia, 1983-5: Fortress Press. I-III. II. *Messiah in Context. Israel's History and Destiny in Formative Judaism.* Second printing: Lanham, 1988: University Press of America. Studies in Judaism series. *The Foundations of Judaism. Method, Teleology, Doctrine.* Philadelphia, 1983-5: Fortress Press. I-III. III. *Torah: From Scroll to Symbol in Formative Judaism.* Second printing: Atlanta, 1988: Scholars Press for Brown Judaic Studies. *The Foundations of Judaism.* Philadelphia, 1988: Fortress. Abridged edition of the foregoing trilogy. *Vanquished Nation, Broken Spirit. The Virtues of the Heart in Formative Judaism.* New York, 1987: Cambridge University Press. Jewish Book Club selection, 1987. Editor: *Judaisms and their Messiahs in the beginning of Christianity.* New York, 1987: Cambridge University Press. [Edited with William Scott Green and Ernest S. Frerichs.] *Judaism in the Matrix of Christianity.* Philadelphia, 1986: Fortress Press. British edition, Edinburgh, 1988, T. & T. Collins. *Judaism and Christianity in the Age of Constantine. Issues of the Initial Confrontation.* Chicago, 1987: University of Chicago Press.
Judaism and its Social Metaphors. Israel in the History of Jewish Thought. N.Y., 1988: Cambridge University Press. *The Incarnation of God: The Character of Divinity in Formative Judaism.* Philadelphia, 1988: Fortress Press. Edited: *The Christian and Judaic Invention of History.* [Edited with William Scott Green]. Atlanta, 1989: Scholars Press for American Academy of Religion. Studies in Religion series. [All of the papers in this collection are worked out within the basic thesis of the documentary history of ideas.]

those histories set forth dimensions of the matrix in which that Judaism, through its writings, is to be situated for broader purposes of interpretation. Documents reveal the system and structure of their authorships, and, in the case of religious writing, out of a document without named authors we may compose an account of the authorship's religion: a way of life, a worldview, a social entity meant to realize both. Read one by one, documents reveal the interiority of intellect of an authorship, and that inner-facing quality of mind inheres even when an authorship imagines it speaks outward, toward and about the world beyond. Even when set side by side, moreover, documents illuminate the minds of intersecting authorships, nothing more.

Then why not simply take at face value a document's *own* claims concerning the determinate situation of its authorship? Readers have already noted innumerable attributions to specific authorities. One obvious mode of determining the matrix of a text, the presently paramount way, as I said, is simply to take at face value the allegation that a given authority, whose time and place we may identify, really said what is attributed to him, and that if a writing says something happened, what it tells us is not what its authorship thought happened, but what really happened. That reading of writing for purposes of not only history, but also religious study, is in fact commonplace. It characterizes all accounts of the religion, Judaism, prior to mine, and it remains a serious option for all those outside of my school and circle.[3] Proof of that fact is to be shown, lest readers who find accommodation in more contemporary intellectual worlds, where criticism and the active intellect reign, doubt my judgment of competing methods and differing accounts. Accordingly, let me characterize the prevailing way of determining the historical and religious matrix of texts, and then proceed to explain my alternate mode for answering the question of what is to be learned, from within a piece of writing, about the religious world beyond.

In historical study, we gain access to no knowledge *a priori*. All facts derive from sources correctly situated, e.g., classified, comprehensively and completely described, dispassionately analyzed, and evaluated. Nothing can be taken for granted. What we cannot

---

[3]That is why people can still read Urbach or Moore as though we learned anything of historical and not merely ad hoc exegetical interest from their compilations of sayings under their various rubrics. In this regard Urbach's various asides are quite interesting, even though not a single account of the history and context of an idea can stand; and the straight historical chapters – e.g., on the social role of sages, on the life of Hillel, on the history of the time – are not only intellectually vulgar, they are a travesty of scholarship, even for the time and within the premises in which they were written.

show, we do not know. These simple dogmas of all historical learning derive not from this writer but go back to the very beginnings of Western critical historical scholarship, to the age of the Renaissance. But all historical and religions-historical scholarship on the documents of the Judaism of the Dual Torah in its formative age, except for mine and for that of a very few others, ignores the canons of criticism that govern academic scholarship. Everyone in the past and many even now take for granted that pretty much everything they read is true – except what they decide is not true.

They cannot and do not raise the question of whether an authorship knows what it is talking about, and they do not address the issue of the purpose of a text: historical or imaginative, for example. For them the issue always is history, namely, what really happened, and that issue was settled, so to speak, at Sinai: it is all true (except, on an episodic basis, what is not true, which the scholars somehow know instinctively). They exhibit the credulity characteristic of the believers, which in the circle of piety is called faith, and rightly so, but in the center of academic learning is mere gullibility. The fundamentalists in the talmudic academies and rabbinical seminaries and Israeli universities take not only as fact but at face value everything in the holy books. "Judaism" is special and need not undergo description, analysis, and interpretation in accord with a shared and public canon of rules of criticism. "We all know" how to do the work, and "we" do not have to explain to "outsiders" either what the work is or why it is important. It is a self-evidently important enterprise in the rehearsal of information. Knowing these things the way "we" know them explains the value of knowing these things.

Scholarship formed on the premise that the sources' stories are to be believed at face value does not say so; rather, it frames questions that implicitly affirm the accuracy of the holy books, asking questions, for example, that can only be answered in the assumption that the inerrant Scriptures contain the answers – therefore, as a matter of process, do not err. By extension holy books that tell stories produce history through the paraphrase of stories into historical language: this is what happened, this is how it happened, and here are the reasons why it happened. If the Talmud says someone said something, he really said it, then and there. That premise moreover dictates their scholarly program, for it permits these faithful scholars to describe, analyze and interpret events or ideas held in the time in which that person lived. Some of these would deny the charge, and all of them would surely point, in their writing, to evidence of a critical approach. But the premise remains the old gullibility. Specifically, the questions they frame to begin with rest on the assumption that the sources respond. The assumption that, if a story refers to a second century rabbi, then the story tells us about the second century, proves routine. And that complete reliance merely on the allegations of sayings and stories constitutes perfect faith in the facticity of fairy tales.

The operative question facing anyone who proposes to translate writing into religion – that is, accounts of "Judaism," as Moore claims to give, or "The Sages," that Urbach imagines he has made for us, is the historical one: How you know exactly what was said and done, that is, the history that you claim to report about what happened long ago? Specifically, how do you know he really said it? And if you do not know that he really said it, how can you ask the questions that you ask, which has as its premise the claim that you can say what happened or did not happen?

The wrong, but commonplace, method is to assume that if a given document ascribes an opinion to a named authority the opinion actually was stated in that language by that sage. On this assumption a much richer history of an idea, not merely of the literary evidences of that idea, may be worked out without regard only to the date of the document at hand. Within this theory of evidence, we have the history of what individuals thought on a common topic. I have already set forth the reason that we cannot proceed to outline the sequence of ideas solely on the basis of the sequence of the sages to whom ideas are attributed. We simply cannot demonstrate that a given authority really said what a document assigns to him. Let me list the range of uncertainty that necessitates this fresh approach, which I have invented.

First, if the order of the documents were fully sound and the contents representative of rabbinical opinion, then the result would be a history of the advent of the idea at hand and the development and articulation of that idea in formative Judaism. We should then have a fairly reliable picture of ideas at hand as these unfolded in orderly sequence. But we do not know that the canonical history corresponds to the actual history of ideas. Furthermore, we cannot even be sure that the order of documents presently assumed in scholarly convention is correct. Second, if a rabbi really spoke the words attributed to him, then a given idea would have reached expression within Judaism *prior* to the redaction of the document. Dividing things up by documents will tend to give a later date and thus a different context for interpretation to opinions held earlier than we can presently demonstrate. Third, although we are focusing upon the literature produced by a particular group, again we have no clear notion of what people were thinking outside of that group. We therefore do not know how opinions held by other groups or by the Jewish people in general came to shape the vision of rabbis. When, for example, we note that there also existed poetic literature and translations of Scriptures characteristic of the synagogue worship, we cannot determine whether the poetry and most translations spoke for rabbis or for some quite different group.

For these reasons I have chosen to address the contextual question within the narrow limits of the canon. That accounts for my formulation of the episteme as "the canonical history of ideas," and explains, also, why I have carefully avoided claiming that a given idea was broadly held only at a given time and place. All I allege is that a given document underscores the presence of an idea for that authorship – that alone. Obviously, if I could in a given formulation relate the appearance of a given idea to events affecting rabbis in particular or to the life of Israel in general, the results would be exceedingly suggestive. But since we do not know for whom the documents speak, how broadly representative they are, or even how comprehensive is their evidence about rabbis' views, we must carefully define what we do and do not know. So for this early stage in research the context in which a given idea is described, analyzed, and interpreted is the canon. But this first step alone carries us to new territory. I hope that in due course others will move beyond the limits which, at the moment, seem to me to mark the farthest possible advance. Now let us turn to the specific case meant to illustrate the method.

Let me now explain in some greater detail the alternative, which I call the documentary history of ideas. It is a mode of relating writing to religion through history through close attention to the circumstance in which writing reached closure. It is accomplished, specifically, by assessing shifts exhibited by a sequence of documents and appealing to the generally accepted dates assigned to writings in explaining those shifts. In this way I propose to confront questions of cultural order, social system and political structure, to which the texts respond explicitly and constantly. Confronting writings of a religious character, we err by asking questions of a narrowly historical character: what did X really say on a particular occasion, and why. These questions not only are not answerable on the basis of the evidence in hand. They also are trivial, irrelevant to the character of the evidence. What strikes me as I review the writings just now cited is how little of real interest and worth we should know, even if we were to concede the historical accuracy and veracity of all the many allegations of the scholars we have surveyed. How little we should know – but how much we should have *missed* if that set of questions and answers were to encompass the whole of our inquiry.

If we are to trace the unfolding, in the sources of formative Judaism, of a given theme or ideas on a given problem, the order in which we approach the several books, that is, components of the entire canon, gives us the sole guidance on sequence, order, and context, that we are apt to find. As is clear, we have no way of demonstrating that authorities to whom, in a given composition, ideas are attributed really said what is assigned to them. The sole fact in hand therefore is that the framers of a given document included in their book sayings imputed to named authorities. Are these dependable? Unlikely on the face of it. Why not? Since the same sayings will be imputed to diverse authorities by different groups of editors, of different books, we stand on shaky ground indeed if we rely for chronology upon the framers' claims of who said what. More important, attributions by themselves cannot be shown to be reliable.

What we cannot show we do not know.[4] Lacking firm evidence, for example, in a sage's own, clearly assigned writings, or even in writings redacted by a sage's own disciples and handed on among them in the discipline of their own community, we have for chronology only a single fact. It is that a document, reaching closure at a given time, contains the allegation that Rabbi X said statement Y. So we know that people at the time of the document reached closure took the view that Rabbi X said statement Y. We may then assign to statement Y a position, in the order of the sequence of sayings, defined by the location of the document in the order of the sequence of documents. The several documents' dates, as is clear, all constitute guesses. But the sequence explained in the prologue, Mishnah, Tosefta, Yerushalmi, Bavli for the exegetical writings on the Mishnah is absolutely firm and beyond doubt. The sequence for the exegetical collections on Scripture Sifra, the Sifrés, Genesis Rabbah, Leviticus Rabbah, the Pesiqtas and beyond is not entirely sure. Still the position of the Sifra and the two Sifrés at the head, followed by Genesis Rabbah, then Leviticus Rabbah, then Pesiqta deR. Kahana and Lamentations Rabbati and some related collections, seems likely.

What are the canonical mainbeams that sustain the history of ideas as I propose to trace that history? A brief reprise of the information given in the Prologue suffices. The formative age of

---

[4]It should be underlined that a British scholar, Hyam Maccoby, maintains exactly the opposite, alleging in a letter to the editor of *Commentary* and in various other writings that there is historical knowledge that we possess *a priori*. We must be thankful to him for making explicit the position of the other side. No historical scholarship known to me concurs with his position on *a priori* historical knowledge; all modern learning in history begins with sources, read *de novo*.

Judaism is the period marked at the outset by the Mishnah, taking shape from sometime before the Common Era and reaching closure at ca. 200 C.E., and at the end by the Talmud of Babylonia, ca. 600 C.E. In between these dates, two streams of writings developed, one legal, explaining the meaning of the Mishnah, the other theological and exegetical, interpreting the sense of Scripture. The high points of the former come with tractate Abot which is the Mishnah's first apologetic, the Tosefta, a collection of supplements ca. 300 C.E., the Talmud of the Land of Israel ca. 400 C.E., followed by the Babylonian Talmud. The latter set of writings comprise compositions on Exodus, in Mekilta attributed to R. Ishmael and of indeterminate date, Sifra on Leviticus, Sifre on Numbers, and another Sifre, on Deuteronomy at a guess to be dated at ca. 300 C.E., then Genesis Rabbah ca. 400 C.E., Leviticus Rabbah ca. 425 C.E., and at the end, Pesiqta de Rab Kahana, Lamentations Rabbati, and some other treatments of biblical books, all of them in the fifth or sixth centuries. These books and some minor related items together form the canon of Judaism as it had reached its definitive shape by the end of late antiquity.

If we lay out these writings in the approximate sequence in which they reached closure beginning with the Mishnah, the Tosefta, then Sifra and its associated compositions, followed by the Talmud of the Land of Israel, and alongside Genesis Rabbah and Leviticus Rabbah, then Pesiqta de Rab Kahana and its companions, and finally the Talmud of Babylonia, we gain what I call "canonical history." This is, specifically, the order of the appearance of ideas when the documents, read in the outlined sequence, address a given idea or topic. The consequent history consists of the sequence in which a given statement on the topic at hand was made (early, middle, or late) in the unfolding of the canonical writings. To illustrate the process, what does the authorship of the Mishnah have to say on the theme? Then how does the compositor of Abot deal with it? Then the Tosefta's compositor's record comes into view, followed by the materials assembled in the Talmud of the Land of Israel, alongside those now found in the earlier and middle ranges of compilations of scriptural exegeses, and as always, the Talmud of Babylonia at the end. In the illustrative exercise that follows we shall read the sources in exactly the order outlined here. I produce a picture of how these sources treat an important principle of the Judaism of the Dual Torah We shall see important shifts and changes in the unfolding of ideas on the symbol under study.

So, in sum, this story of continuity and change rests upon the notion that we can present the history of the treatment of a topical program in the canonical writings of that Judaism. I do not claim that the documents represent the state of popular or synagogue opinion. I do not know whether the history of the idea in the unfolding official texts corresponds to the history of the idea among the people who stand behind those documents. Even less do I claim to speak about the history of the topic or idea at hand outside of rabbinical circles, among the Jewish nation at large. All these larger dimensions of the matter lie wholly beyond the perspective of this book. The reason is that the evidence at hand is of a particular sort and hence permits us to investigate one category of questions and not another. The category is denied by established and universally held conventions about the order in which the canonical writings reached completion. Therefore we trace the way in which matters emerge in the sequence of writings followed here.

We trace the way in which ideas were taken up and spelled out in these successive stages in the formation of the canon. Let the purpose of the exercise be emphasized. *When we follow this procedure, we discover how, within the formation of the rabbinical canon of writings, the idea at hand came to literary expression and how it was then shaped to serve the larger purposes of the nascent canonical system as a whole.* By knowing the place and uses of the topic under study within the literary evidences of the rabbinical system, we gain a better understanding of the formative history of that system. What do we not learn? Neither the condition of the people at large nor the full range and power of the rabbinical thinkers' imagination comes to the fore. About other larger historical and intellectual matters we have no direct knowledge at all. Consequently we claim to report only what we learn about the canonical literature of a system evidenced by a limited factual base. No one who wants to know the history of a given idea in all the diverse Judaisms of late antiquity, or the role of that idea in the history of all the Jews in all parts of the world in the first seven centuries of the Common Era will find it here.

In order to understand the documentary method we must again underline the social and political character of the documentary evidence presented. These are public statements, preserved and handed on because people have adopted them as authoritative. The sources constitute a collective, and therefore official, literature. All of the documents took shape and attained a place in the canon of the rabbinical movement as a whole. None was written by an individual in such a way as to testify to personal choice or decision. Accordingly, we cannot provide an account of the theory of a given individual at a particular time and place. We have numerous references to what a given individual said about the topic at hand. But these references do not reach us in the authorship of that person, or even in his language.

They come to us only in the setting of a *collection* of sayings and statements, some associated with names, other unattributed and anonymous. The collections by definition were composed under the auspices of rabbinical authority – a school or a circle. They tell us what a group of people wished to preserve and hand on as authoritative doctrine about the meaning of the Mishnah and Scripture. The compositions reach us because the larger rabbinical estate chose to copy and hand them on. Accordingly, we know the state of doctrine at the stages marked by the formation and closure of the several documents.

We follow what references we find to a topic in accord with the order of documents just now spelled out. In this study we learn the order in which ideas came to expression in the canon. We begin any survey with the Mishnah, the starting point of the canon. We proceed systematically to work our way through tractate Abot, the Mishnah's first apologetic, then the Tosefta, the Yerushalmi, and the Bavli at the end. In a single encompassing sweep, we finally deal with the entirety of the compilations of the exegeses of Scripture, arranged, to be sure, in that order that I have now explained. Let me expand on the matter of my heavy emphasis on the order of the components of the canon. The reason for that stress is simple. We have to ask not only what documents viewed whole and all at once ("Judaism") tell us about our theme. In tracing the order in which ideas make their appearance, we ask about the components in sequence ("history of Judaism") so far as we can trace the sequence. Then and only then shall we have access to issues of *history*, that is, of change and development. If our theme makes its appearance early on in one form, so one set of ideas predominate in a document that reached closure in the beginnings of the cannon and then that theme drops out of public discourse or undergoes radical revision in writings in later stages of the canon, that fact may make considerable difference. Specifically, we may find it possible to speculate on where, and why a given approach proved urgent, and also on the reasons that that same approach receded from the center of interest.

In knowing the approximate sequence of documents and therefore the ideas in them (at least so far as the final point at which those ideas reached formal expression in the canon), a second possibility emerges. What if – as is the case – we find pretty much the same views, treated in the same proportion and for the same purpose, yielding the same message, early, middle, and late in the development of the canon? Then we shall have to ask why the literature remains so remarkably constant. Given the considerable shifts in the social and political condition of Israel in the land of Israel as well as in Babylonia over a period of more than four hundred years, that evident stability in the teachings for the effective life will constitute a considerable fact for analysis and interpretation. History, including the history of religion, done rightly thus produces two possibilities, both of them demanding sustained attention. Things change. Why? Things do not change. Why not? We may well trace the relationship between the history of ideas and the history of the society that holds those same ideas. We follow the interplay between society and system – world view, way of life, addressed to a particular social group – by developing a theory of the relationship between contents and context, between the world in which people live and the world which people create in their shared social and imaginative life. When we can frame a theory of how a system in substance relates to its setting, of the interplay between the social matrix and the mode and manner of a society's world-view and way of life, then we may develop theses of general intelligibility, theories of why this, not that, of why, and why no and how come.

The story of continuity and change rests upon the notion that we can present the history of the treatment of a topical program in the canonical writings of that Judaism. I do not claim that the documents represent the state of popular or synagogue opinion. I do not know whether the history of the idea in the unfolding official texts corresponds to the history of the idea among the people who stand behind those documents. Even less do I claim to speak about the history of the topic or idea at hand outside of rabbinical circles, among the Jewish nation at large. All these larger dimensions of the matter lie wholly beyond the perspective of this book. The reason is that the evidence at hand is of a particular sort and hence permits us to investigate one category of questions and not another. The category is defined by established and universally held conventions about the order in which the canonical writings reached completion. Therefore we trace the way in which matters emerge in the sequence of writings followed here. We trace the way in which ideas were taken up and spelled out in these successive stages in the formation of the canon. When we follow this procedure, we discover how, within the formation of the rabbinical canon of writings, the idea at hand came to literary expression and how it was then shaped to serve the larger purposes of the nascent canonical system as a whole.

My documentary method for the study of Judaism yields concrete results, and I have published extensive accounts of them. Here I give an example of the result of the method I have outlined. For that example, I take the documentary history of the single critical symbol of the Judaism of the Dual Torah, namely, (the) Torah. That documentary history traces the story of how "the Torah" lost its capital letter and definite article and ultimately became "torah." What for nearly a millennium had been a particular scroll or book came to serve as a symbol of an entire system. When a rabbi spoke of torah, he no longer meant only a particular object, a scroll and its contents. Now he used the work to encompass a distinctive and well-defined world view and way of life. Torah had come to stand for something one does. Knowledge of the Torah promised not merely information about what people were supposed to do, but ultimate redemption or salvation.

In the Judaism of the Dual Torah as it emerged from its formative age., everything was contained in that one thing, "Torah." When we speak of "torah," or "the Torah," in rabbinical literature of late antiquity, we no longer denote a particular book, on the one side, or the contents of such a book, on the other. Instead, we connote a broad range of clearly distinct categories of noun and verb, concrete fact and abstract relationship alike. "Torah" stands for a kind of human being. It connotes a social status and a sort of social group. It refers to a type of social relationship. It further denotes a legal status and differentiates among legal norms. As symbolic abstraction, the word encompasses things and persons, actions and status, points of social differentiation and legal and normative standing, as well as "revealed truth." In all, the main points of insistence of the whole of Israel's life and history come to full symbolic expression in that single word. If people wanted to explain how they would be saved, they would use the word Torah. If they wished to sort out their parlous relationships with gentiles, they would use the world Torah. Torah stood for salvation and accounted for Israel's this-worldly condition and the hope, for both individual and national alike, of life in the world to come. For the kind of Judaism under discussion, therefore, the word Torah stood for everything. The Torah symbolized the whole, at once and entire. When, therefore, we wish to describe the unfolding of the definitive doctrine of Judaism in its formative period, the first exercise consists in paying close attention to the meanings imputed to a single word. Every detail of the religious system at hand exhibits essentially the same point of insistence, captured in the simple notion of the Torah as the generative symbol, the total, exhaustive expression of the system as a whole.

If we start back with the Mishnah, which later on formed the oral part of the one whole Torah, written and oral, revealed by God to Moses at Sinai, we look in vain for a picture of the Mishnah as (part of) the Torah. For the Mishnah provided no account of itself. Unlike biblical law codes, the Mishnah begins with no myth of its own origin. It ends with no doxology. Discourse commences in the middle of things and ends abruptly. What follows from such laconic mumbling is that the exact status of the document required definition entirely outside the framework of the document itself. The framers of the Mishnah gave no hint of the nature of their book, so the Mishnah reached the political world of Israel without a trace of self-conscious explanation or any theory of validation. The framers of the Mishnah nowhere claim, implicitly or explicitly, that what they have written forms part of the Torah, enjoys the status of God's revelation to Moses at Sinai, or even systematically carries forward secondary exposition and application of what Moses wrote down in the wilderness. Later on, I think two hundred years beyond the closure of the Mishnah, the need to explain the standing and origin of the Mishnah led some to posit two things. First, God's revelation of the Torah at Sinai encompassed the Mishnah as much as Scripture. Second, the Mishnah was handed on through oral formulation and oral transmission from Sinai to the framers of the document as we have it.

As for the Mishnah itself, however, it contains not a hint that anyone has heard any such tale. The earliest apologists for the Mishnah, represented in Abot and the Tosefta alike, know nothing of the fully realized myth of the Dual Torah of Sinai. Only the two Talmuds reveal that conception – alongside their mythic explanation of where the document came from and why it should be obeyed. So the Yerushalmi marks the change. In any event, the absence of explicit expression of such a claim in behalf of the Mishnah requires little specification. It is just not there. A survey of the uses of the word Torah in the Mishnah, to be sure, provides us with an account of what the framers of the Mishnah, founders of what would emerge as rabbinic Judaism, understood by that term. But it will not tell us how they related their own ideas to the Torah, nor shall we find a trace of evidence of that fully articulated way of life – the use of the word Torah to categorize and classify persons, places, things, relationships, all manner of abstractions – that we find fully exposed in some later redacted writings.

The next document in sequence beyond the Mishnah, Abot, The Fathers, draws into the orbit of Torah-talk the names of authorities of the Mishnah. But Abot does not claim that the Mishnah forms part of the Torah, any more than the document imputes supernatural standing to sages, as we saw in Chapter Seven. Nor, obviously, does the tractate know the doctrine of the two Torahs. Only in the Talmuds do we begin to find clear and ample evidence of that doctrine. Abot, moreover, does not understand by the word Torah much more than the framers of the Mishnah do. Not only does the established classification scheme remain intact, but the sense essentially replicates already familiar usages, producing no innovation. On the contrary, I find a diminution in the range of meanings. Yet Abot in the aggregate does differ from the Mishnah. The sixty-two tractates of the Mishnah contain Torah-sayings here and there. But they do not fall within the framework of Torah-discourse. They speak about other matters entirely. Abot, by contrast, says a great deal about Torah-study. The claim that Torah-study produces direct encounter with God forms part of Abot's thesis about the Torah. In Abot, Torah is instrumental. The figure of the sage, his ideals and conduct, forms the goal, focus and center. To state matters simply: Abot regards study of Torah as what a sage does. The substance of Torah is what a sage says. That is so whether or not the saying relates to scriptural revelation. The content of the sayings attributed to sages endows those sayings with self-validating status. The sages usually do not quote verses of Scripture and explain them, nor do they speak in God's name. Yet, it is clear, sages talk Torah. What follows? It is this: if a sage says something, what he says is Torah. More accurately, what he says falls into the classification of Torah. Accordingly Abot treats Torah-learning as symptomatic, an indicator of the status of the sage, hence, as I said, as merely instrumental. The instrumental status of the Torah, as well as of the Mishnah, lies in the net effect of their composition: the claim that through study of the Torah sages enter God's presence. So study of Torah serves a further goal, that of forming sages. The theory of Abot pertains to the religious standing and consequence of the learning of the sages. To be sure, a secondary effect of that theory endows with the status of revealed truth things sages say. But then it is because they say them, not because they have heard them in an endless chain back to Sinai. The fundament of truth is passed on through sagacity, not through already formulated and carefully memorized truths. That is shy the single most important word in Abot also is the most common, the word "says."

The Mishnah is held in the Yerushalmi to be equivalent to Scripture (Y. Hor. 3:5). But the Mishnah is not called Torah. Still, once the Mishnah entered the status of Scripture, it would take but a short step to a theory of the Mishnah as part of the revelation at Sinai – hence, Oral Torah. In the Yerushalmi we find the first glimmerings of an effort to theorize in general, not merely in detail, about how specific teachings of Mishnah relate to specific teachings of Scripture. The citing of scriptural prooftexts for Mishnah propositions, after all, would not have caused much surprise to the framers of the Mishnah; they themselves included such passages, though not often. But what conception of the Torah underlies such initiatives, and how to Yerushalmi sages propose to explain the phenomenon of the Mishnah as a whole? The following passage gives us one statement. It refers to the assertion at M. Hag. 1:8D that the laws on cultic cleanness presented in the Mishnah rest on deep and solid foundations in the Scripture.

Y. Hagigah 1:7

[V A] The laws of the Sabbath [M. 1:8B]: R. Jonah said R. Hama bar Uqba raised the question [in reference to M. Hag. 1:8D's view that there are many verses of Scripture on cleanness], "And lo, it is written only, 'Nevertheless a spring or a cistern holding water shall be clean; but whatever touches their carcass shall be unclean (Lev. 11:36). And from this verse you derive many laws. [So how can M. 8:8D say what it does about many verses for laws of cultic cleanness?]"

[B] R. Zeira in the name of R. Yohanan: "If a law comes to hand and you do not know its nature, do not discard it for another one, for lo, many laws were stated to Moses at Sinai, and all of them have been embedded in the Mishnah."

The truly striking assertion appears at B. The Mishnah now is claimed to contain statements made by God to Moses. Just how these statements found their way into the Mishnah, and which passages of the Mishnah contain them, we do not know. That is hardly important, given the fundamental assertion at hand. The passage proceeds to a further, and far more consequential, proposition. It asserts that part of the Torah was written down, and part was preserved in memory and transmitted orally. In context, moreover, that distinction must encompass the Mishnah, thus explaining its origin as part of the Torah. Here is a clear and unmistakable expression of the distinction between two forms in which a single Torah was revealed and handed on at Mount Sinai, part in writing, part orally.

While the passage below does not make use of the language, Torah-in-writing and Torah-by-memory, it does refer to "the written" and "the oral." I believe myself fully justified in supplying the word Torah in square brackets. The reader will note, however, that the word Torah likewise does not occur at K, L. Only when the passage reaches its climax, at M, does it break down into a number of categories – Scripture, Mishnah, Talmud, laws, lore. It there makes the additional point that everything comes from Moses at Sinai. So the fully articulated theory of two Torahs (not merely one Torah in two forms) does not reach final expression in this passage. But short of explicit allusion to Torah-in-writing and Torah-by-memory, which (so far as I am able to discern) we find mainly in the Talmud of Babylonia, the ultimate theory of Torah of formative Judaism is at hand in what follows.

Y. Hagigah 1:7

[V D] R. Zeirah in the name of R. Eleazar: "'Were I to write for him my laws by ten thousands, they would be regarded as a strange thing' (Hos. 8:12). Now is the greater part of the Torah written down? [Surely not. The oral part is much greater.] But more abundant are the

[E]	matters which are derived by exegesis from the written [Torah] than those derived by exegesis from the oral [Torah]." And is that so?
[F]	But more cherished are those matters which rest upon the written [Torah] than those which rest upon the oral [Torah]....
[J]	R. Haggai in the name of R. Samuel bar Nahman, "Some teachings were handed on orally, and some things were handed on in writing, and we do not know which of them is the more precious. But on the basis of that which is written, 'And the Lord said to Moses, Write these words; in accordance with these words I have made a covenant with you and with Israel' (Ex. 34:27), [we conclude] that the ones which are handed on orally are the more precious."
[K]	R. Yohanan and R. Yudan b. R. Simeon — One said, "If you have kept what is preserved orally and also kept what is in writing, I shall make a covenant with you, and if not, I shall not make a covenant with you."
[L]	The other said, "If you have kept what is preserved orally and you have kept what is preserved in writing, you shall receive a reward, and if not, you shall not receive a reward."
[M]	[With reference to Deut. 9:10: "And on them was written according to all the words which the Lord spoke with you in the mount,"] said R. Joshua b. Levi, "He could have written, 'On them,' but wrote, 'And on them.' He could have written, 'All,' but wrote, 'According to all.' He could have written, 'Words,' but wrote 'The words.' [These then serve as three encompassing clauses, serving to include] Scripture, Mishnah, Talmud, laws, and lore. Even what an experienced student in the future is going to teach before his master already has been stated to Moses at Sinai."
[N]	What is the Scriptural basis for this view?
[O]	"There is no remembrance of former things, nor will there be any remembrance of later things yet to happen among those who come after" (Qoh. 1:11).
[P]	If someone says, "See, this is a new thing," his fellow will answer him, saying to him, "this has been around before us for a long time."

Here we have absolutely explicit evidence that people believed part of the Torah had been preserved not in writing but orally. Linking that part to the Mishnah remains a matter of implication. But it surely comes fairly close to the surface, when we are told that the Mishnah contains Torah-traditions revealed at Sinai. From that view it requires only a small step to the allegation that the Mishnah is part of the Torah, the oral part. To define the category of the Torah as a source of salvation, as the Yerushalmi states matters, I point to a story that explicitly states the proposition that the Torah constitutes a source of salvation. In this story we shall see that because people observed the rules of the Torah, they expected to be saved. And if they did not observe, they accepted their punishment. So the Torah now stands for something more than revelation and life of study, and (it goes without saying) the sage now appears as a holy, not merely a learned, man. This is because his knowledge of the Torah has transformed him. Accordingly, we deal with a category of stories and sayings about the Torah entirely different from what has gone before.

Y. Taanit 3:8

[II A] As to Levi ben Sisi: troops came to his town. He took a scroll of the Torah and went up to the roof and said, "Lord of the ages! If a single word of this scroll of the Torah has been nullified [in our town], let them come up against us, and if not, let them go their way."

[B] Forthwith people went looking for the troops but did not find them [because they had gone their way].

[C] A disciple of his did the same thing, and his hand withered, but the troops whet their way.

[D] A disciple of his disciple did the same thing. His hand did not wither, but they also did not go their way.

[E] This illustrates the following apophthegm: You can't insult an idiot, and dead skin does not feel the scalpel.

What is interesting here is how taxa into which the word Torah previously fell have been absorbed and superseded in a new taxon. The Torah is an object: "He took a scroll...." It also constitutes God's revelation to Israel: "If a single word...." The outcome of the revelation is to form an ongoing way of life, embodied in the sage himself: "A disciple of his did the same thing...." The sage plays an intimate part in the supernatural event: "His hand withered...." Now can we categorize this story as a statement that the Torah constitutes a particular object, or a source of divine revelation, or a way of life? Yes and no. The Torah here stands not only for the things we already have catalogued. It represents one more thing which takes in all the others. Torah is a source of salvation. How so? The Torah stands for, or constitutes, the way in which the people Israel saves itself from marauders. This straightforward sense of salvation will not have surprised the author of Deuteronomy.

In the canonical documents up to the Yerushalmi, we look in vain for sayings or stories that fall into such a category. True, we may take for granted that everyone always believed that, in general, Israel would be saved by obedience to the Torah. That claim would not have surprised any Israelite writers from the first prophets down through the final redactors of the Pentateuch in the time of Ezra and onward through the next seven hundred years. But, in the rabbinical corpus from the Mishnah forward, the specific and concrete assertion that by taking up the scroll of the Torah and standing on the roof of one's house, confronting God in heaven, a sage in particular could take action against the expected invasion – that kind of claim is not located, so far as I know, in any composition surveyed so far.

Still, we cannot claim that the belief that the Torah in the hands of the sage constituted a source of magical, supernatural, and hence salvific power, simply did not flourish prior, let us say, to ca. 400 C.E. We cannot show it, hence we do not know it. All we can say with assurance is that no stories containing such a viewpoint appear in any rabbinical document associated with the Mishnah. So what is critical here is not the generalized category – the genus – of conviction that the Torah serves as the source of Israel's salvation. It is the concrete assertion – the speciation of the genus – that in the hands of the sage and under conditions specified, the Torah may be utilized in pressing circumstances as Levi, his disciple, and the disciple of his disciple, used it. That is what is new. This stunningly new usage of Torah found in the Yerushalmi emerges from a group of stories not readily classified in our established categories. All of these stories treat the word Torah (whether scroll, contents, or act of study) as source and guarantor of salvation. Accordingly, evoking the word Torah forms the centerpiece of a theory of Israel's history, on the one side, and an account of the teleology of the entire system, on the other. Torah indeed has ceased to constitute a specific thing or even a category or classification when stories about studying the Torah yield not a judgment as to status (i.e., praise for the learned man) but promise for supernatural blessing now and salvation in time to come.

The key to the first Talmud's theory of the Torah lies in its conception of the sage, to which that theory is subordinate. Once the sage reaches his full apotheosis as Torah incarnate, then, but only then, the Torah becomes (also) a source of salvation in the present concrete formulation of the matter. That is why we traced the doctrine of the Torah in the salvific process by elaborate citation of stories about sages, living Torahs, exercising the supernatural power of the Torah, and serving, like the Torah itself, to reveal God's will. Since the sage embodied the Torah and gave the Torah, the Torah naturally came to stand for the principal source of Israel's salvation, not merely a scroll, on the one side, or a source of revelation, on the other. The history of the symbolization of the Torah proceeds from its removal from the framework of material objects, even from the limitations of its own contents, to its transformation into something quite different and abstract, quite distinct from the document and its teachings. The Torah stands for this something more, specifically, when it comes to be identified with a living person, the sage, and endowed with those particular traits that the sage claimed for himself. While we cannot say that the process of symbolization leading to the pure abstraction at hand moved in easy stages, we may still point to the stations that had to be passed in sequence. The word Torah reached the apologists for the Mishnah in its long-established meanings: Torah-scroll, contents of the Torah-scroll. But even in the Mishnah itself, these meanings provoked a secondary development, status of Torah as distinct from other (lower) status, hence, Torah-teaching in contradistinction to scribal teaching. With that small and simple step, the Torah ceased to denote only a concrete and material thing – a scroll and its contents. It now connoted an abstract matter of status. And once made abstract, the symbol entered a secondary history beyond all limits imposed by the concrete object, including its specific teachings, the Torah-scroll.

I believe that Abot stands at the beginning of this process. In the history of the word Torah as abstract symbol, a metaphor serving to sort out one abstract status from another regained concrete and material reality of a new order entirely. For the message of Abot, as we saw, was that the Torah served the sage. How so? The Torah indicated who was a sage and who was not. Accordingly, the apology of Abot for the Mishnah was that the Mishnah contained things sages had said. What sages said formed a chain of tradition extending back to Sinai. Hence it was equivalent to the Torah. The upshot is that words of sages enjoyed the status of the Torah. The small step beyond, I think, was to claim that what sages said was Torah, as much as what Scripture said was Torah. And, a further small step (and the steps need not have been taken separately or in the order here suggested) moved matters to the position that there were two forms in which the Torah reached Israel: one [Torah] in writing, the other [Torah] handed on orally, that is, in memory. The final step, fully revealed in the Talmud at hand, brought the conception of Torah to its logical conclusion: what the sage said was in the status of the Torah, was Torah, because the sage was Torah incarnate. So the abstract symbol now became concrete and material once more. We recognize the many, diverse ways in which the Talmud stated that conviction. Every passage in which knowledge of the Torah yields power over this world and the next, capacity to coerce to the sage's will the natural and supernatural worlds alike, rests upon the same viewpoint. The first Talmud's theory of the Torah carries us through several stages in the processes of the symbolization of the word Torah. First transformed from something material and concrete into something abstract and beyond all metaphor, the word Torah finally emerged once more in a concrete aspect, now as the encompassing and universal mode of stating the whole doctrine, all at once, of Judaism in its formative age.

The documentary history of the symbol, Torah, raises more questions than it settles. For once we recognize that shifts and turnings in the treatment of a fixed topic or symbol characterize the movement from one writing to the next, we want to explain change. And, in the nature of things, we wonder what has happened in the world beyond that has led to the reconsideration of the generative symbol of a system such as this one. Identifying the documentary matrix of an idea or a symbol directs our attention not to, but beyond, the sequence of writings. We want to ask about the world beyond the system. In other studies I have addressed that question; it would carry me far afield to deal with it here. It suffices at this point simply to observe that, in light of what has been said, any account of an idea, myth, issue, conception – emotions, incarnation, for example – that takes for granted all sources exist on a timeless plain and takes at face value all attributions simply has nothing of value to teach for those interested in the history of religion and of religious ideas. I repeat, that does not mean bibliographical studies will omit all reference to these works, even though they now form mere curiosities. But it does mean that we no longer have to take seriously and argue with results that derive from premises that no longer hold true. So no, we no longer have to read Moore or Urbach or Schechter.

EPILOGUE

9

The Language and Structure of the Babylonian Talmud: Its Influence on its Readers' Mode of Thought

Jhonatan Rotberg
Brown University

The specific literary traits of a document can be used as clues to (partly) reconstruct its authors' unstated intentions and concerns for the audience's response. By discovering and analyzing the literary traits of the Babylonian Talmud (Bavli), we shall see that one of the authorship's main objectives was the development of its audience's skills of orderly, systematic and thus critical thinking. To achieve this, three methods were employed. First, the Bavli seeks to the engage reader's mind through the use of intellectual provocation. Second, the symmetrical structure of its debates motivates the reader to reflect on the arguments in an orderly manner. And third, to achieve such symmetry, the Bavli makes highly efficient use its language and excludes of any unrelated material. We take up for our exemplary case the opening lines of the Babylonian Talmud's treatment of Mishnah-tractate Berakhot 8:1, that is, b. Ber. 51b-52a.

Firstly, the Bavli seeks to engage the reader's mind by turning him into an active, rather than passive participant of the exchanges. For example, after settling the first argument of Berakhot 8:1, the Talmud traps the reader into questioning an assumption of the given issue.

> And is it the reasoning of the House of Shammai that the blessing of the day is more important?
> Babylonian Talmud Berakhot 51b

This is assumed of the House of Shammai because it reasons that the blessing of the day comes before that of the wine (Berakhot 8:1). The assumption, however, is immediately contested by a passage which puts the *Havdala* (blessing of the day) last.

> But has a Tanna not taught: "He who enters his house at the close of the Sabbath blesses over the wine and the light and the spices and afterward he says *Havdalah*. And if he has only one cup, he leaves it for after the food and then says the other blessing in order after it."

For the reader who is not yet aware, the following statement explicitly emphasizes the need to test given assumptions.

> But lo, on what account [do you say] this is the view of the House of Shammai? Perhaps it is the House of Hillel's [opinion].

Although this assumption is eventually proven true using a different set of evidence, this process prompts its audience to engage within the discourse. This implies the questioning and close analysis of information that could have otherwise easily been taken for granted.

Through the use of this kind of intellectual provocation, the Bavli makes its reader realize the importance of actively reflecting on the stated arguments. By doing this, the reader assimilates more from the Bavli than by merely following the arguments as given, and gradually penetrates deeper into the text itself. The importance of actively participating and thus penetrating within a Talmudic discourse lies in ultimately decoding the authorship's intentions and thoughts.

Next, the Bavli's authorship presents its audience with a highly formalized and symmetric document. This type of structure forces the reader to map out the arguments and to reflect about them in a well patterned manner. In the following example (Mishna's Berakhot 8:3), the Bavli makes this evident by symmetrically stating each Houses' arguments followed by a series of rebuttal and counter-rebuttal statements First, the Bavli quotes the reasoning of the House of Shammai, who openly contends that of the House of Hillel:

> The House of Shammai say, "He wipes his hands on the napkin and lays it on the table, for if you say, 'on the cushion,' [that view is wrong, for it is a precautionary] decree lest the liquids which are on the napkin become unclean on account of the cushion and go back and render the hands unclean."

Followed by rebuttals and answers:

> – And will not the cushion [itself] render the napkin unclean?
> – A vessel cannot make a vessel unclean.
> – And will not the cushion [itself] make the man unclean?

– A vessel cannot make a man unclean.

Following, the Bavli swaps Houses, but obeys an identical pattern.

And the House of Hillel say, '"On the cushion," for if you say "on the table" [that opinion is wrong, for it is a] decree lest the liquids become unclean on account of the table and go and render the food unclean.'

Again, followed by rebuttal and answer:

– But will not the table render the food which is on it unclean?

– We here deal with a table which is unclean on the second remove, and something unclean on the second remove does not render something unclean on the third remove in respect to unconsecrated food, except by means of liquids [which are always unclean on the first remove].

In this, as in many other samples, the Bavli presents parallel structures for both counterparts' opinion: Give rule, disprove opponent followed by a series of rebuttal(s) and answer(s) (with an eventual convergence toward a solution). This example illustrates an array of clashing thoughts in an organized and parallel structure. This proves the Babylonian authorship's intention to force the reader into thinking about a set of complex arguments in an orderly manner. Consequently, this kind of exposure develops in its audience a clear and systematic mode of thought to be exercised throughout the document.

Lastly, because the Babylonian Talmud is a highly edited and crafted document, we should expect to find much significance in its well chosen language. In its discourse, it does not waste a single word, nor does it digress into opinions irrelevant to the current issue. The Bavli's selection and use of language, therefore, reflects a deep concern for conciseness and objectivity. Observing the conclusion of the current argument in Berakhot 8:3:

What [principle] do they dispute?

The House of Shammai reckon that it is prohibited to make use of a table unclean in the second remove, as a decree on account of those who eat Heave-offering [which is rendered unfit by an object unclean in the second remove].

And the House of Hillel reckon that it is permitted to make use of a table unclean in the second remove, for those who eat Heave-offering [the priests] are careful.

We see that, although no translation can perfectly convey the original text's use of language, the cited passage shows the thrift and directness in which the Talmud articulates the Houses' convictions. In the original Hebrew only 11 words (30+ in English) are used to voice each House's ruling and reason. Moreover, the use of adjectives is highly restricted, and superfluous words or phrases are largely omitted. In short, the Bavli is efficient and direct in its presentation of arguments and debates.

Because of the sages' desire for symmetry, their concern with conciseness and objectivity serves as a means toward perfection of structure. To achieve a symmetric structure in its debates they needed the strict exclusion of any unrelated idea, for extraneous material would unbalance the structure's equilibrium. Similarly, the use of adverbs or adjectives would bias the presentation, and prevent the reader from discerning a perfectly balanced dialogue. Without any intrusions or value judgements, then, the Bavli achieves conciseness and objectivity while striving for a perfect equilibrium of presentation and structure.

By first engaging, and then exemplifying a highly systematic mode of discourse to the reader, the sages of the Bavli sought to develop him into a tools of systematic and critical thinker. By working outwards from the text, this study has illustrated the process in which the Babylonian Talmud's structure and language can be used as basis for inference regarding the authorship's means to attain their goal. Because the Babylonian sages understood that the thorough understanding of the wisdom within their text called for a critical assessment of its arguments, they sought to immerse the reader into the text, and to illustrate the process of orderly and systematic discourse.

Index

Al-Biruni 46
Aristotle, Aristotelian 138-141
Ashkenazi (Jews) 25, 27, 59
Aufrecht, Walter 67
Babylonian Talmud 153, 182, 197, 199
Baghdadi (Jews) 11, 17, 28, 30, 39, 44, 45
Bar Kokhba 169, 170
Barzillay, Ezra, *see also* Haddad, Ezra 12
Bavli 87, 89-91, 95, 108, 114, 150, 153, 181, 184, 197-200
Bloch, Renée 160
Bousset, Wilhelm 160
Brauer, E. 13, 17, 18, 20, 36, 37, 45, 47, 54, 55, 60
Brooks, Roger 67
Brown, R. E. 72,
Cadbury, H. J. 73
Caro, Joseph 14, 33
Charles, R. H. 160
Chen, D. 76, 78
Chiat, M. J. (S.) 67, 75, 76, 78, 79
Chorazin 75
Christ 17, 26, 67, 68, 89

Christian(s) 7, 12, 50-52, 55, 61, 62, 72, 73, 89, 159, 170, 176
Christianity 21, 73, 89, 115, 128, 168, 176
circumcise, circumcised, circumcision 47, 59, 60, 116
Cohen 12, 35, 46
comparative Midrash 124, 125, 130, 160
Conzelmann, H. 73
Corbo, V. 75, 78
creation 17-19, 29, 42, 57, 146, 158
de Haas, J. 4
diaspora, diasporan 22, 71-74
Dion, Paul-Eugéne 68
Dor 71
Drower, E. S., *see also* Stevens, E. S. 3-8, 11, 26, 43, 54
Dual Torah 86, 89, 90, 107, 113, 121, 173, 174, 176, 178, 182, 185-187
Egypt 18, 29, 51, 52, 55, 68, 69, 72, 80
Elbogen, I. 16, 37
Encyclopaedia Judaica 158, 159
Exodus 18, 31, 37, 45, 90, 182

Ezra 51, 58, 62, 191
Foerster, G. 75, 76, 78, 79
Galilee 71-76, 78-81
Gamla 75, 76, 78, 79
Gentile(s) 5, 13, 14, 19, 46, 96, 100, 186
Goitein, S. D. 4, 12, 15
gospel(s) 72, 89, 105, 106, 110, 114, 115, 133, 134
Grabbe, Lester L. 68, 70
Green, William Scott 131, 176
Gressmann, Hugo 160
Griffiths, J. Gwyn 68, 80
Groh, Dennis 67
Gutmann, J. 67, 75, 76, 78, 79
Hackforth-Jones, M. 7, 63
Haddad, Ezra, *see also* Barzillay, Ezra 12, 27, 39
Haenchen, E. 73
Haim, Joseph 16, 21, 39
Halivni, David Weiss 122
Hasidism 90
Heer, M. D. 158
Heinemann, Joseph 38, 160
Hoenig, S. 67
Hooke, S. H. 31
Horbury, Wm. 174
Howard, Delton Thomas 139
Hüttenmeister,.F. 75, 76, 78, 79
Iranian (Jews) 19
Israel 7, 10, 12, 19, 32, 37, 41-43, 45, 51, 52, 62, 63, 67, 79, 87, 92, 100, 129, 149, 155, 157, 158, 176, 180, 182, 184, 187, 191, 193
Israeli(s) 5, 6, 156-158, 178

Jackson, F. J. Foakes 73
Jacobs, Louis 32, 137-139, 141-147
Jerusalem 4, 7, 12-18, 22, 31, 33-36, 38, 39, 41, 43, 44, 51, 54, 55, 57, 60, 69-77, 79-81, 116, 155, 158, 165, 174
Jesus 67, 68, 72, 89, 170
Jewish Encyclopaedia 5, 28
Josephus 69, 71, 72
Judea 51, 70-76, 78, 80
Kabbalism, Kabbalistic 5, 12, 39, 41, 50
Kabbalist(s) 15-17, 25, 34, 38, 39, 41, 54, 56
Kadushin 164, 173, 174
Kimelman, R. 72
Kurdish (Jews) 16, 17, 30, 36, 51, 55, 59
Lake, K. 73
Lehmann, O. 6
Levine, A. J. 67
Levine, L. I. 67, 75, 76, 78, 79
Loewe, H. 174, 175
Maccoby, Hyam 181
Mandaean(s) 3, 7, 8, 16, 18, 20, 26, 29, 32, 43, 50, 52, 55, 61
Maoz, Z. 76, 78-80
Marmorstein, E. 4-8, 164
Martyn, J. L. 72
Masada 75-79
Michaeli, T. 76, 78, 79
Midrash 35, 42, 87, 106, 124, 125, 127, 130, 134, 152, 160, 166, 176
Migdal 75, 79

Index

Mirsky, Norman 76
Mishnah, mishnaic 14, 16, 17, 31, 42, 52, 53, 58, 70, 87-91, 95, 99, 102, 106, 108, 112, 114, 116, 118, 123, 126, 134, 141, 157, 166, 168, 170, 181, 182, 184, 186-193
Mishnah-Tosefta 163, 165, 168, 170, 171
Montefiore, C. G. 174, 175
Moore, George Foot 159, 160, 173-175, 177, 179, 194
Nathan of Gaza 39
New Year 3, 22, 25, 27-29, 42, 52
New Year for Trees 38, 41
Oesterley, W. O E. 12, 46
Oral Torah 188
Orthodox Jews 4, 5, 22, 28, 47, 56
Orthodox Judaism 157, 165, 172
Ovadiah, A. 76, 78, 79
Palestine 3, 17, 31, 41, 42, 62, 63, 67-72, 74, 80, 150
Palestinian (Jews) 62, 67, 70-72, 75, 76, 160
Passover 3, 10, 17, 18, 23, 30, 31, 37, 43, 46-48, 50, 54-58, 69, 144
Pentateuch 6, 36, 37, 90, 191
Pentecost 10, 31, 57
Purim 6, 30, 43, 46, 47
Qal Wa-Homer 138-141
Qumran 71, 78, 160
Rabbi(s) 6, 9, 12, 13, 21, 22, 30, 32, 33, 38-40, 42, 50, 60, 89-91, 126, 127, 128, 141, 147, 153, 158, 160-163, 165, 168, 169, 170, 171, 175, 176, 179, 180, 181, 186

rabbinic, rabbinical 9, 10, 15, 31, 54, 70, 72, 85, 87, 90, 92, 98, 109, 112-114, 120-126, 131, 151, 157-159, 160, 166, 168, 170, 171, 173-175, 178, 179, 183-187, 191, 192
ritual meal 23, 33, 34, 42, 48
Rivkin, Ellis 67
Robinson, Th. E. 46
Rosh Hashana 22, 38
Sabbatai Zevi 39
Sabbath 8, 9, 12-21, 27, 31, 33, 35, 50, 115, 117, 118, 142, 151, 189, 198
sage(s) 89-91, 102, 105, 106, 110, 115, 116, 128, 133, 134, 145, 151, 152, 155, 156, 158, 160, 161, 164, 165, 175, 177, 179, 187, 188, 191-193, 200
Sanders, E. P. 72
Sassoon, Albert 5
Sassoon, David 6
Schechter, Solomon 173-175, 194
Schiffman, L. H. 72
Scholem, G. 16, 39, 41
Schürer, Emil 26, 67, 68
scriptural 32, 91, 92, 99, 102, 142-144, 147, 182, 188, 190
Scripture 36, 69, 89, 90, 92-102, 105, 111, 114, 119, 121, 123-125, 127, 131, 133, 138, 147, 181, 182, 184, 187-190, 193
secular meal 23, 25
Segal, J. B. 7
Sephardic 6, 22, 25, 33
Shabbath 17

Sifra 70, 90, 95, 96, 98-100, 121, 181, 182
Sifré 90, 92, 95
Stegner, William R. 67
Steinsaltz, Adin 149-153
Stevens, E. S., *see also* Drower, E. S. 3, 54
syllogism, syllogistic 88, 119, 130, 138-141
synagogue 5, 6, 8, 12, 16, 19, 20, 22, 25, 27-32, 35-37, 43-45, 57-59, 67-81, 90, 117, 180, 183, 185
Tabernacles 29-31, 37, 43, 59
Talmud(s) 12-18, 26, 31, 41, 48, 57, 70, 87, 89, 99, 104, 114, 123, 132, 137-147, 149-153, 157, 162, 163, 166, 178, 182, 187, 189, 190, 193, 197, 199
talmudic 8, 30, 32, 52, 56, 110, 114, 126, 127, 137-139, 141, 142, 144, 147, 150-152, 158-162, 165-169, 178, 198
Temple 16, 31, 35, 56, 67, 69-71, 73, 74, 77, 80, 139, 158, 160, 170

Tiberius 71
Torah 10, 28, 32, 35, 36, 58, 59, 80, 86, 89, 90, 94, 102, 107, 113, 116-118, 121, 127-129, 131, 141, 168, 173, 174, 176, 178, 182, 185-194
Torah-scroll 193
Torah-study 90, 118, 188
Tosefta 31, 70, 77, 90, 102, 123, 166, 181, 182, 184, 187
Urbach, Ephraim E. 155-167, 169, 172-175, 177, 179, 194
Vermes, Geza 67, 68, 160
Yadin, Y. 76-78
Yeivin, Z. 75
Yemeni (Jews) 17, 20, 48
Yerushalmi 90, 95, 181, 184, 187, 188, 190-192
Yom Kippur 4, 29-31
Zohar 10, 17, 21, 22, 28, 35, 42, 56-58, 163
Zoroastrian(s) 7, 16, 21, 29, 32, 57

www.ingramcontent.com/pod-product-compliance
Lightning Source LLC
Chambersburg PA
CBHW031626160426
43196CB00006B/304